IMAGES
*of America*

# LOCK HAVEN

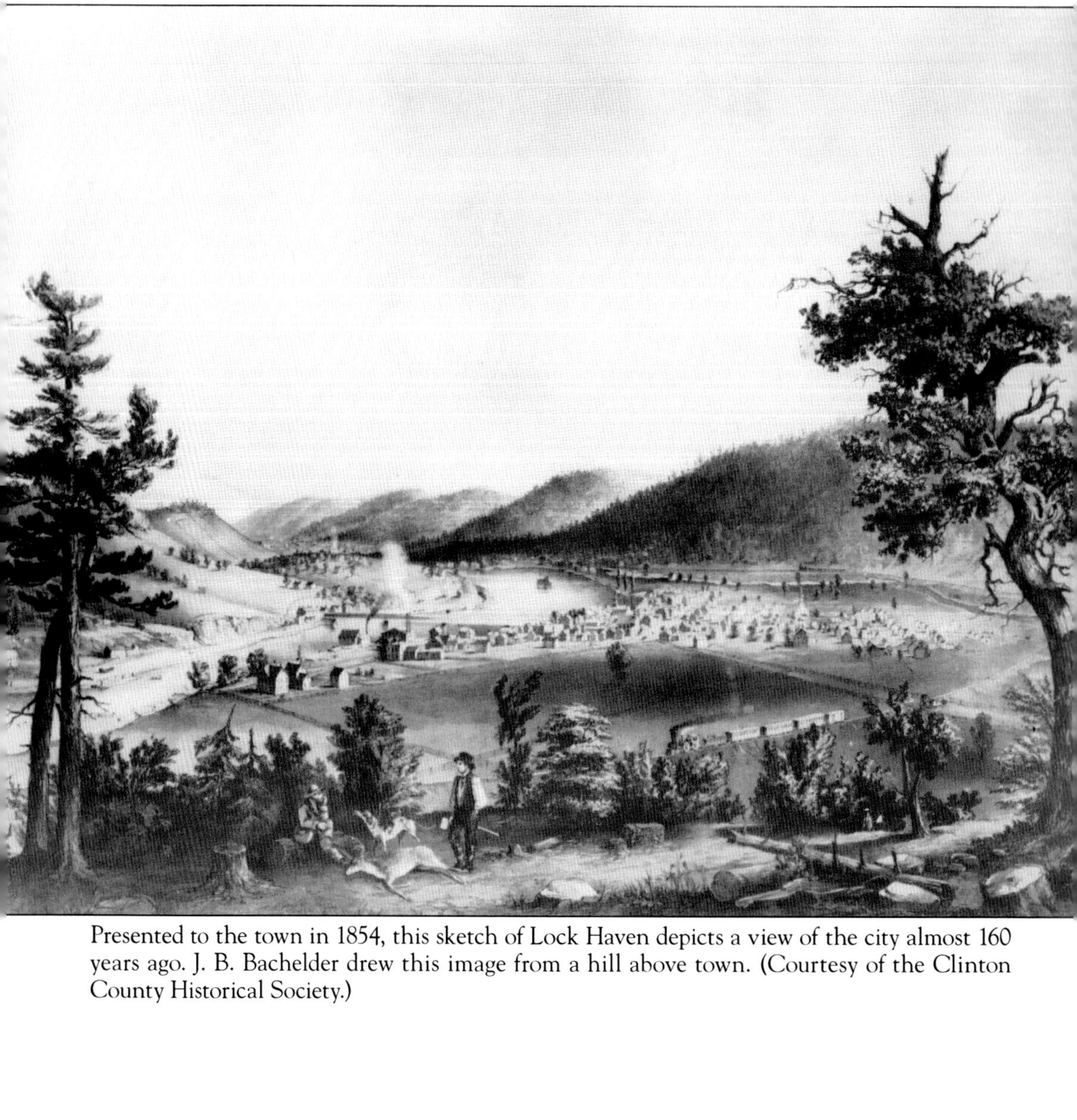

Presented to the town in 1854, this sketch of Lock Haven depicts a view of the city almost 160 years ago. J. B. Bachelder drew this image from a hill above town. (Courtesy of the Clinton County Historical Society.)

**On the Cover:** George Kreamer, one of Lock Haven's mayors, makes his way across the west branch of the Susquehanna River. Before bridges, residents crossed the river by ferry. In 1838, a ferry was started at East Water Street in Lock Haven to Lockport. J. P. Huling, owner of the Washington House, managed the Lock Haven end and Judge Hanna managed the Lockport side. (Courtesy of the Anne Halenbake Ross Library.)

IMAGES
*of America*

# LOCK HAVEN

Maria J. Boileau

ARCADIA
PUBLISHING

ISBN 978-0-7385-7417-2

Published by Arcadia Publishing
Charleston, South Carolina

Printed in the United States of America

Library of Congress Control Number: 2010934148

For all general information, please contact Arcadia Publishing:
Telephone 843-853-2070
Fax 843-853-0044
E-mail sales@arcadiapublishing.com
For customer service and orders:
Toll-Free 1-888-313-2665

Visit us on the Internet at www.arcadiapublishing.com

*This book is dedicated to the volunteers, past and present, who have given their time and talent preserving the history of Lock Haven and Clinton County. You have made all the difference in preserving the beauty of the community. Thank you.*

# CONTENTS

# ACKNOWLEDGMENTS

There are hundreds of volunteers and paid employees who have been involved with the Clinton County Historical Society and the Annie Halenbake Ross Library over the years, so it is difficult to name just a few. The Clinton County Historical Society is dedicated to preserving the history of our community. Lou Bernard, curator, and Anne McCloskey, executive director, offered all of their research at the Heisey Museum for this book. Both Anne and Lou are dedicated to the care and keeping of the museum and were willing to share their valuable time and expertise. It is obvious that they both love this community and their work.

I also wish to thank the volunteers and paid staff at the Annie Halenbake Ross Library, especially Diane Whitaker, director, and J. A. Babay, assistant director, who shared their offices, computers, files, and valuable time to help with this book. They are truly dedicated to the growth and sustainability of our community library.

In addition, photographs were provided by the Hope Hose Fire Company, the City of Lock Haven, Citizens Hose Fire Company, and the Bland J. Rossman Post 1630 VFW in Lock Haven. There is a treasure trove of photographs available at these organizations and many thanks go to their employees and members for sharing their history for this book.

A special thanks to Erin Vosgien for her patience and assistance during this project. And thank you to my husband, John, and my children, Danny and Julie, for your love and support.

# INTRODUCTION

Situated between the beautiful West Branch of the Susquehanna River and the Bald Eagle Creek, Lock Haven was home for the Lenni Lenape Indians. One of the most historic sites was the Great Island located just east of Lock Haven. Surrounded by water and offering rich farmland, this area became a meeting point and home for many tribes. The Great Island can be found on old maps before early settlers arrived.

William Reed was one of the early settlers in 1773. Reed built a log cabin on East Water Street that he named Reed's Fort, surrounding it with a stockade. Reed's Fort was the last in a series of strong points extending up the West Branch Valley from Sunbury built to protect settlers against Indian attacks. Because of the conflict with the Indians, Reed's Fort was evacuated in 1778 during what was referred to as the "Great Runaway." It was not until 1783 that families returned to their homes.

In 1833, Jerry Church and his brother Willard Church recognized the potential of the area when they negotiated with Dr. Henderson of Huntingdon to purchase 200 acres of farmland for $20,000. Church named the town "Lockhaven," for the canal lock and the haven the town had become as a home for river boatmen. Lock Haven was incorporated in 1834 with a population of about 700. It became a borough in 1840 and was made a city in 1876.

The city grew rapidly due to a number of events including its selection as the county seat and the building of a courthouse in 1844. The completion of the canal in 1834 stimulated the lumber industry in Clinton County. And in 1849, the West Branch Boom, a device by which logs could be stored as they floated down the river from the upper tributaries, was completed in Lock Haven. The industry grew rapidly with the completion of the boom in Lock Haven, Williamsport, and other points along the river.

The West Branch Boom made Lock Haven the first market for timber rafts on the West Branch of the Susquehanna River. Lumbermen from eastern Pennsylvania came to purchase rafts of timber.

The collective cutting capacity of the Lock Haven Mills was 100 million board feet per year, and the lumber industry in the area eventually included 13 mills. Most of the large, beautiful homes located in the Water Street Historic District were built by families who prospered from over 50 years of lumbering in Clinton County.

But by the end of the century, the lumber industry was declining; persistent flood damage to the log booms and the canal and depletion of the forest finally put an end to an era for the city. Fortunately, other industries were established, providing a new economic base for Lock Haven as it entered the 20th century. Furniture, paper, firebricks, and silk were all produced in the city.

Much like other rural cities and towns along the river, the City of Lock Haven has seen a number of boom and bust cycles through its history. Changes in the manufacturing industry around the country had a significant impact on Lock Haven.

In 1938, the Piper Aircraft Corporation began producing small planes on the site of the old silk mills. Piper Aircraft remained one of the city's largest employers until a combination of a major flood and an ownership struggle resulted in the relocation of the company to Florida in the 1980s.

Lock Haven's many churches and distinct neighborhoods gave the town a unique identity and sense of place. As Lock Haven developed, churches were constructed replacing home services and meetinghouses. Churches offered a source of strength for families. Art and entertainment thrived throughout the years. Lifelong residents can tell stories about church buildings and former places of entertainment. Lock Haven had created a sense of place. Photographs taken by early photographers like John W. C. Floyd offered hundreds of views of life during the late 1800s.

The river, which brought both wealth and prosperity, also brought destruction of those individual communities and the loss of the very identity that made Lock Haven what it is today. Time and again it was the people of this community who showed their strength and determination and continually worked on revitalization efforts.

It is the communities of Lock Haven—the communities in business and fraternal organizations, communities of faith, neighborhood communities with strong cultural heritages, and communities bound by service to each other and to this country—that have truly formed Lock Haven's identity.

Today Lock Haven remains the largest city in Clinton County with an estimated population of 9,000. While there is still a manufacturing presence in the city, major employers represent the educational, health, and social services sectors. Home to major employers such as First Quality Tissue and Lock Haven Hospital, Lock Haven is once again forming its identity.

Established in 1870, Lock Haven University, originally the Central State Normal School, is now one of the largest employers in the city. The university hosts approximately 4,500 students each year and offers 57 undergraduate degree programs and three graduate programs.

Capitalizing on the resources and beauty of the community, tourism is becoming a growing industry. The area offers an increasing number of outdoor events and festivals with access to scenic views, hiking, boating, and numerous other outdoor recreational activities.

Lock Haven is a unique find, offering the beauty of the river, the mountains, and a rich architecture. And Lock Haven's identity can be still be found in its communities and in the people determined to revitalize Main Street while maintaining a unique history and sense of place.

# *One*

# Jerry Church's "Lockhaven"

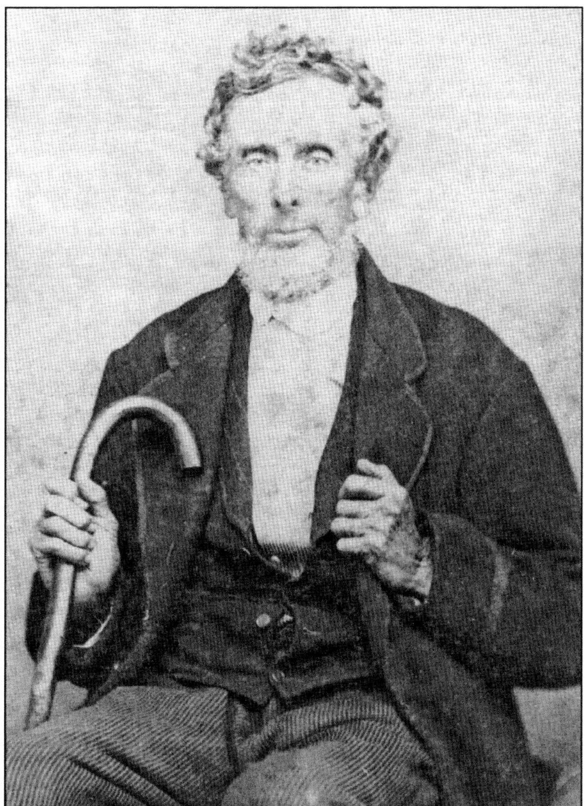

Lock Haven's founder, Jeremiah Church, was described as a traveler, spectator, and adventurer. To his family, he was kindly, a great storyteller and friend to all. Although he only remained in Lock Haven until 1845, his contributions can be seen in early photographs. Church described the progress of the town after 10 years: "it is a beautiful village and a place of considerable business." (Courtesy of Annie Halenbake Ross Library.)

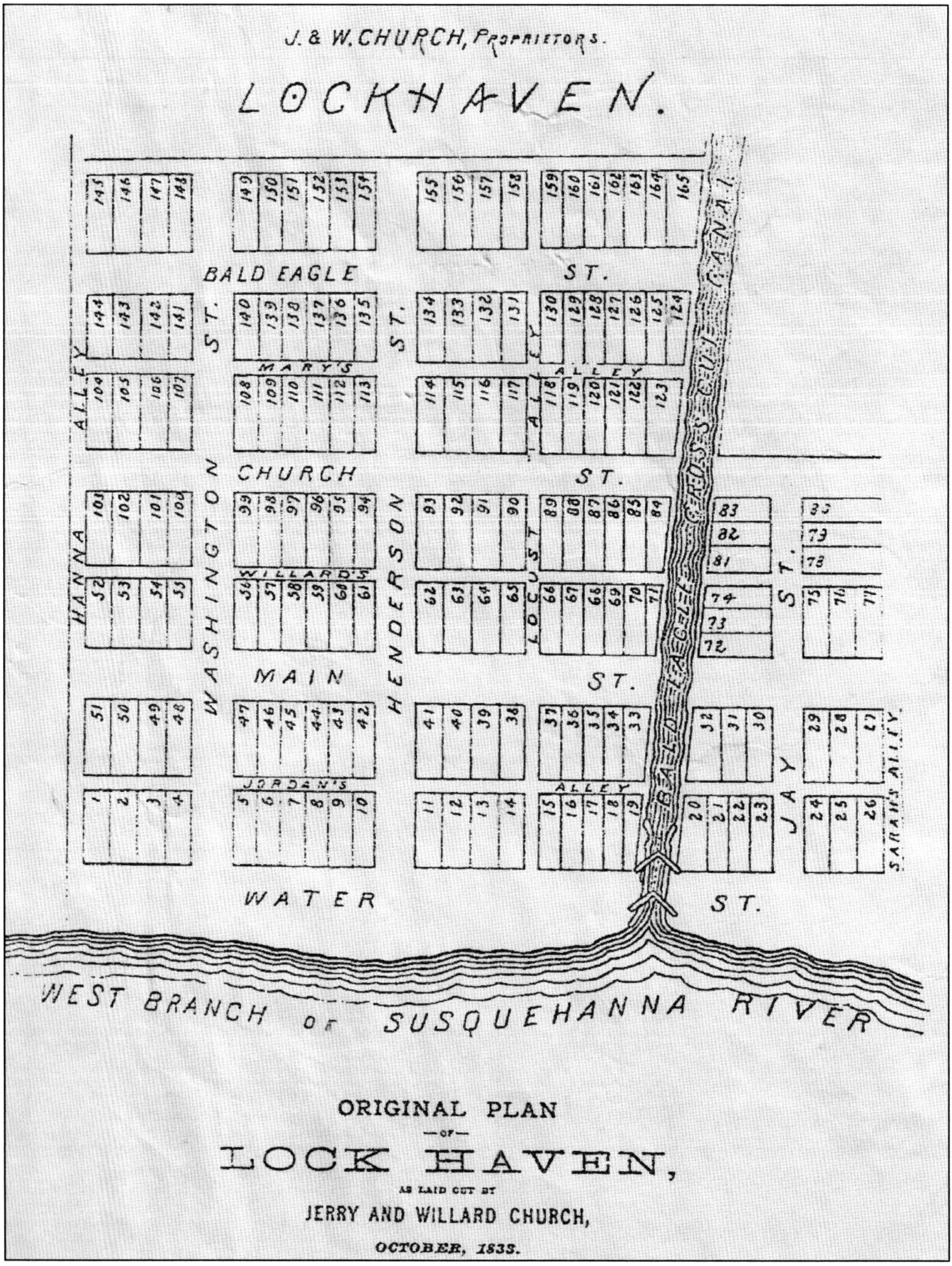


Pictured here, the original plan for Lock Haven as designed by Jerry and Willard Church included 165 lots. Church paid a total of $20,000 to Dr. John Henderson of Huntingdon: $5,000 when he took possession, with the balance to be paid in two years. A $50 bill was paid to bind their agreement. Church, ready to start the new town, plotted out the map in October 1833. The lots were made available at a public auction in November with the title and possession to be given the following April. The lots sold quickly enough that Church was able to pay off all debt a year early. (Courtesy of the Clinton County Historical Society.)

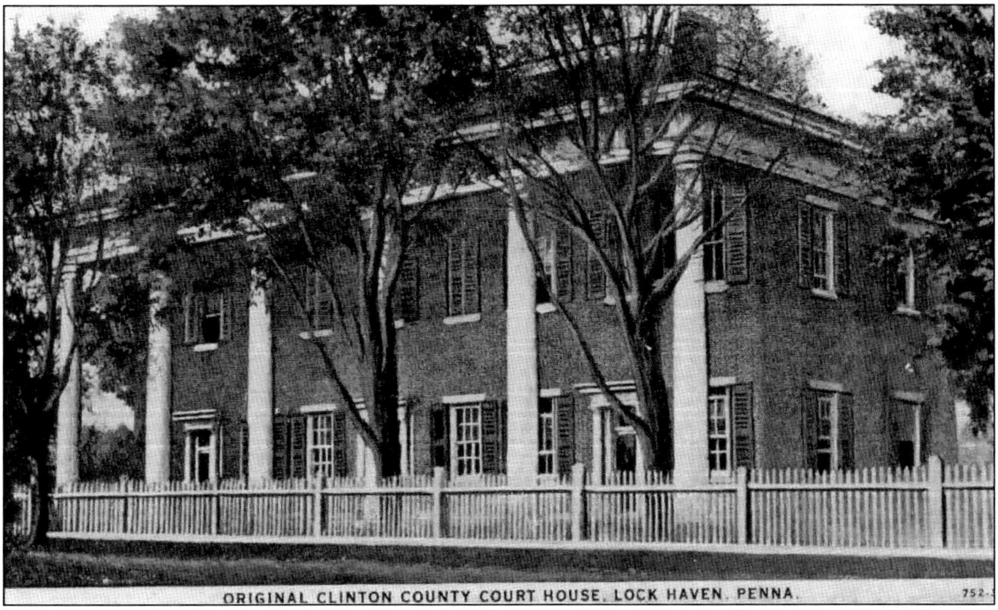


John Morehead and G. Hower Jr. and Company were the contractors for the county's first courthouse, which was completed in 1843 for $12,703.60. The addition of a fence and "necessary," along with some extras, brought the cost to $13,558.85. This building was the Clinton County Courthouse for 26 years. It was built on the land where Robb Elementary School now stands. (Courtesy of Annie Halenbake Ross Library.)

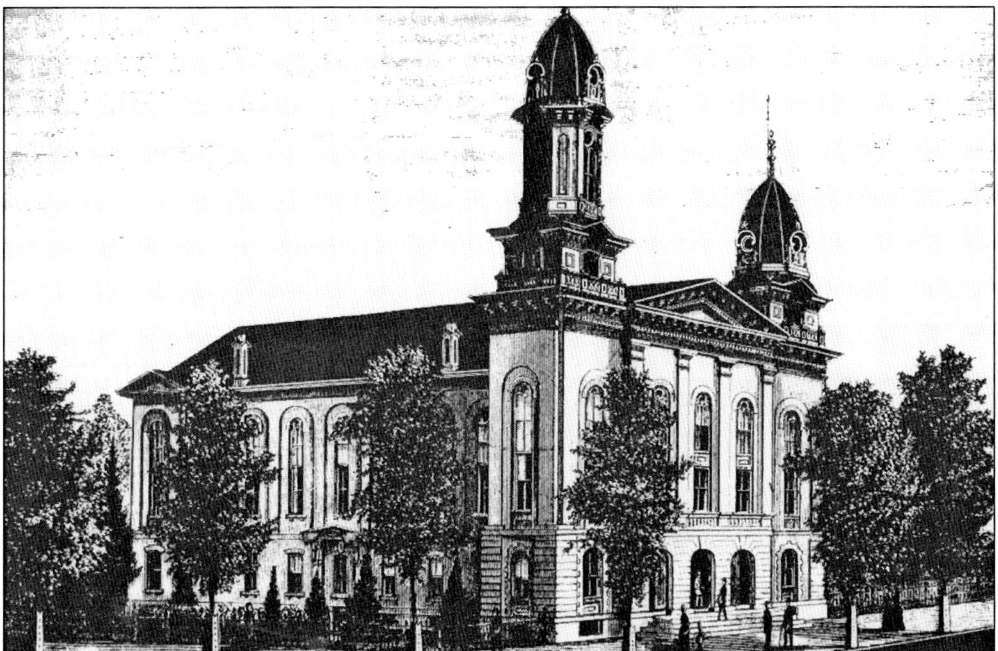

The first meeting of the Clinton County Commissioners in the new Clinton County Courthouse was held on February 8, 1869. Located at the corner of Jay and Water Streets, the final cost of this building was $102,464. Samuel Sloan and Addison Hutton of Philadelphia were the architects. (Courtesy of Annie Halenbake Ross Library.)

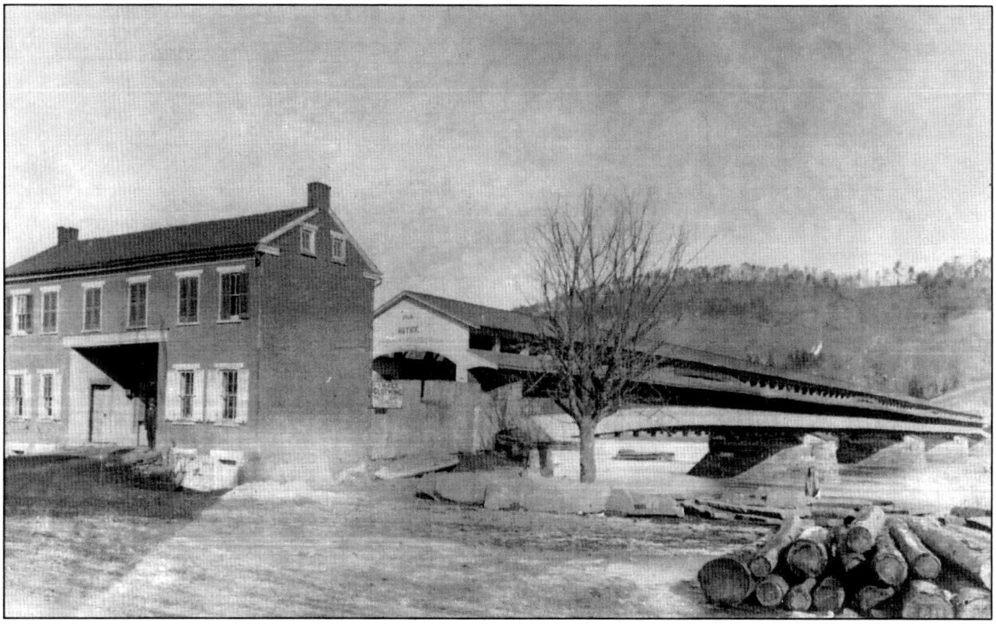

The old wooden covered bridge that crossed the river at Jay Street was built in 1852 and cost $25,000. The two-story brick Toll House was located on the Lock Haven side of the river and stood immediately at the end of the bridge. The bridge was destroyed in a fire in 1919 and was replaced by a steel structure resting on three piers and two abutments. (Courtesy of the Clinton County Historical Society.)

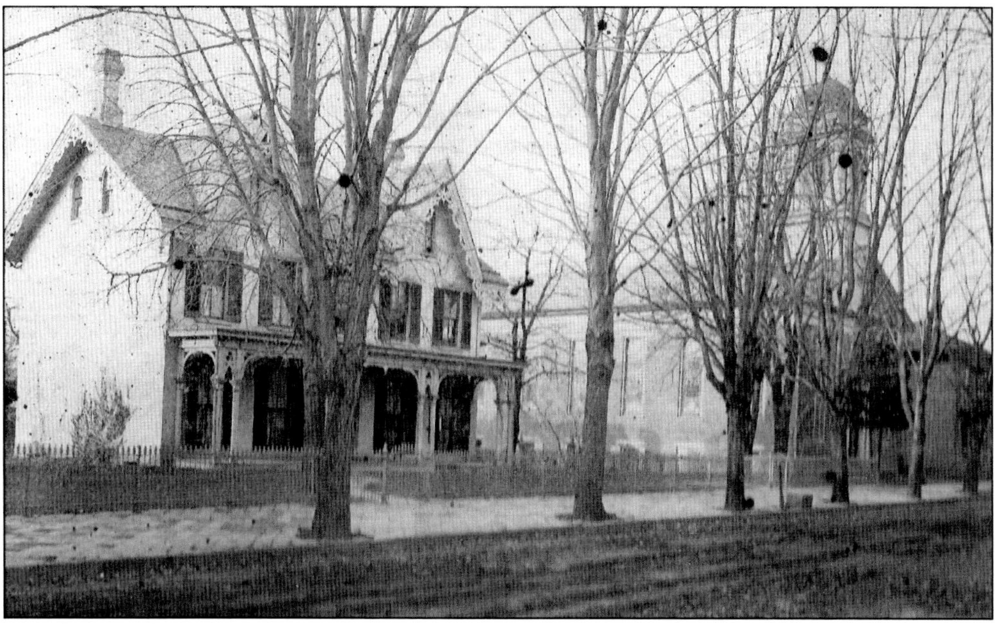

Dr. John Henderson of Huntingdon County built this farmhouse in 1833 for his 200-acre farm. In 1834, Jerry Church purchased the farm and laid out the town of Lock Haven. John and Walter Devling obtained the property in 1834 and operated a popular tavern there. This house has served as a farmhouse, tavern, and doctor's office and is now home to the Heisey Museum. (Courtesy of the Clinton County Historical Society.)

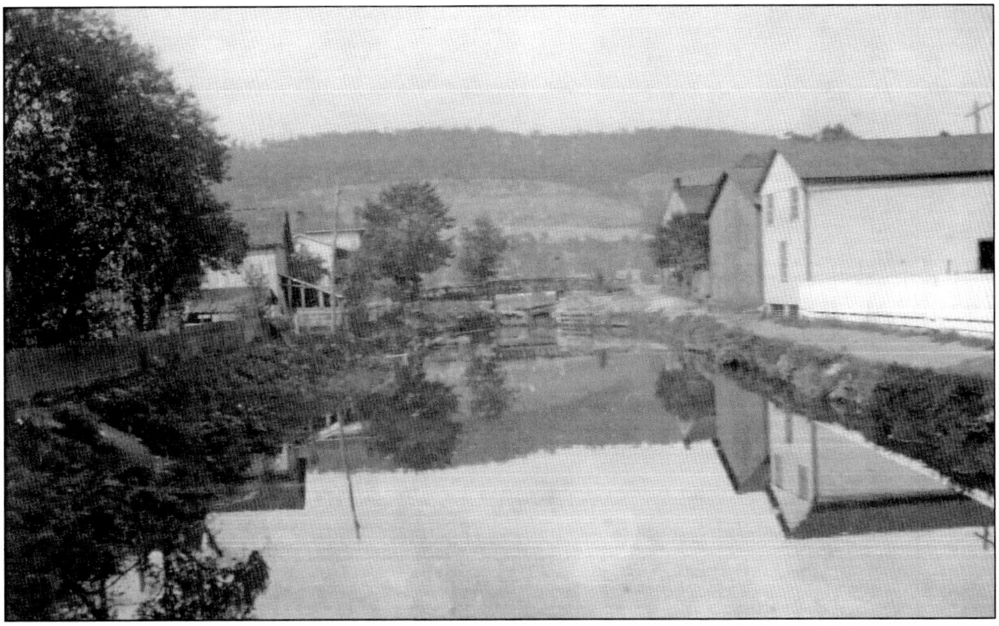

The West Branch Canal opened in 1834. Pictured here is a view of the Bald Eagle crosscut canal from East Main Street. The Bald Eagle crosscut canal ran from the West Branch through Lock Haven and Flemington to Bald Eagle Creek. Canal boats carried passengers, mail, and cargo. The canal was used very little after the 1889 flood. (Courtesy of the Clinton County Historical Society.)

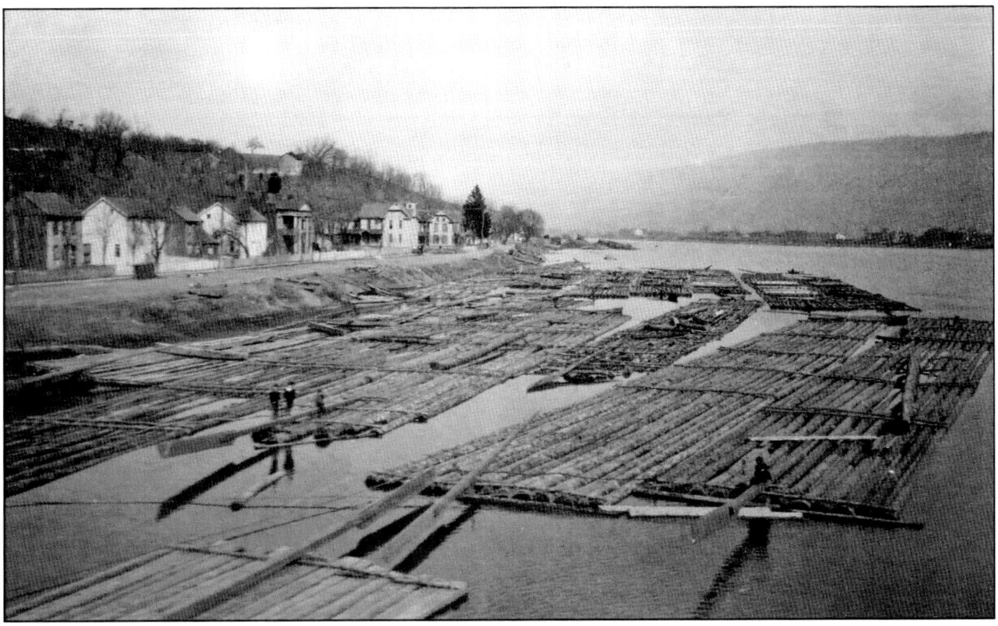

Oak, white pine, hemlock, maple, and cherry trees populated the county in its early years. The West Branch of the Susquehanna River became a highway for transporting this vast wealth as it was harvested. As the lumber industry grew, log rafts filled the river. These rafts, constructed of logs placed side by side and fastened with lash poles, were used to transport logs and lumber. (Courtesy of the Annie Halenbake Ross Library.)

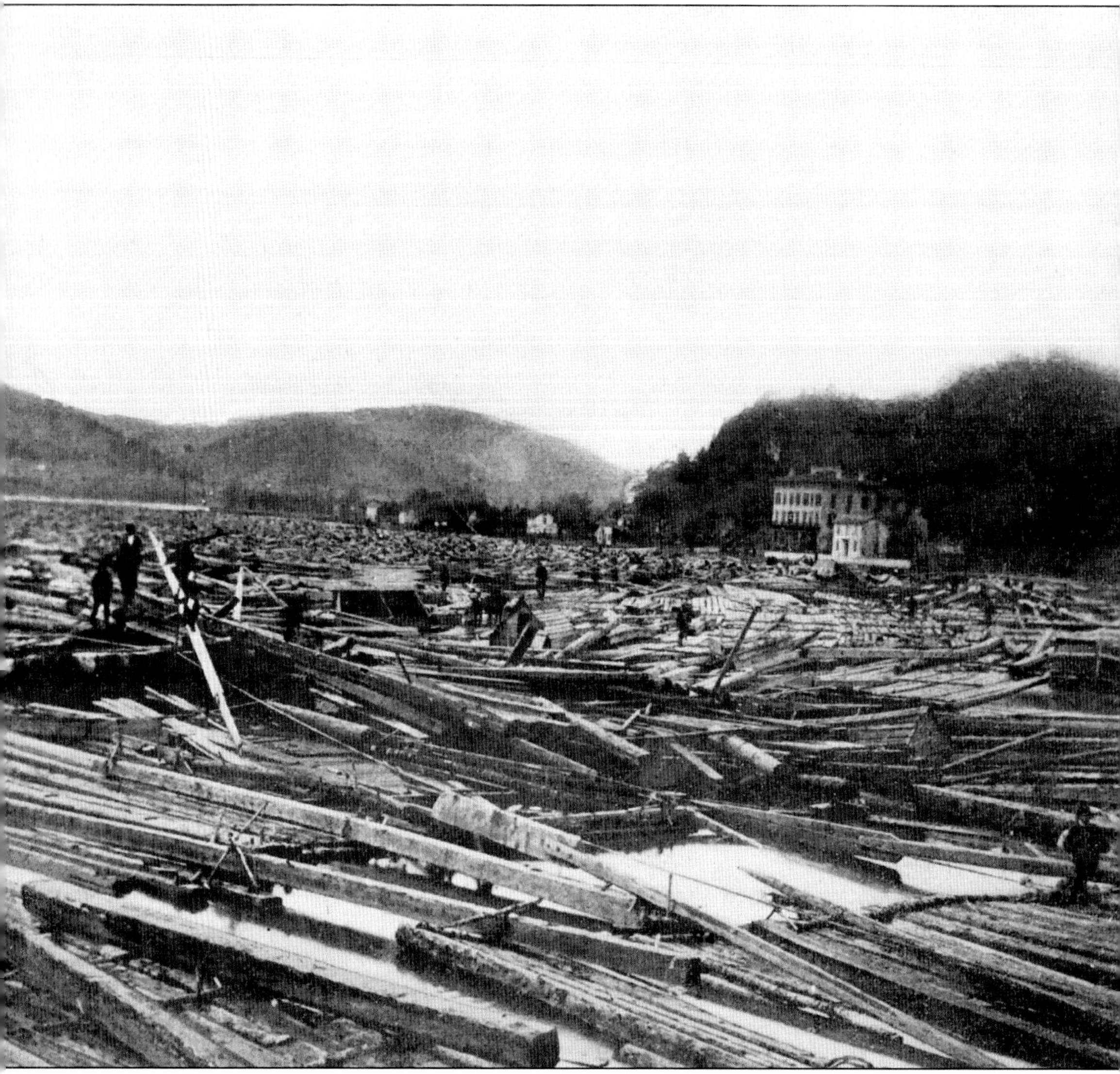

At the height of the lumber season, hundreds of rafts floated down the river at once. Jams were a challenge for log drivers and breaking log jams called for great strength. The greatest log jam occurred in 1874 when a raft too big to pass through became wedged and caused all river traffic to stop. More than 200 rafts and thousands of logs were jammed. A crew led by Joe Colberth worked to break the jam. When the logjam broke, thousands of feet of lumber were released and were caught downriver at the Williamsport boom. (Courtesy of the Annie Halenbake Ross Library.)

# *Two*

# ALL IN A DAY'S WORK

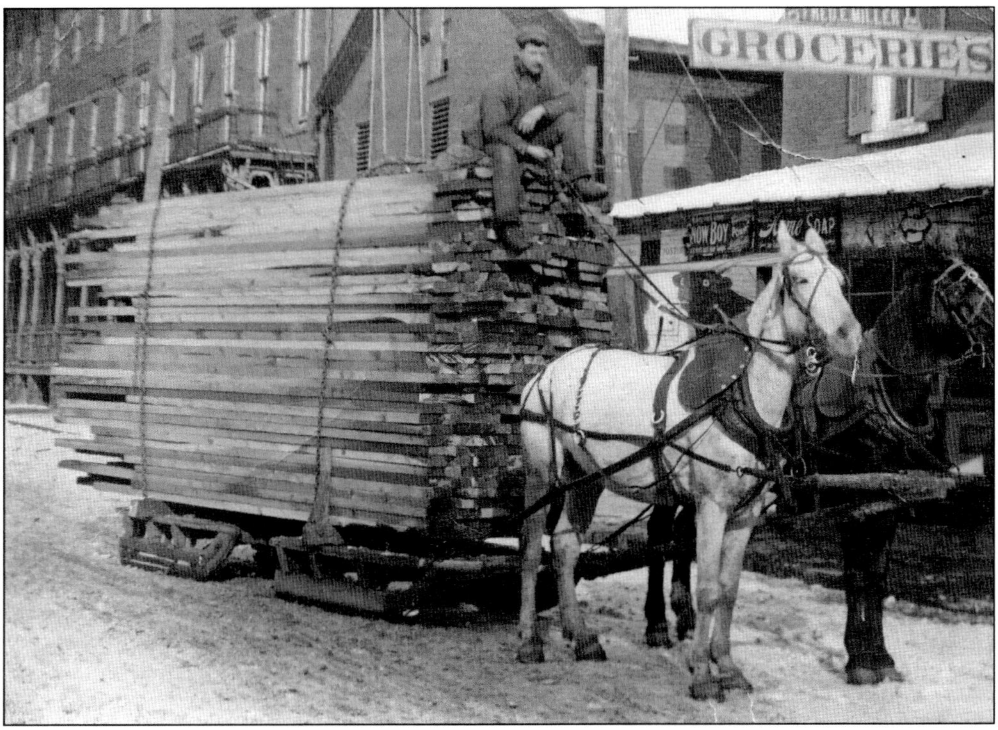


In the earliest days, when Lock Haven was a lumber center, workers called "boom rats" sorted timber in the river, branding it and sending it on for delivery to sawmills. Lock Haven became a town of sawmills, iron foundries, and tanneries. Merchants' ads boasted well-stocked stores, modern goods, fair prices, and courteous service. While the nature of work evolved over time, the work ethic of the community remained strong. (Courtesy of the Clinton County Historical Society.)

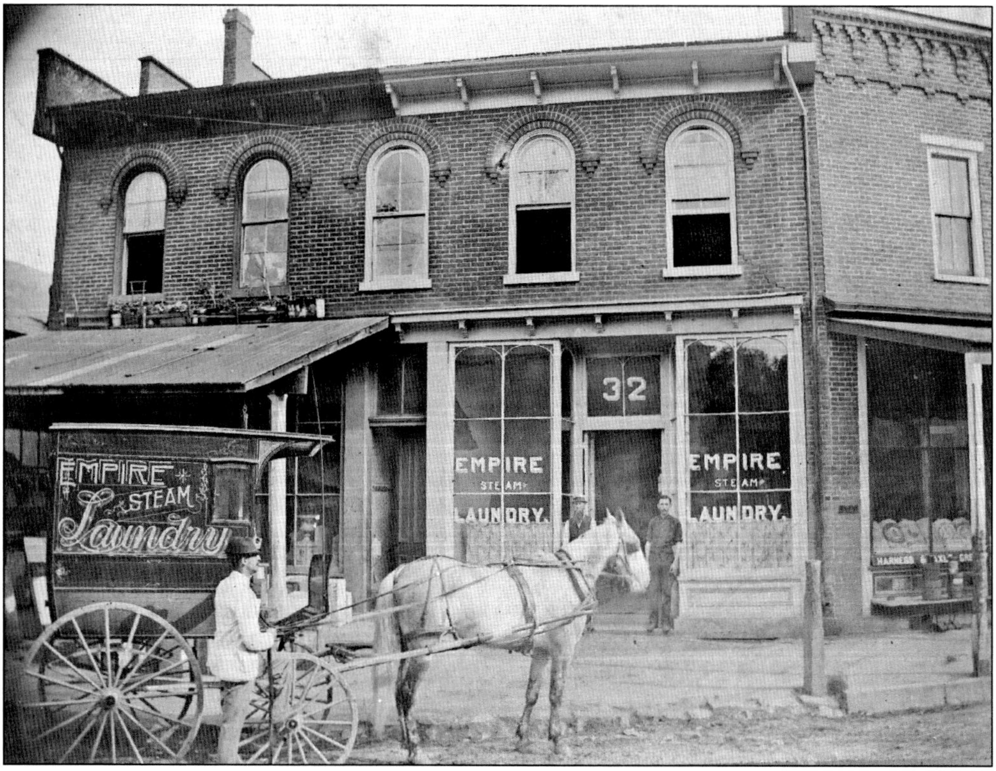


Lock Haven Steam Laundry opened in 1902 on Corning Street and was owned and operated by P. P. Rittman and Harry T. Rittman, natives of Lock Haven. The business had 35 employees, two delivery wagons, and served all the hotels in town. (Courtesy of the Annie Halenbake Ross Library.)

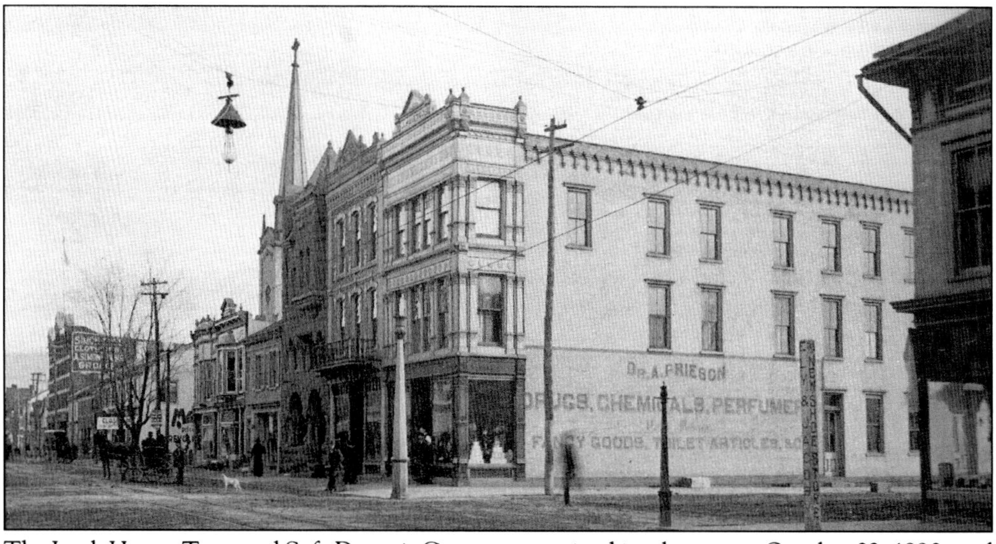

The Lock Haven Trust and Safe Deposit Company received its charter on October 22, 1890, and began business in January 1891. The bank was located in a brownstone building on East Main Street near Vesper Street. The bank can be seen in this picture—it is the third building from the corner. (Courtesy of the Annie Halenbake Ross Library.)

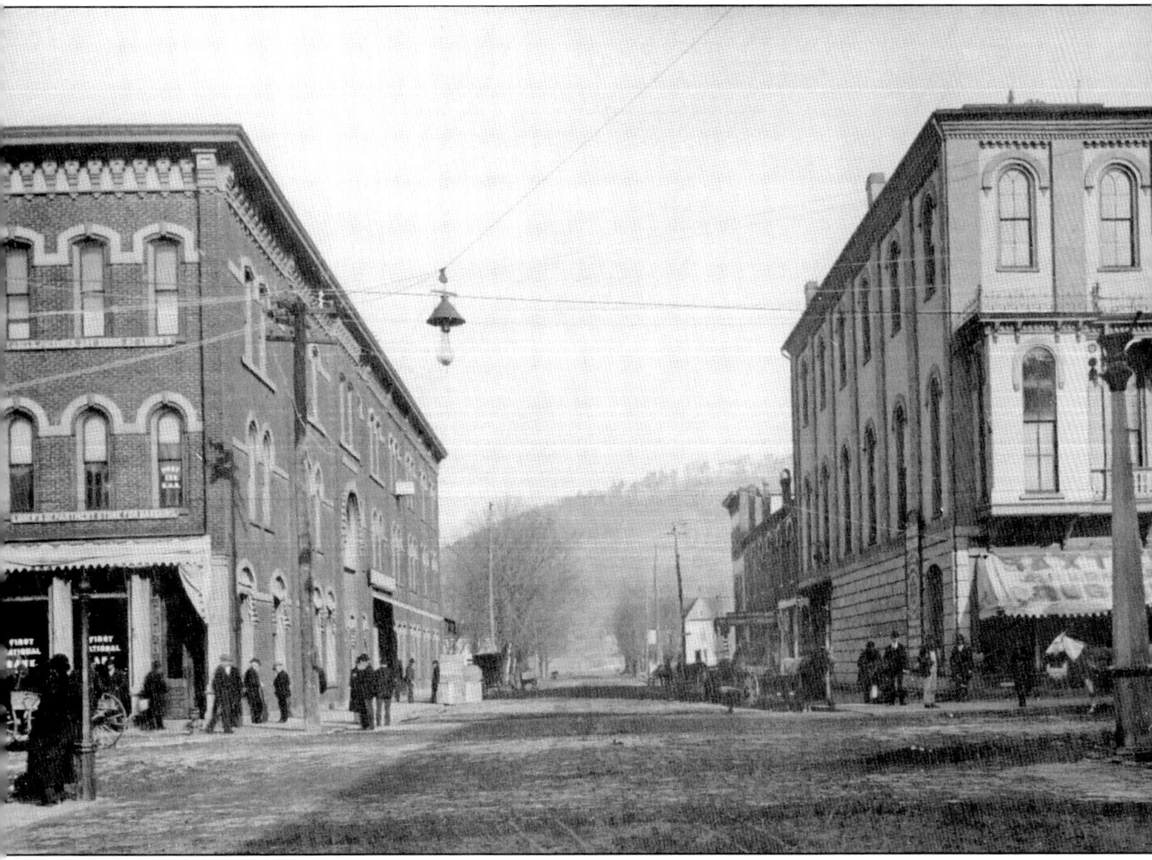

The original capital for the First National Bank of Lock Haven was $100,000. When this sum had been raised, it had to be taken to Washington to secure the bank's charter, because at that time the money could not be sent by express or bank draft. With the money in his possession, the president of the bank, T. C. Kintzing, put it in a carpetbag and drove with it to his home where the family guarded it all night. The next day he took a train at Chathams Run station, which was not as busy as the Lock Haven train station. In Washington, Kintzing deposited the currency in the U.S. Treasury and received all new bills. Kintzing returned to Lock Haven and the bank opened for business on October 15, 1864, in a building on East Water Street between Grove and Jay Streets. The bank relocated to the Exchange Building, seen on the left in this picture, at the corner of Main and Vesper Streets. (Courtesy of the Clinton County Historical Society.)

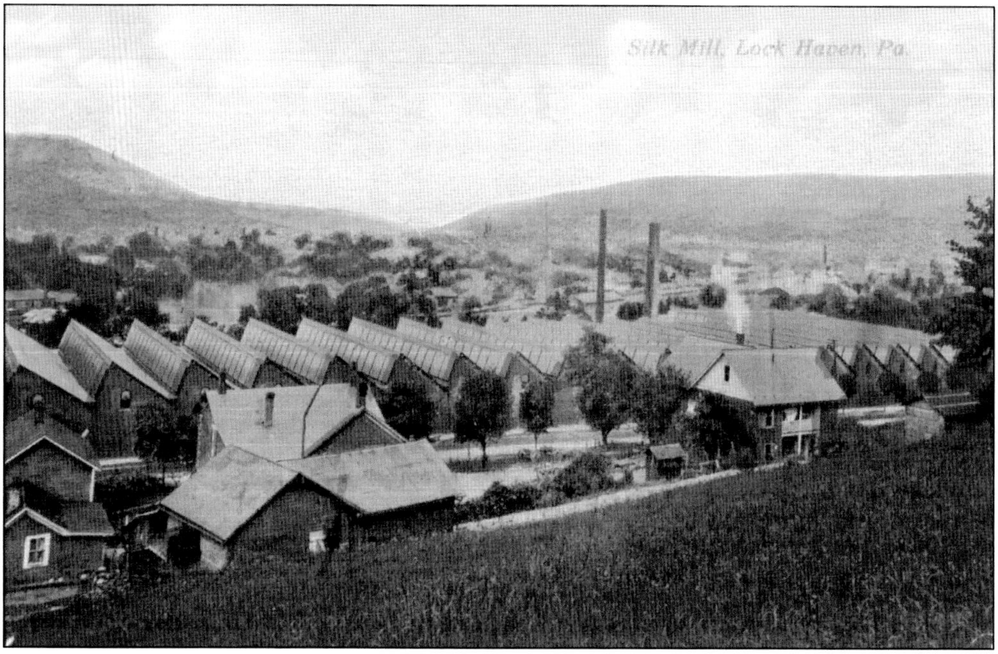


Established in 1898, the Lock Haven Silk Mills Etc. was located on Fairview Street. The main office was located in Bloomsburg, Pennsylvania. In 1902, the company employed 400 people and produced about 4,000 yards of finished silk each day. (Courtesy of the Annie Halenbake Ross Library.)

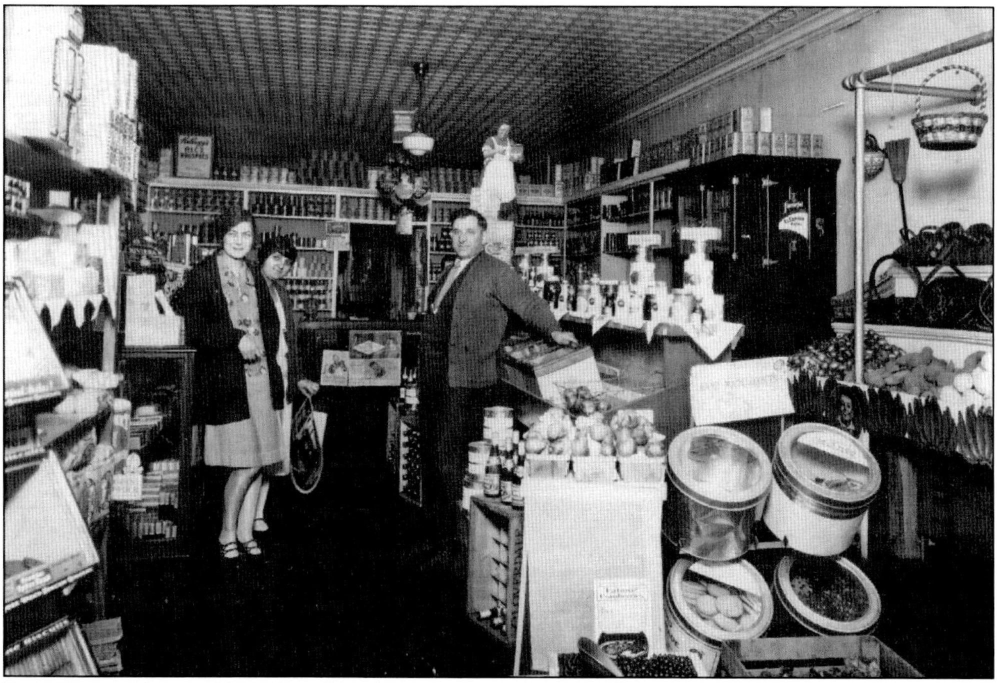

Everyday staples could be found at this grocery store owned and operated by Anthony Reitano. This downtown business was located on Bellefonte Avenue in the 1920s. (Courtesy of the Annie Halenbake Ross Library.)

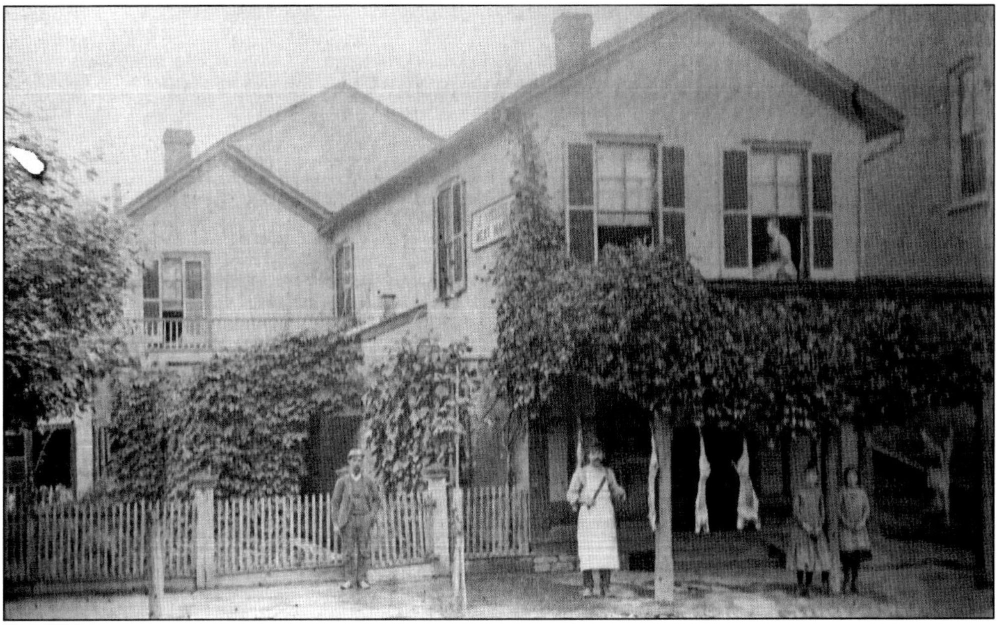

Nitsche's Meat Market was a landmark on East Main Street in Lock Haven for many years. Nitsche's was operated by John Nitsche and then by his son William. The frame building on East Main Street opposite the Roxy Theater was razed in 1931. William Nitsche opened the first meat market in the village at this stand. The picture is dated 1886. (Courtesy of the Annie Halenbake Ross Library.)

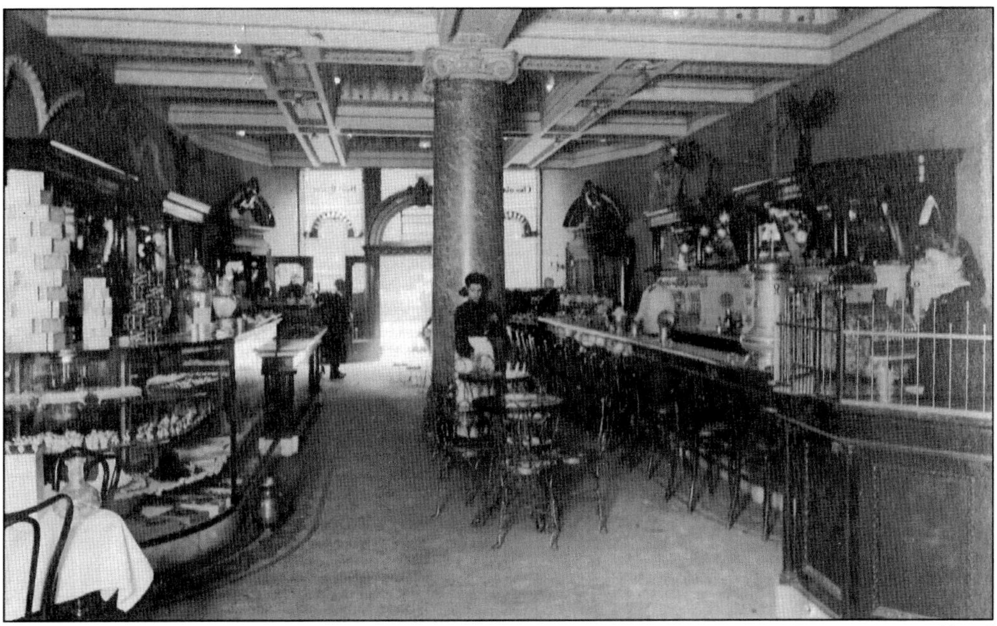

In 1906, B. C. Achenbach and Sons was established at 121 East Main Street. The company offered an ice cream and catering business. Products included cakes, pastry rolls, and confectioneries. They also catered weddings, banquets, parties, and social functions. The business's ice cream bar logo is still embedded in the sidewalk in front of this building today. (Courtesy of the Annie Halenbake Ross Library.)

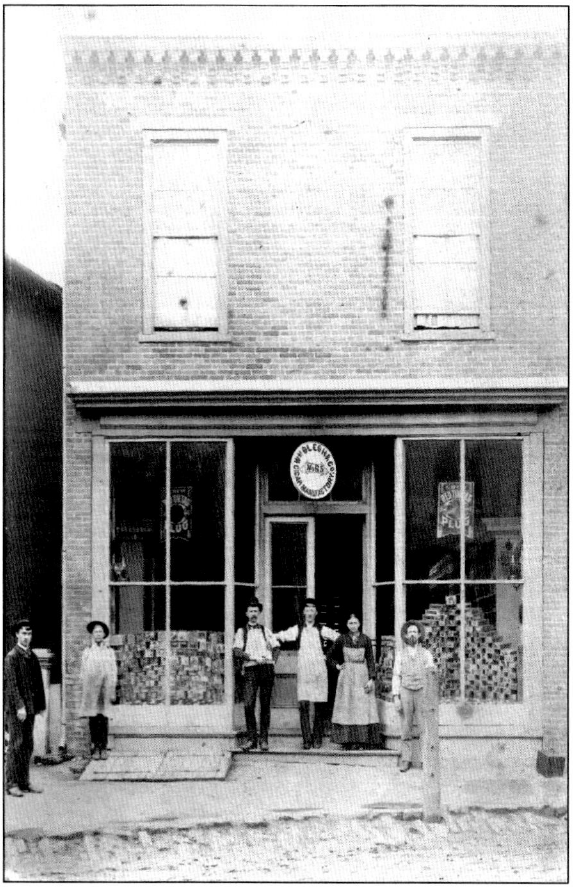

By 1872, there were six cigar businesses in Lock Haven. Sixty cigar makers and several sales agents were employed at the cigar manufacturer operated by Allen Sterner. Located at 119 East Main Street, the business was established by William Sterner in 1865. The factory and retail store offered all the leading brands of cigars, tobaccos, and supplies. Allen Sterner was later a city alderman and mayor of Lock Haven. (Courtesy of the Annie Halenbake Ross Library.)

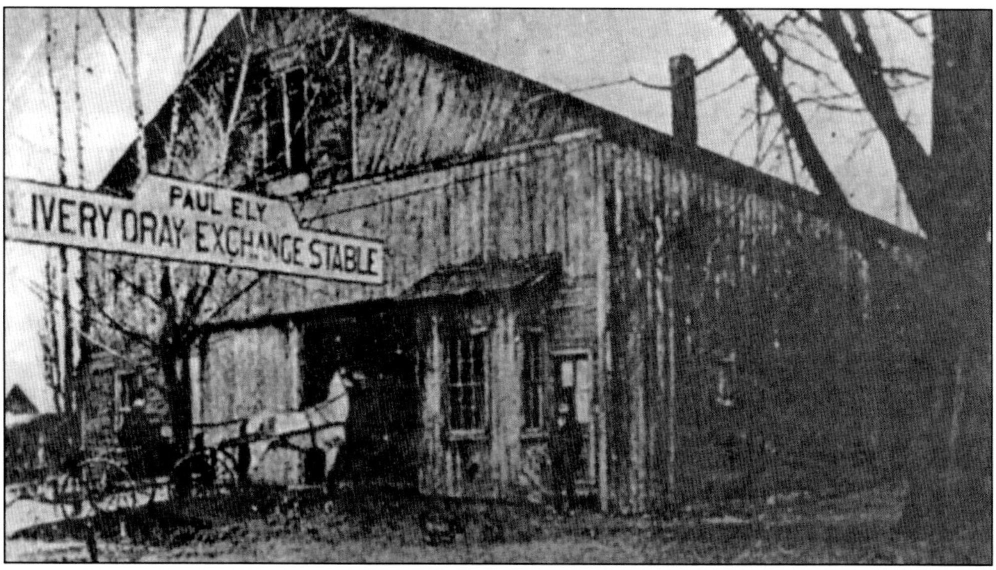


Pictured here, the Paul Ely Livery Dray and Exchange stable was located on North Vesper Street at the river. In the late 1800s when traveling salesmen and others traveled in town, they hired a horse and buggy from the local livery stable. (Courtesy of the Annie Halenbake Ross Library.)

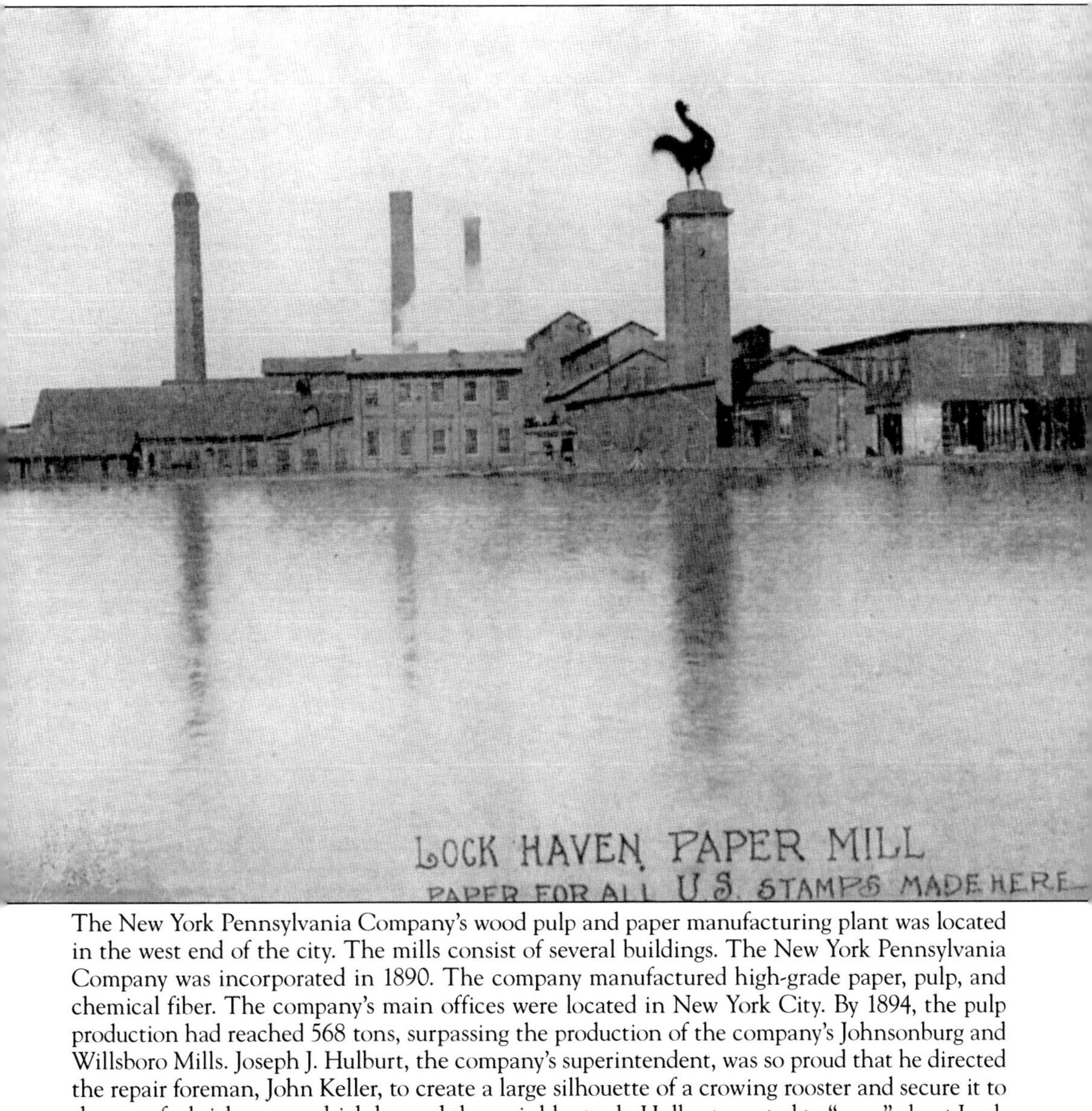


The New York Pennsylvania Company's wood pulp and paper manufacturing plant was located in the west end of the city. The mills consist of several buildings. The New York Pennsylvania Company was incorporated in 1890. The company manufactured high-grade paper, pulp, and chemical fiber. The company's main offices were located in New York City. By 1894, the pulp production had reached 568 tons, surpassing the production of the company's Johnsonburg and Willsboro Mills. Joseph J. Hulburt, the company's superintendent, was so proud that he directed the repair foreman, John Keller, to create a large silhouette of a crowing rooster and secure it to the top of a brick tower, which housed the sprinkler tank. Hulburt wanted to "crow" about Lock Haven's success. (Courtesy of the Annie Halenbake Ross Library.)

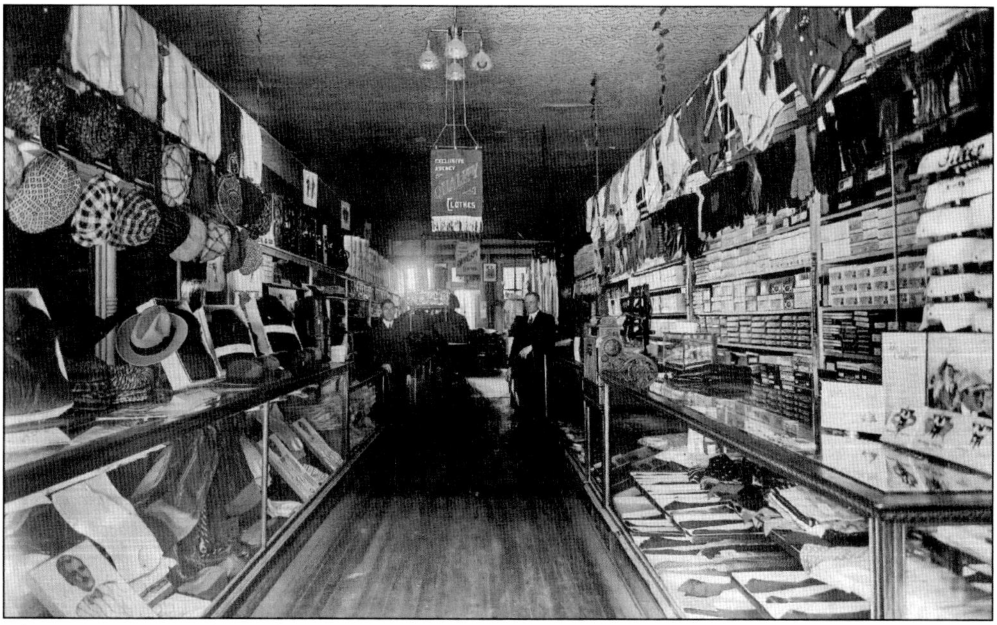

The Hurwitz Store, located at 127 East Main Street, offered all types of men's clothing. There's very little room behind the counter for all of the shirt boxes. This store offered everything from long underwear to gloves, shirts, ties, and hand-tailored clothes. Notice the ornate cash register on the right counter. Pictured here are John Forsht and Israel S. Hurwitz. (Courtesy of the Annie Halenbake Ross Library.)

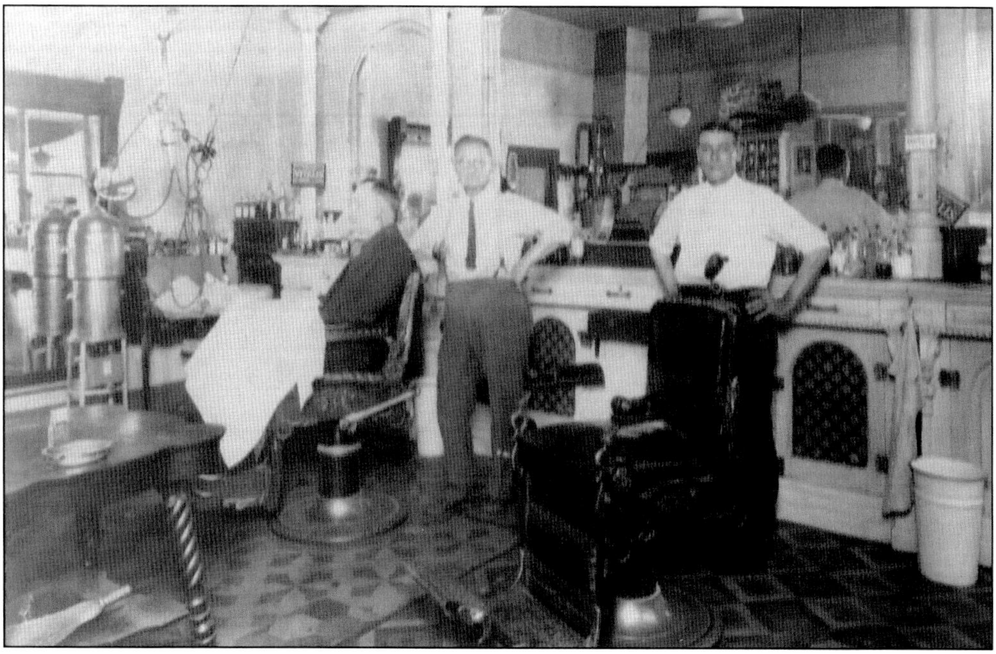

Heimer's Barbershop was located on Vesper Street in downtown Lock Haven. This view of the barbershop was taken after the shop had been remodeled. Harry H. Gramley, an apprentice, is seen at one of the chairs. Heimer's was reported to be one of the oldest continuously operated barbershops in town. (Courtesy of the Annie Halenbake Ross Library.)

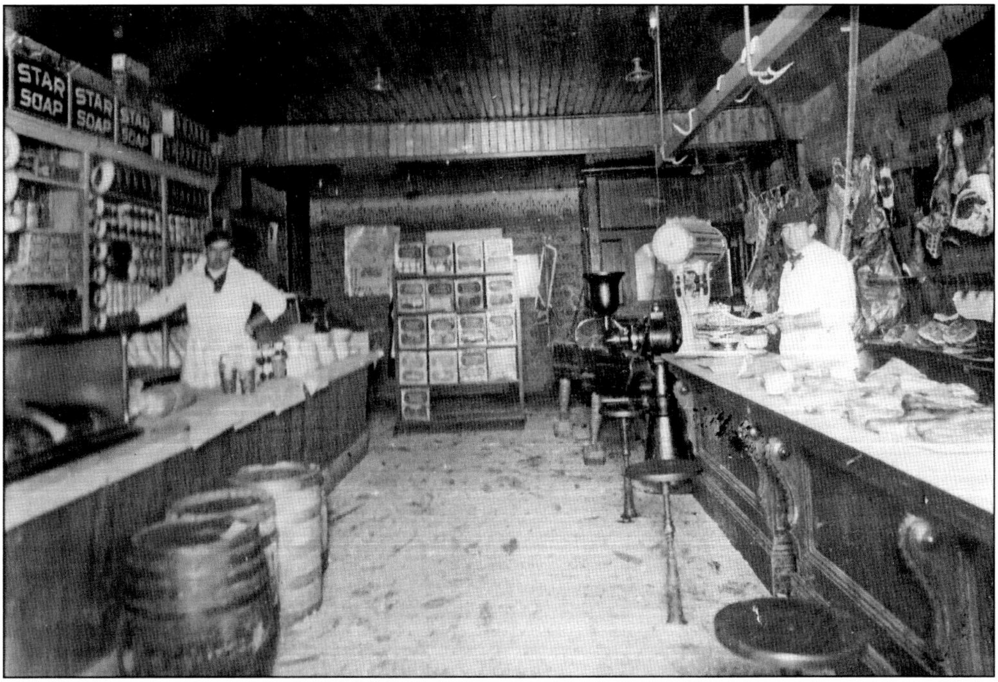


Butcher shops have come a long way since the Conklin Grocery-Butcher Shop on Henderson Street in 1912. Earle Conklin is on the left and Ollie Conklin is on the right. Notice the cuts of meat behind the counter ready for sale. (Courtesy of the Annie Halenbake Ross Library.)

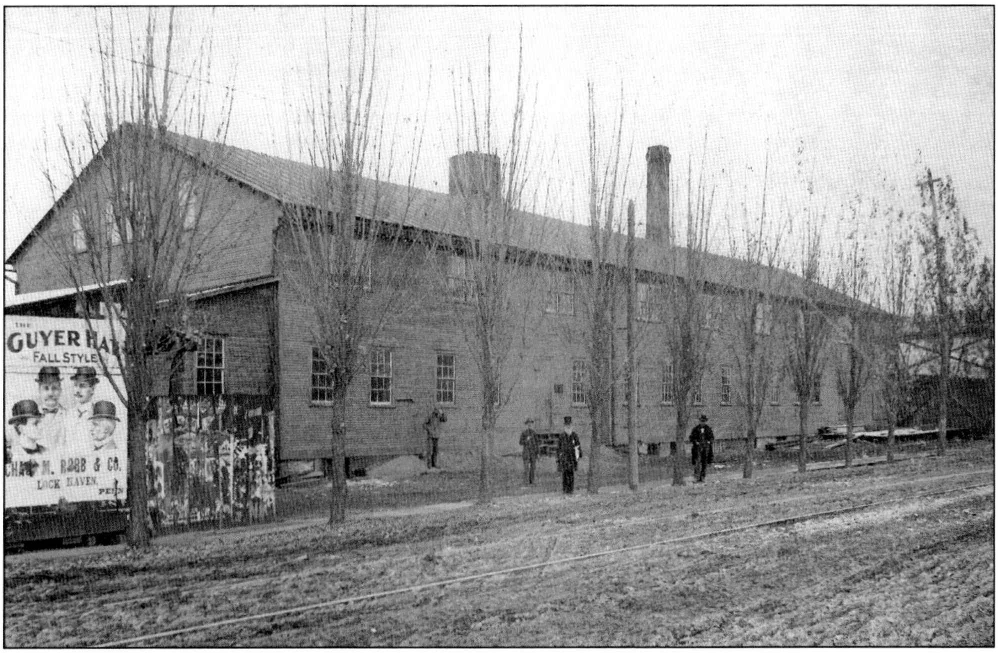


Hipple and Kintzing Planing Mill once occupied this site on Bellefonte Avenue in the Commerce Street area on the north side of the street. This picture taken in 1906 includes Ernest J. Herman, a foreman who specialized in reading blueprints and was known as "the colonel." (Courtesy of the Annie Halenbake Ross Library.)

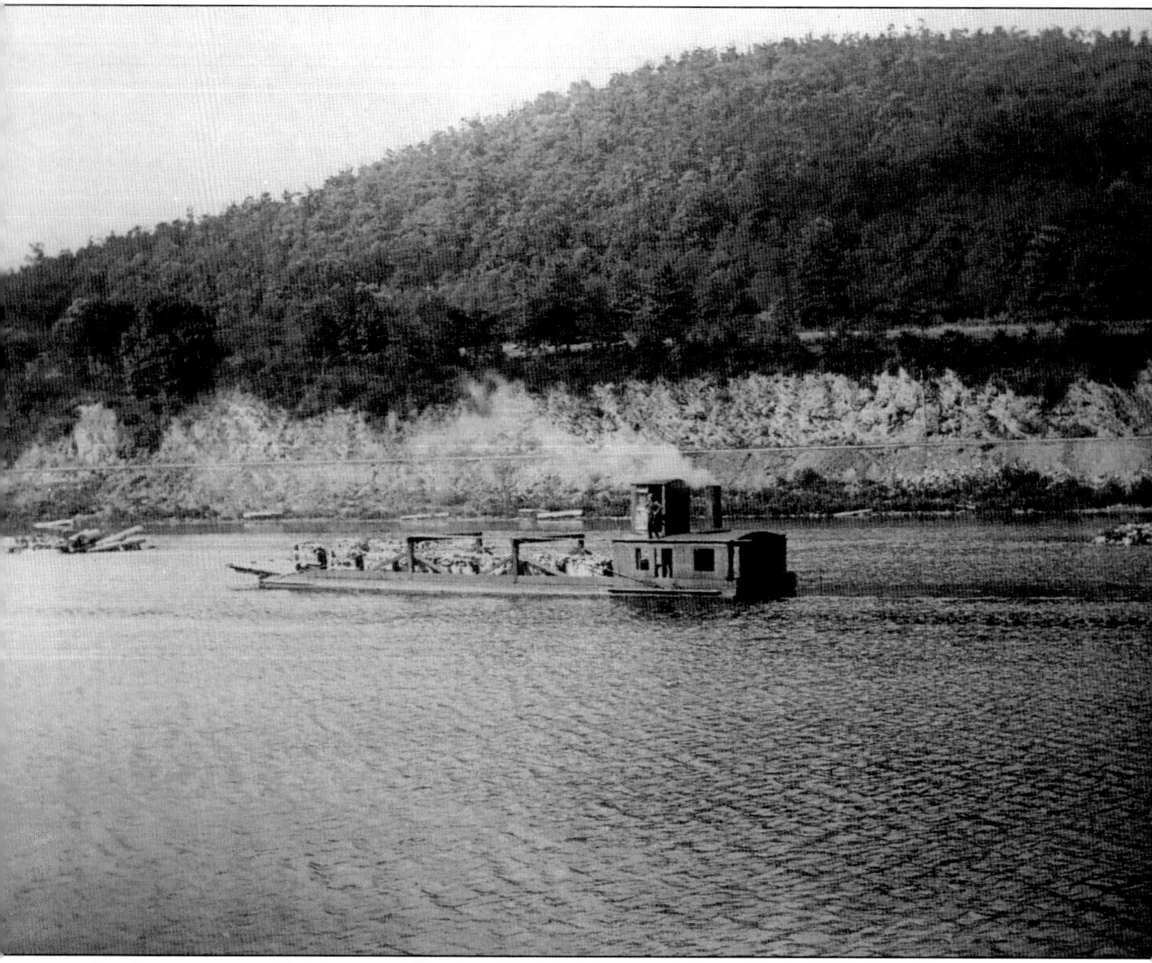

In this picture, a clay barge makes its way on the West Branch of the Susquehanna River from Queens Run Fire Brick Company. The company, organized in 1887, held 5,000 acres of fire clay mines in Queens Run. The barge was used to transport the clay to their plants in the city of Lock Haven. The company produced fire bricks and shipped them all across the country. In 1892, they produced 30,000 bricks per day and employed 160 people. (Courtesy of the Annie Halenbake Ross Library.)

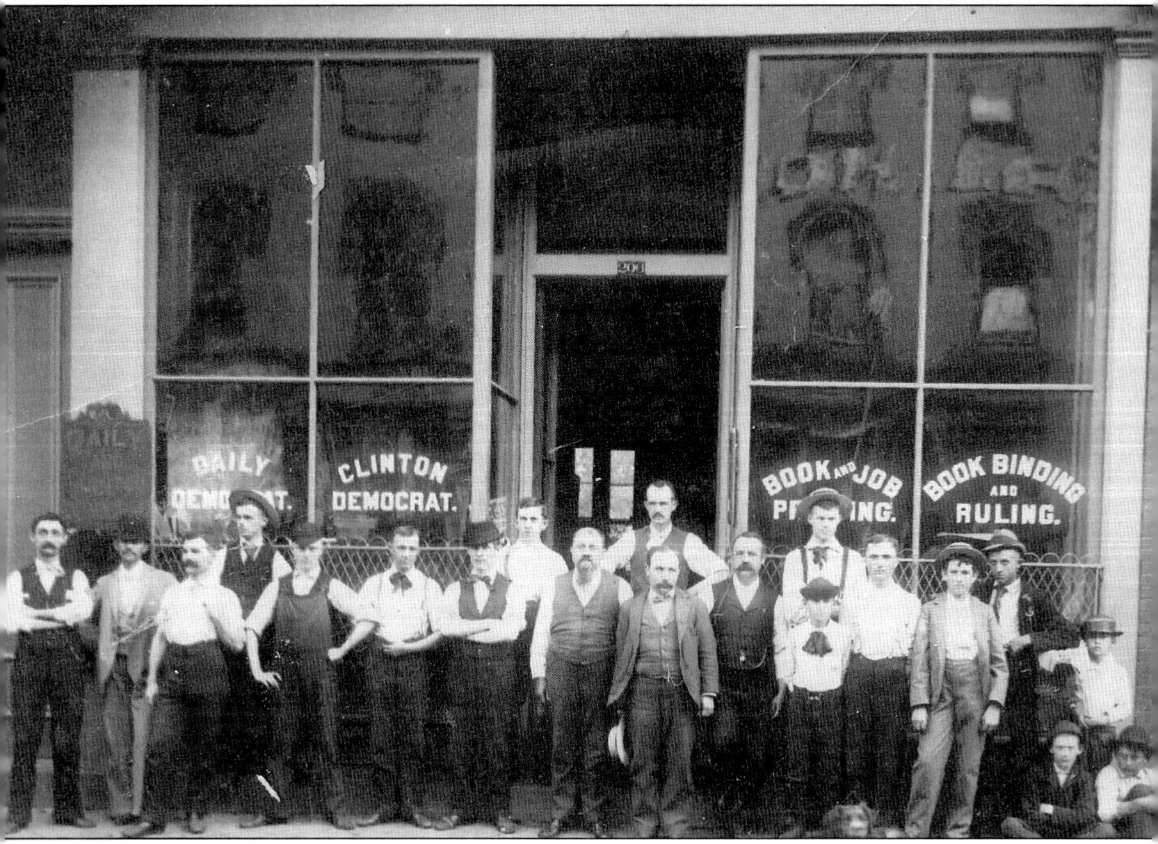


The first newspaper published in Clinton County was the *Eagle*, but in 1839 the name was changed to the *Clintonian*. A series of newspapers were published in the county including the *Clinton County Whig*, the *Clinton Tribune*, the *Tribune*, the *Watchman*, the *Lock Haven Press*, and the *Clinton County Democrat*. In 1845, the *Clinton Democrat* was established, and it remained in business until 1921. H. L. Dieffenbach merged the *Clinton County Democrat* and the *Clinton Democrat*, two rival newspapers, in 1845. Seen here are the employees of the newspaper. In 1892, the company offered a weekly four-page, 32-column sheet and a daily, four-page, 28-column sheet paper. Both papers were dedicated to supporting the principles of the Democratic Party. George Bowman established the *Clinton Republican* in 1863, which was considered the leading supporter of the Republican Party. (Courtesy of the Annie Halenbake Ross Library.)

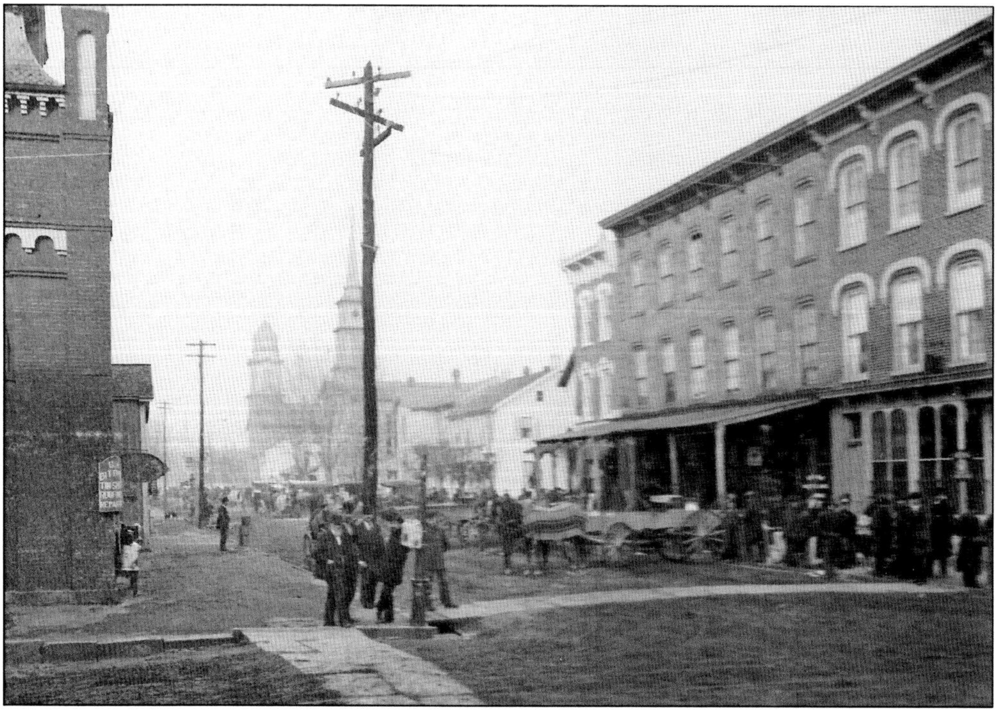

The Lock Haven Market House was built in 1868 on Grove and East Church Streets. In 1872, the city created a free curb market on Grove Street from Main to Bald Eagle Streets and Church Street from Grove to Vesper Streets. The Lock Haven outdoor market on Grove and East Church Streets is seen here. Also pictured at the 1940 Lock Haven curb market was Betty Shilling (below) selling her poultry. During market day in the early 1900s, the sidewalks were crowded with farm wagons. (Both, courtesy of the Annie Halenbake Ross Library.)

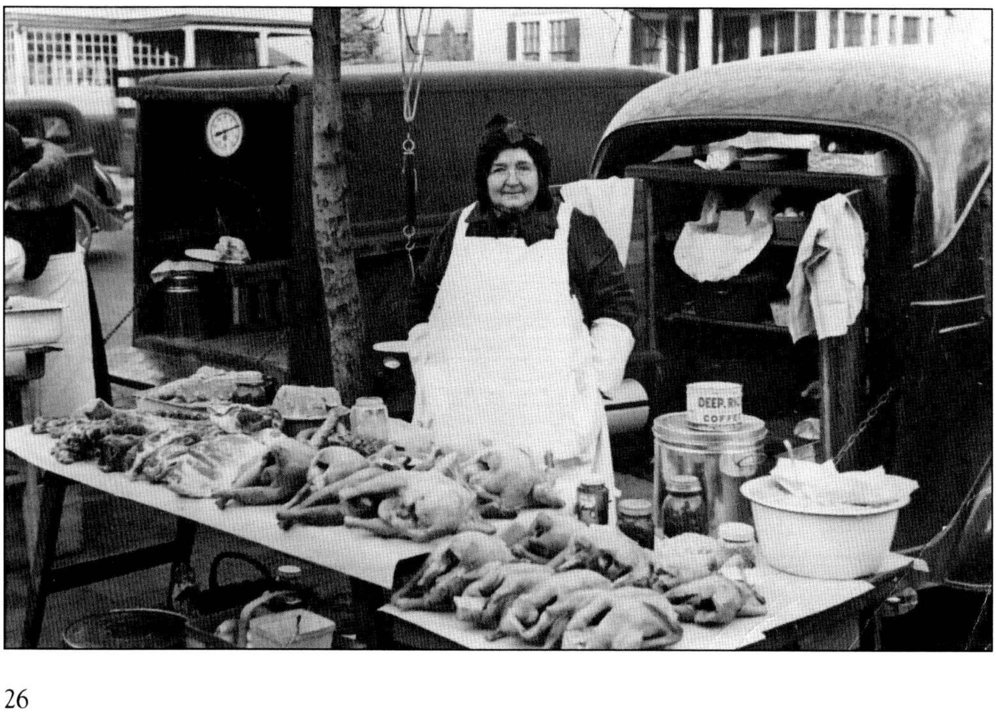

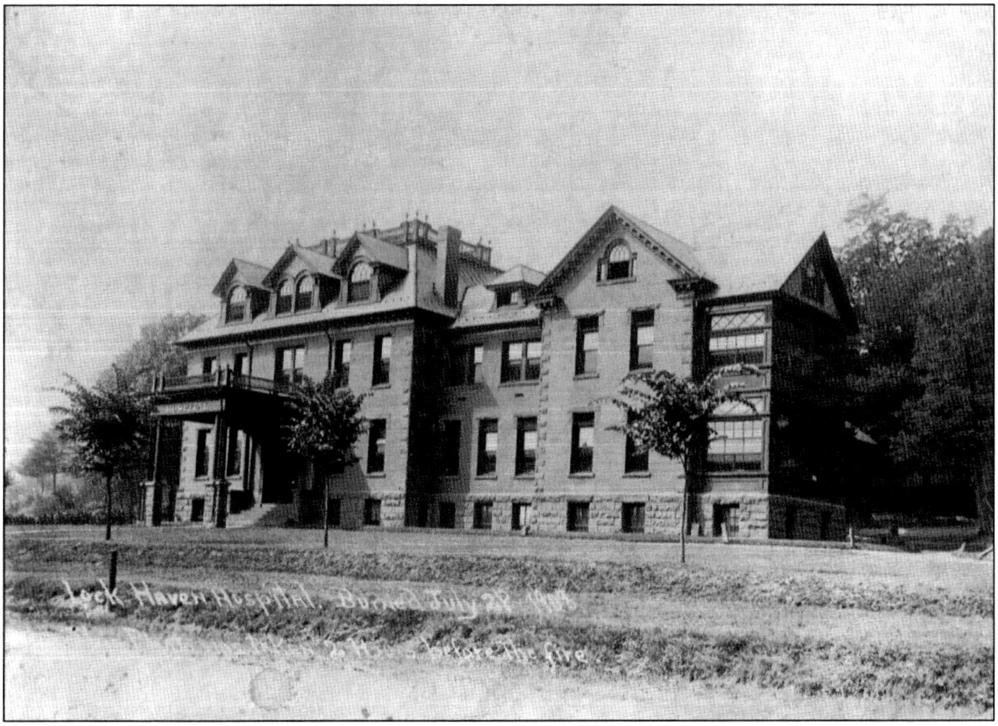


Lock Haven Hospital opened in a farmhouse on September 7, 1897. Dr. Rita B. Church was the superintendent. A training school was set up almost at once, and one pupil matriculated for a two-year course beginning in September 15, 1897. A new building was constructed on land donated by Wilson Kistler. The hospital was ready to receive patients on May 30, 1903. Cornelia Happersett was the superintendent from 1905 to 1908. On July 28, 1908, the hospital burned to the ground. The nurses' determination to save their patients from the fire resulted in the loss of their wardrobes and possessions. The hospital was totally remodeled in 1924 with modern equipment, an x-ray, and a heliotherapy department. (Both, courtesy of the Annie Halenbake Ross Library.)

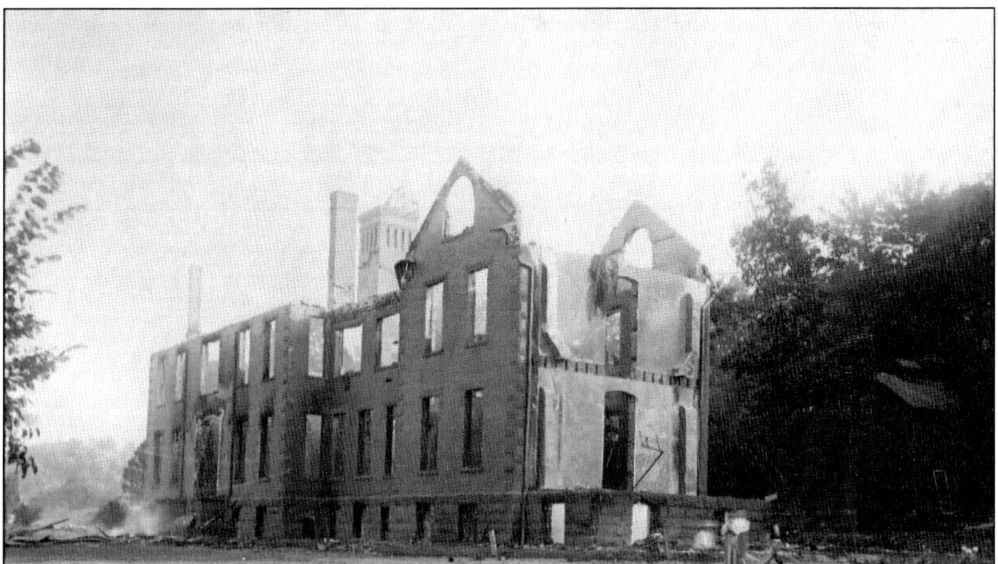

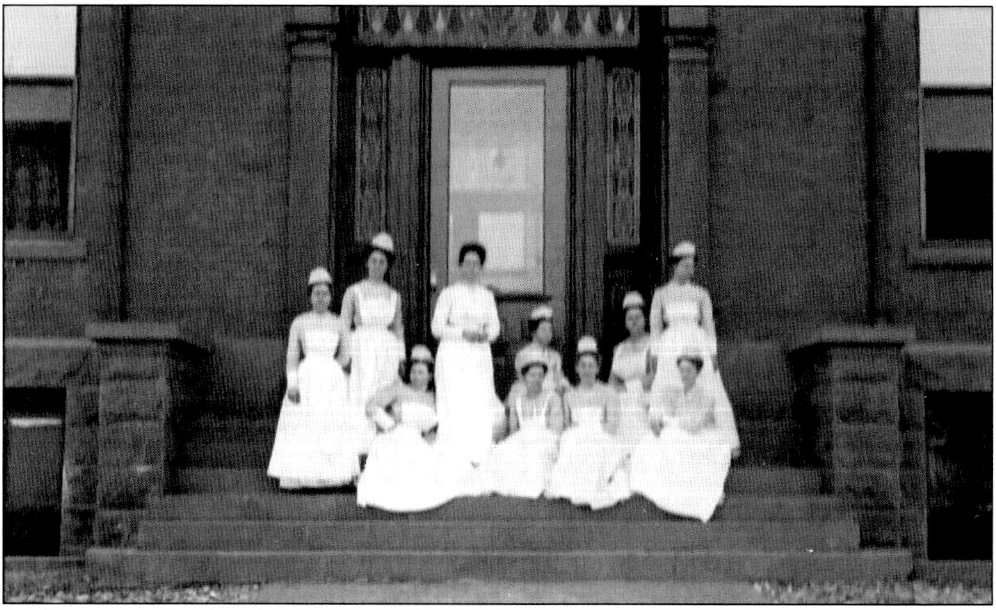

Student nurses stand on the steps at Lock Haven Hospital in the early 1900s. Mrs. Chamberlain, the superintendent, stands in the center. The hospital's nursing school closed in 1936 due to the Depression. Graduate nurses staffed the hospital from that time until October 1943, when the school of nursing was established. The first four classes admitted to the reestablished school were aided by a federal grant from the U.S. Cadet Nurse Corps. Once World War II came to an end, so did the cadet funds. (Courtesy of the Annie Halenbake Ross Library.)

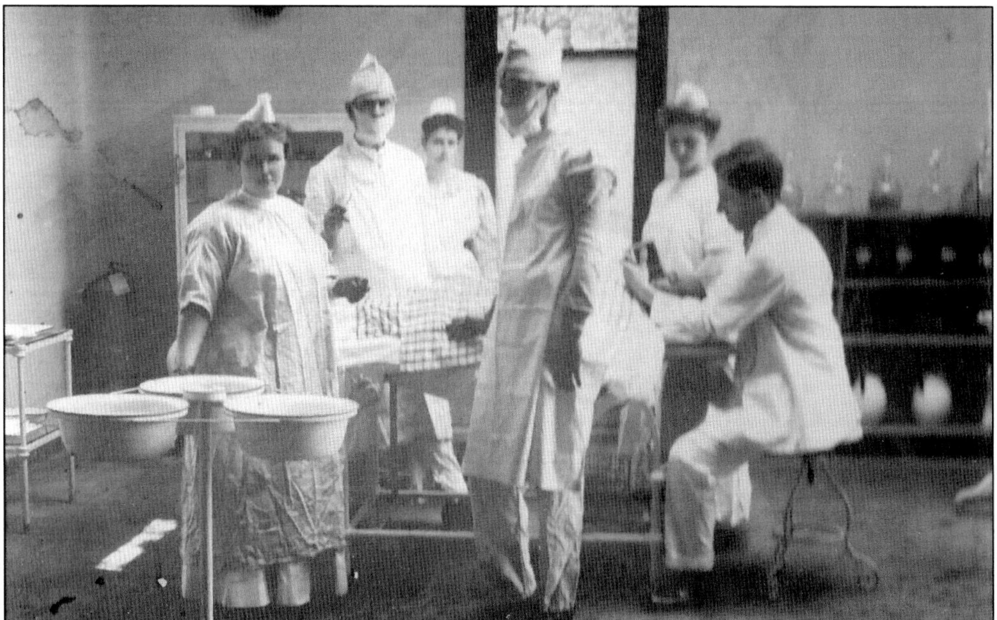

Dr. F. P. Ball came to Lock Haven with his family in 1860, and attended city schools until 1872. He graduated from the University of Pennsylvania in Philadelphia in 1877. He returned to Lock Haven and married M. Louise Mackey in 1883. Dr. Ball is seen here in the operating room as surgeon in the early days of Lock Haven Hospital. (Courtesy of the Annie Halenbake Ross Library.)

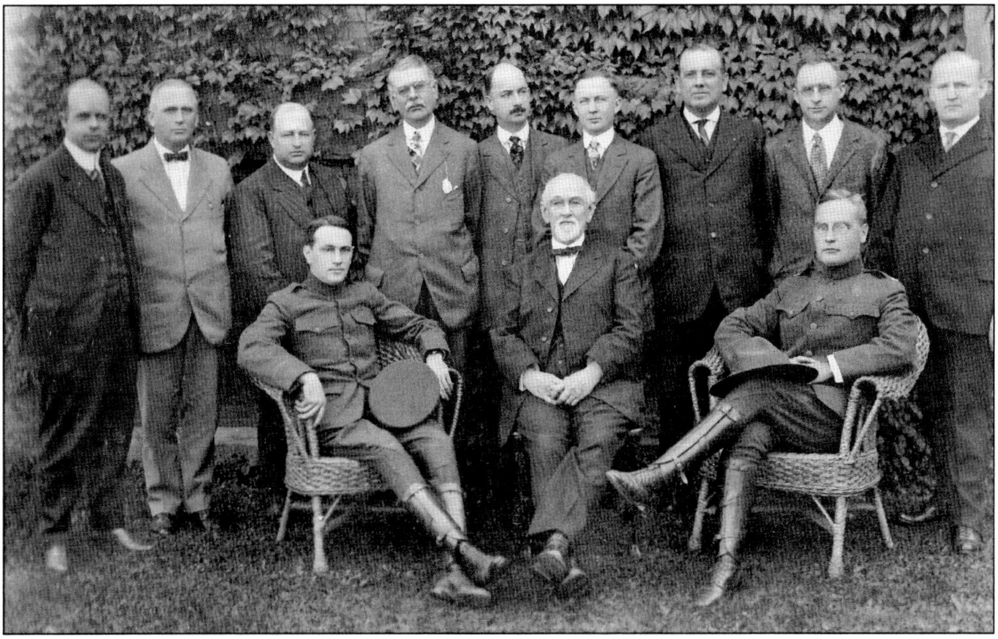

This photograph of local medical practitioners was made about the time the United States entered World War I. Pictured here are, from left to right, (first row) Dr. James L. Lubrecht, Dr. R. B. Watson, and Dr. George D. Green; (second row) Dr. William E. Welliver, Dr. Joseph M. Corson, Dr. John B. Critchfield, Dr. Frank P. Ball, Dr. E. C. Blackburn, Dr. C. B. Kirk, Dr. P. McDowell Tibbins, Dr. Saylor J. McGhee, and Dr. A. B. Painter. (Courtesy of the Annie Halenbake Ross Library.)

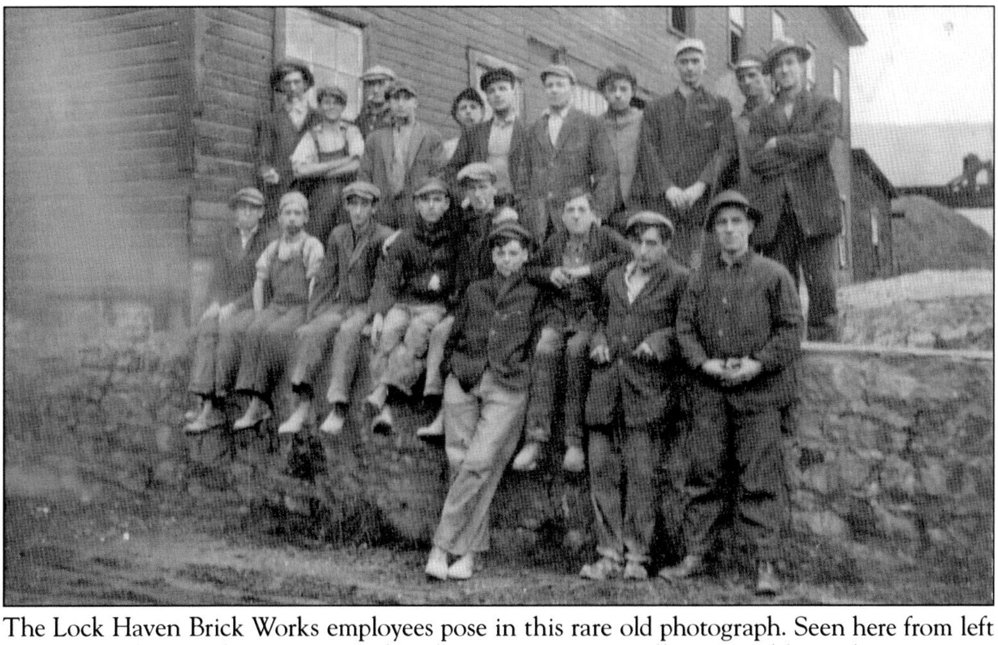

The Lock Haven Brick Works employees pose in this rare old photograph. Seen here from left to right are: (first row) Cons Herr, Edward Bennett, George Zell, Lee Muthler, Jack Carrington, George Litz, Ernest Probst, William Zell, and Frank Stringfellow; (second row) unidentified, Joe Rayhorn, Ezra Myers, Charles Zell, unidentified, David Saiers, Harry Saiers, Clarence Litz, Thomas Maggs, Harry Litz, and Joe Remick. (Courtesy of the Annie Halenbake Ross Library.)

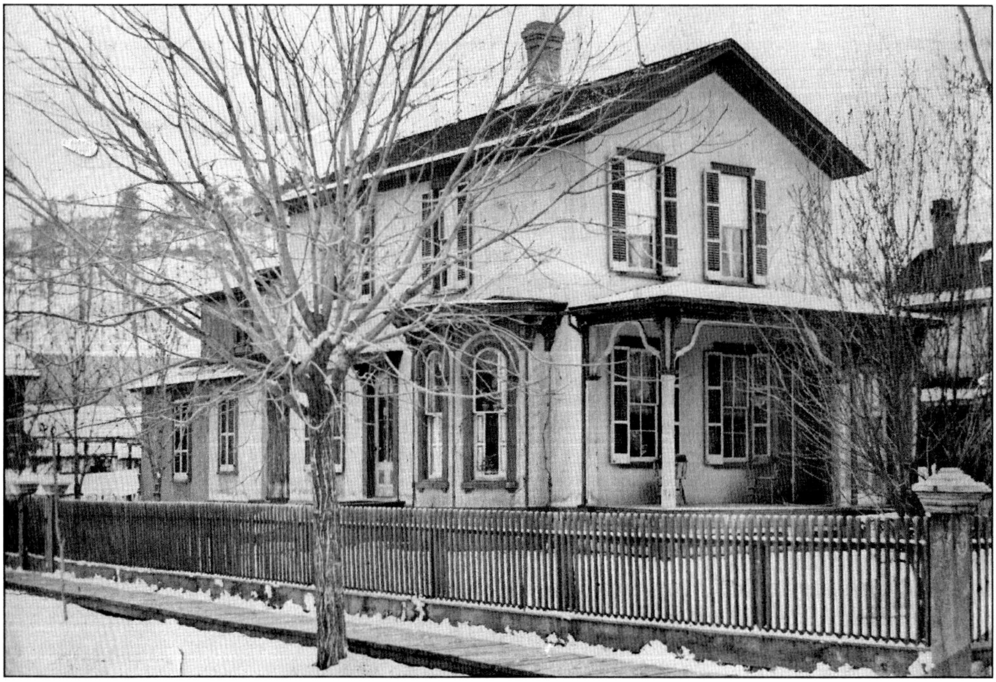

In 1887, this house was the home of the J. F. Clark family, who operated a bookstore in the Opera House Block. In 1920, the house was sold to P. P. Griffin, and would become the location of the Lock Haven Chair Factory. The home was cut in two and transported a short distance down Fifth Street, where the two sections were placed on new foundations. (Courtesy of the Annie Halenbake Ross Library.)

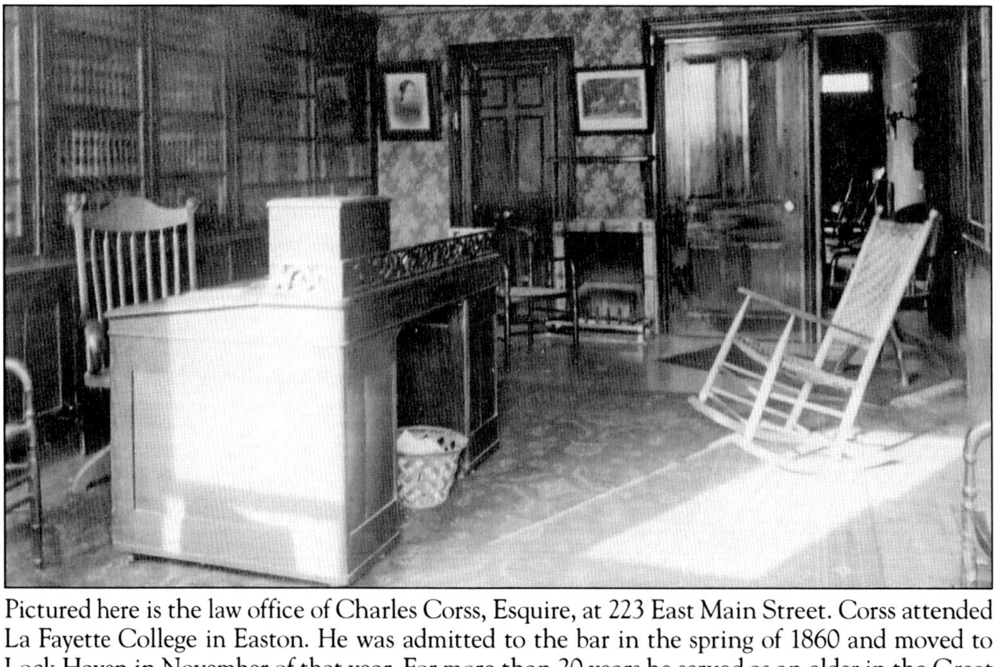

Pictured here is the law office of Charles Corss, Esquire, at 223 East Main Street. Corss attended La Fayette College in Easton. He was admitted to the bar in the spring of 1860 and moved to Lock Haven in November of that year. For more than 20 years he served as an elder in the Great Island Presbyterian Church. (Courtesy of the Annie Halenbake Ross Library.)

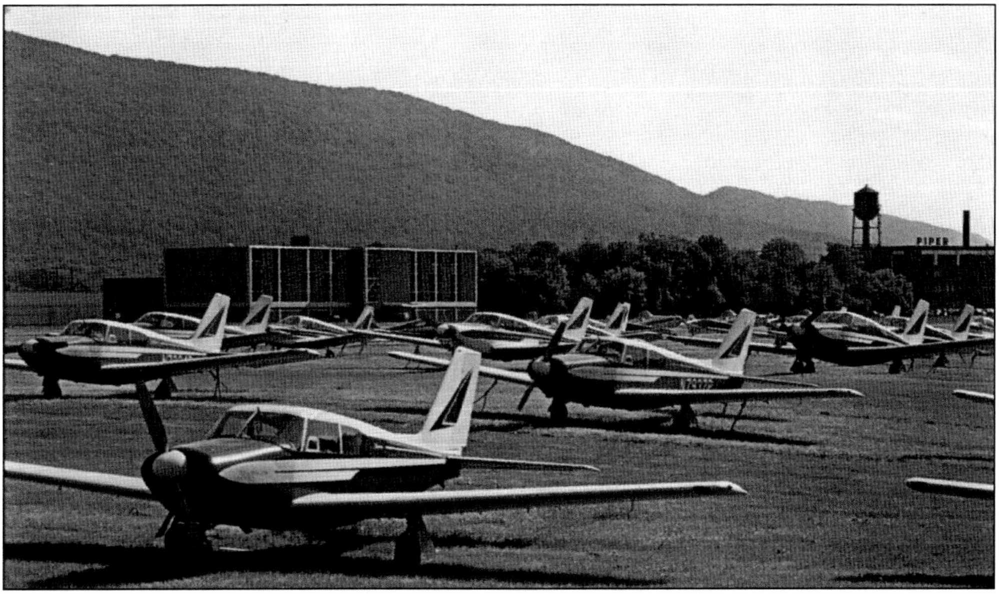


William T. Piper purchased the Taylor Brothers Aircraft Corporation in late 1930 and located Piper Aircraft Corporation in Lock Haven in 1937. Piper Aircraft Corporation became the world's leading manufacturer of general aviation aircraft. The company remained in Lock Haven until 1984 and produced a number of popular aircraft including the "Cub" and a series of planes bearing Native American names such as Aztec, Cherokee, Cheyenne, Comanche, Navajo, and Pawnee. (Courtesy of the Annie Halenbake Ross Library.)

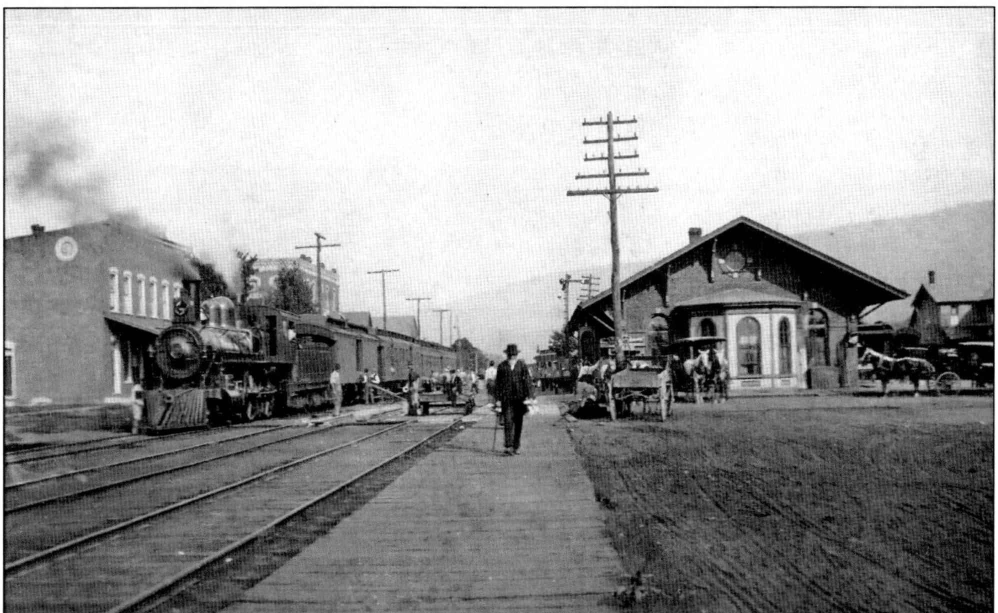

The Lock Haven station of the Pennsylvania Railroad, located at Henderson Street, hosted 20 trains per day. Trains traveled to Erie and Buffalo and east to Harrisburg. The train station was torn down. Seen here is a steam engine pulling a coal tender, mail car, and two passenger cars. (Courtesy of the Annie Halenbake Ross Library.)

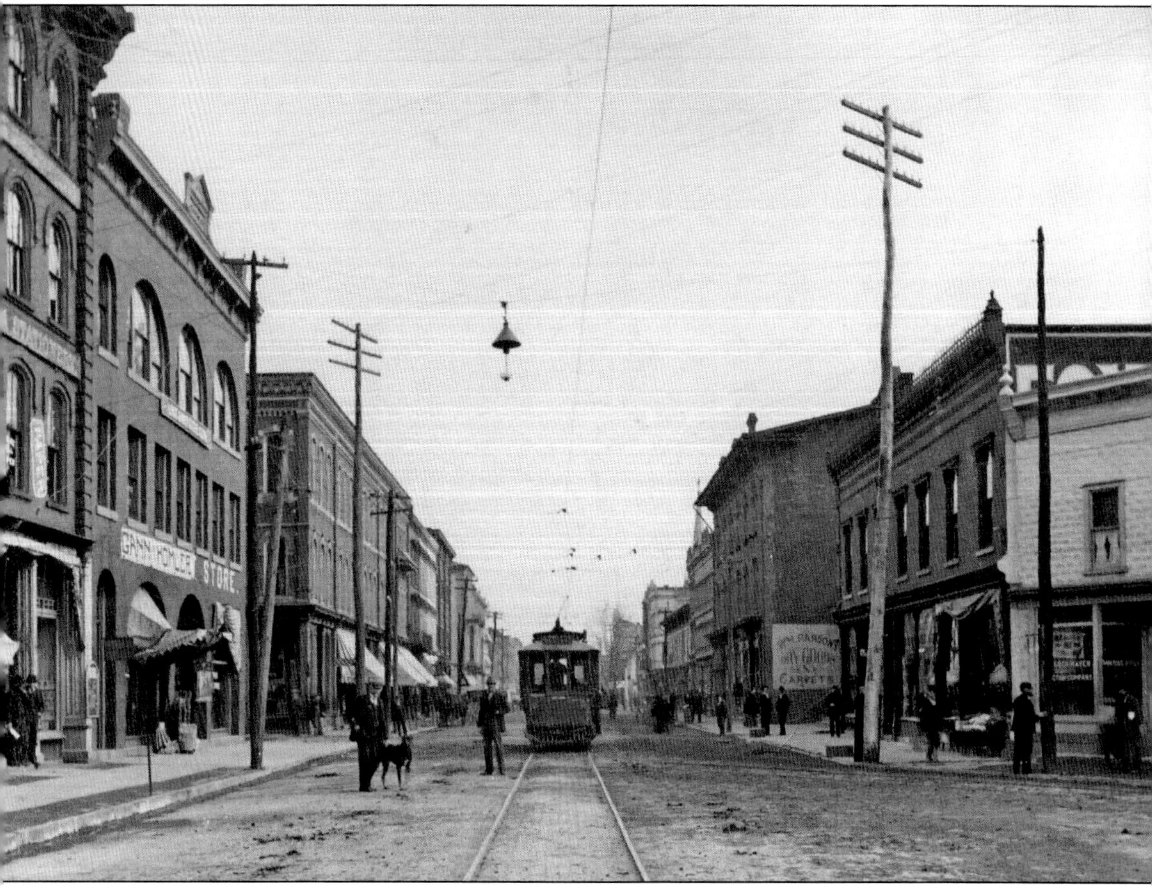


Trolley service began Saturday, December 14, 1894, in Lock Haven. On that first day of service, almost 800 citizens had their first ride on the cars. The wage for a conductor was 15¢ per hour. The trolley started at Clinton and Henderson Streets, which was only a half block from the railroad station. The line ran from Henderson to Main Streets and then up Bellefonte, passing railroad stations, prominent hotels, and business houses toward the south ward, where the road passed the paper mills, clay works, and other industries, and then along Route 220 to Mill Hall. The fare was 5¢ for the entire length of the line. The trolley also hauled all sorts of items including mail that traveled from the Lock Haven Post Office to Flemington and Mill Hall twice a day. The trolley cars were replaced by buses in the late 1920s. (Courtesy of the Clinton County Historical Society.)

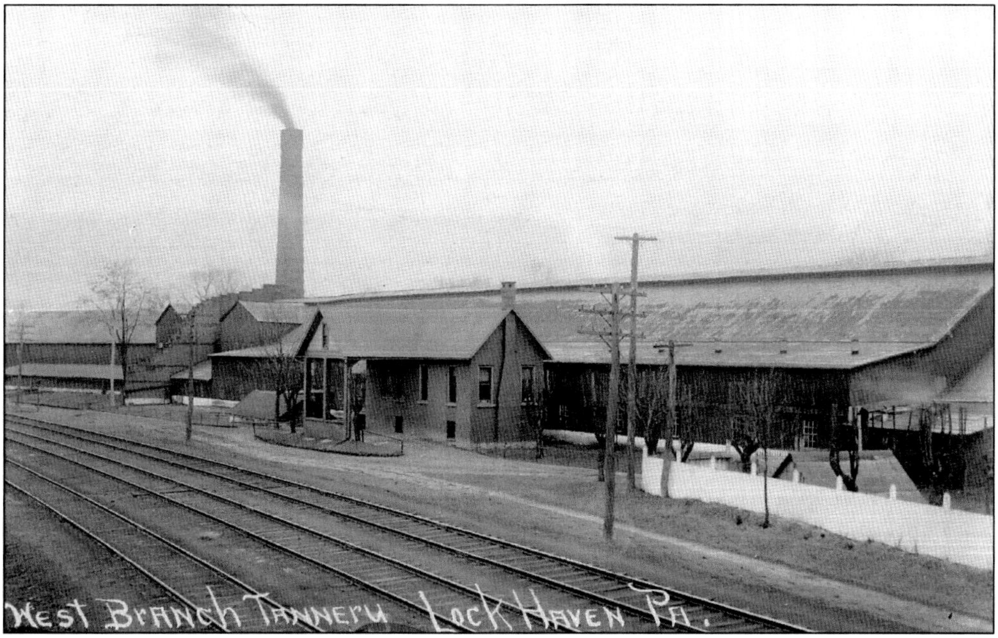


Built in 1870, the West Branch Tannery, Kistler, Lesh and Company was established by the Kistler Brothers. Located between Fourth and Sixth Streets, the plant was destroyed by fire and rebuilt. The company produced sole leather. By 1940, the tannery produced over 300 hides per day. (Courtesy of the Annie Halenbake Ross Library.)

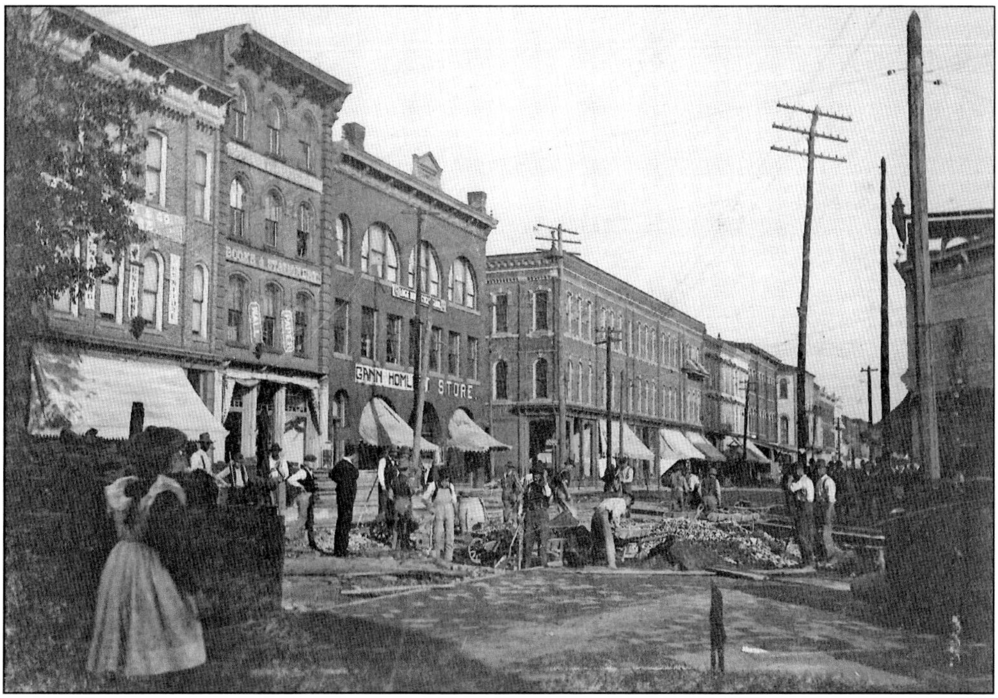

By 1896, all the plank roads had disappeared. Plank roads and sidewalks were replaced by flagstone, brick, and patent paving. Here workers are paving Bellefonte Avenue in the early 1900s. The street lights were installed in 1913. (Courtesy of the Annie Halenbake Ross Library.)

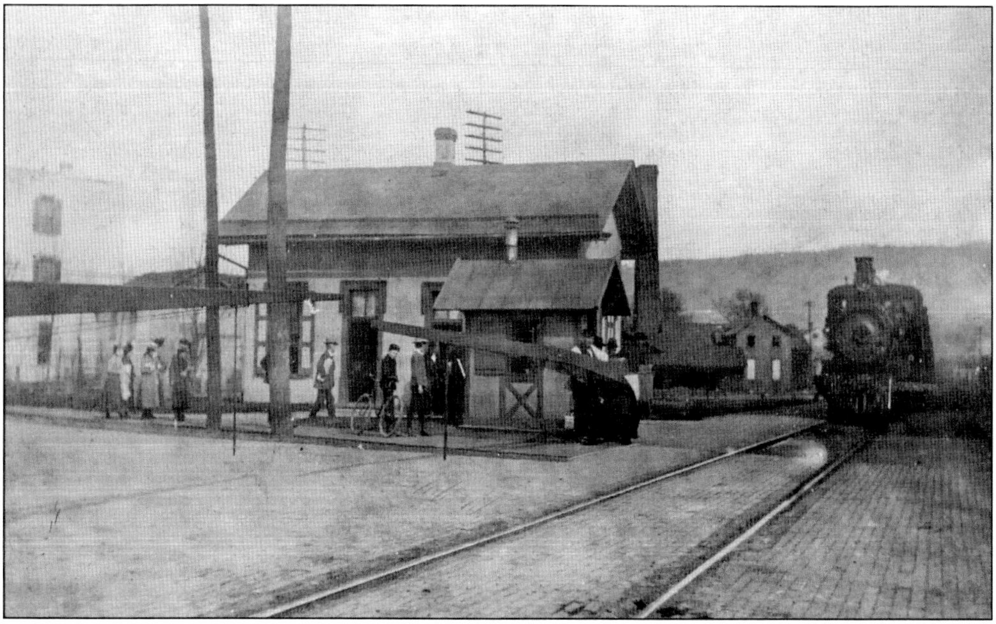

Passengers purchase tickets as the train arrives at the station on Bellefonte Avenue. In 1859, the Philadelphia and Erie Railroad was located in Lock Haven. The railroad was so vital to the community that the business district moved from Water Street to Main and Church Streets. A short walk from the train station to town made shopping that much easier. (Courtesy of the Annie Halenbake Ross Library.)

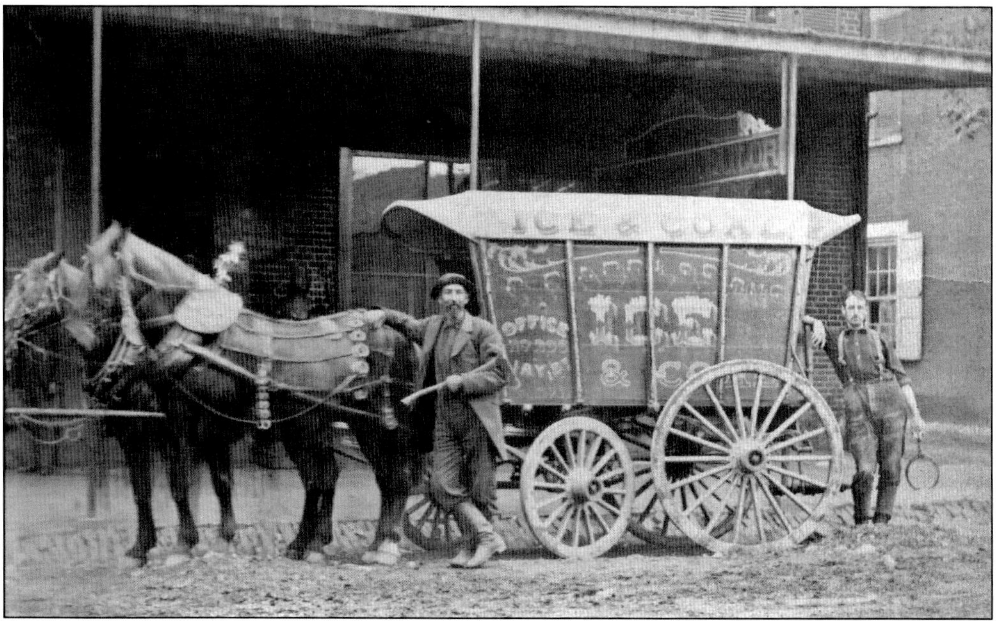

Ice and coal were important resources for businesses and residences in Lock Haven in the late 1800s. This delivery truck driver holds an axe in the crook of his arm, a necessary tool for his trade. Ice was cut from the river and layered with sawdust to keep it from melting. The business office was located on Jay Street, as advertised on the side of the wagon. (Courtesy of the Annie Halenbake Ross Library.)

# *Three*

# PLACES TO STAY AND PLAY

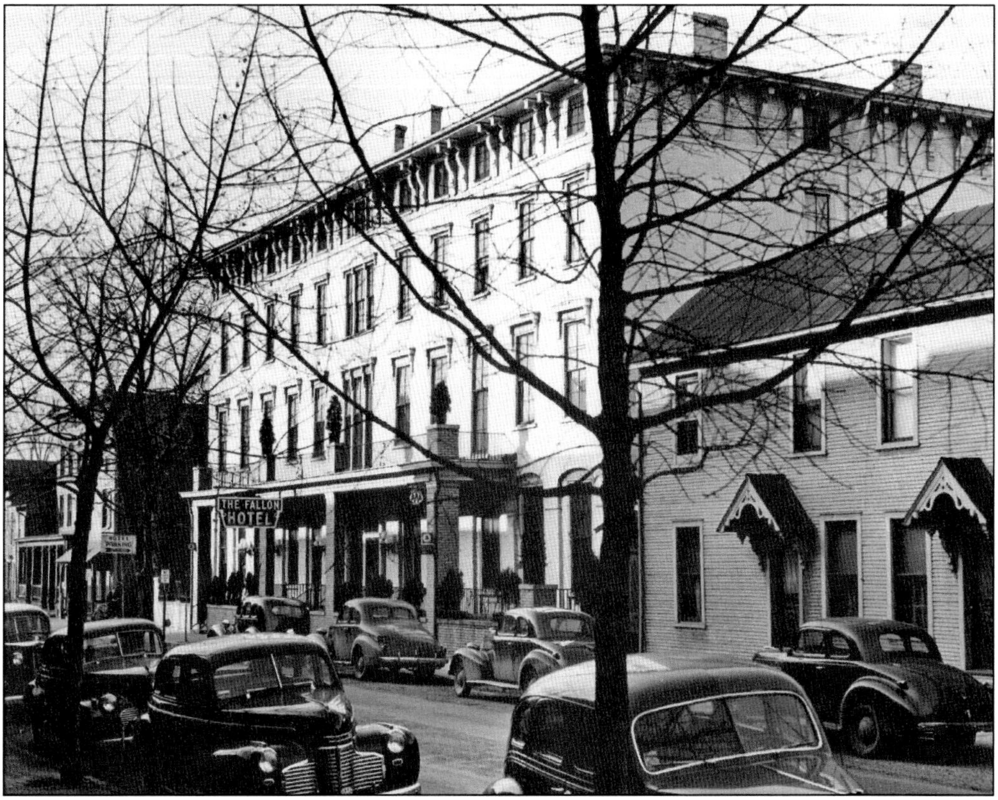


Lock Haven was once home to over 40 hotels. Early establishments were constructed to host elaborate musical and theatrical performances. Many of these buildings contained ornate decorations, and proprietors enjoyed great success. Floods and economic hardship lead to the removal of some of these buildings. Seen here is the Fallon Hotel, financed by Maria Christina, Queen of Spain in 1855, under the direction of John and Christopher Fallon. Originally the hotel could accommodate 400 guests. (Courtesy of the Annie Halenbake Ross Library.)

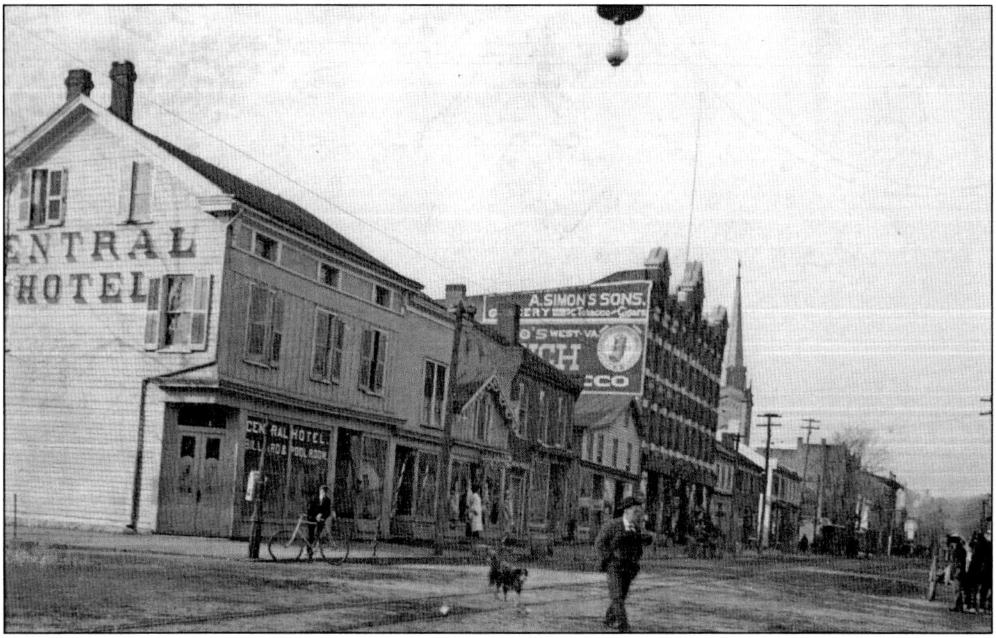


Located at the corner of Main and Grove Streets, the Central Hotel had 21 sleeping rooms with accommodations for 50 guests. It was used as a dwelling by Dr. Lichtenthaler Sr. for about five years and then purchased in 1870 by the Simon Brothers who remodeled and improved it. Its first proprietor was Peter Meitzler. The building was razed in 1923 and the site is now occupied by the Masonic Temple. (Courtesy of the Annie Halenbake Ross Library.)

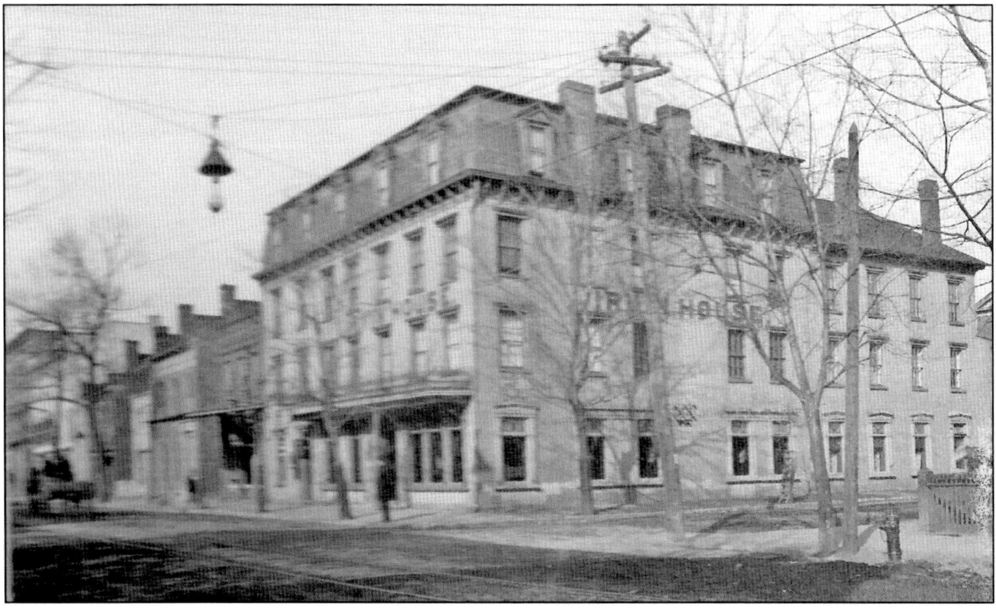

The Irvin House (formerly the Mansion House) was built by John Moorehead in 1838. Moorehead sold the building to William Barker, who operated a hotel called the Mansion House. Dr. Irvin then purchased it and renamed it the Irvin House. The Irvin Hotel was razed in 1973 after the 1972 flood as part of Lock Haven's post flood redevelopment project. (Courtesy of the Annie Halenbake Ross Library.)

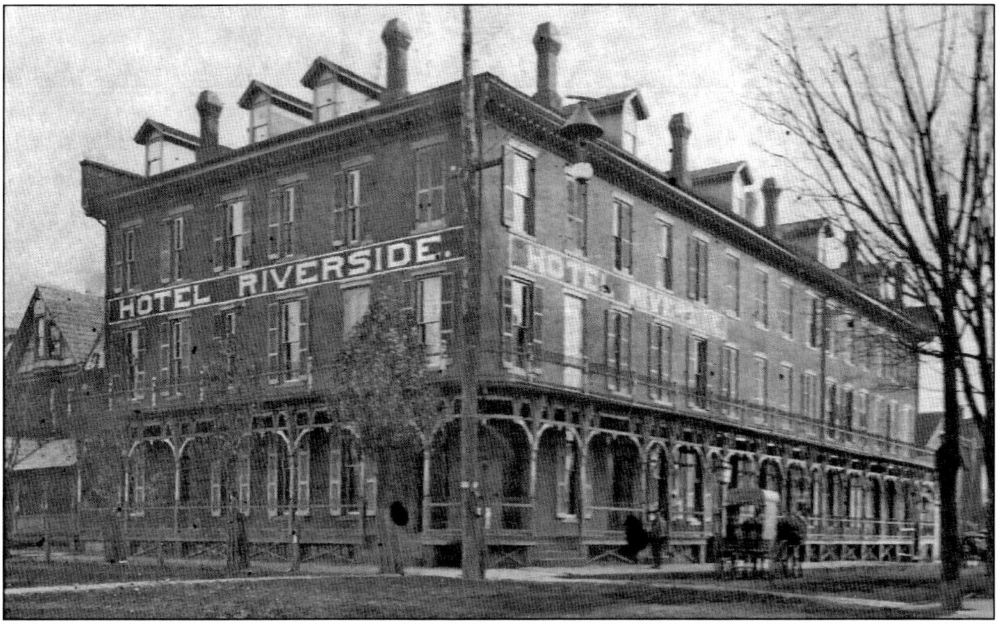


The Montour House was erected in 1834 on the first lot sold by Jerry Church. In 1891, Peter Meitzler purchased the hotel and renamed it Hotel Meitzler. The house contained 50 sleeping rooms with accommodations for 100 guests. The hotel had broad double verandas running across the front and street sides. In 1892, it was renamed the Hotel Riverside. (Courtesy of the Annie Halenbake Ross Library.)

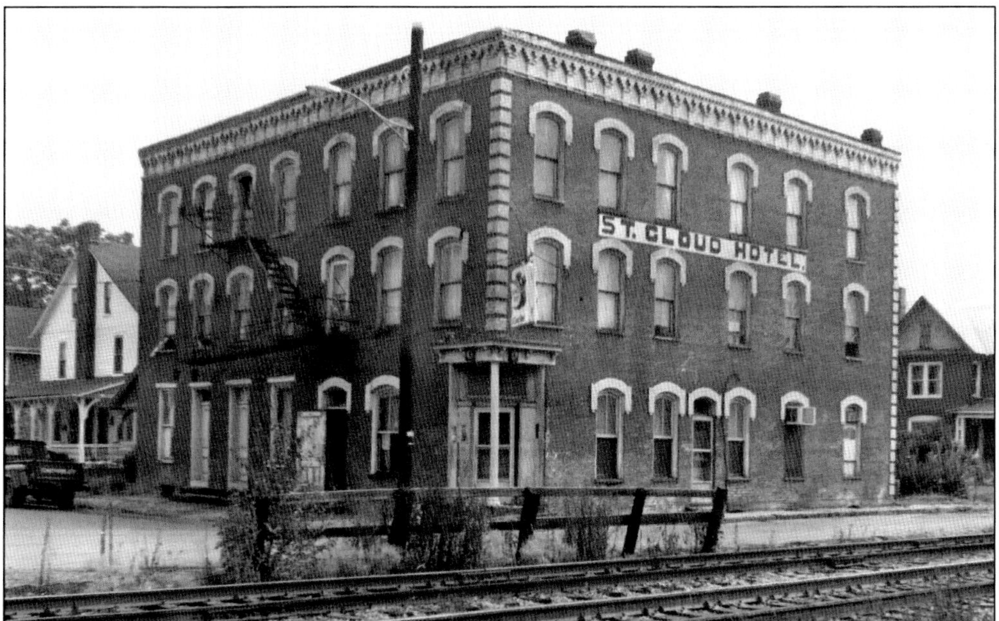


Situated opposite the railroad station on Clinton and Washington Streets, the St. Cloud Hotel was established in the 1880s. The hotel contained 20 guest rooms and offered parlors, writing rooms, and a dining room bar. This large three-story brick building was built by Daniel Gross in 1885. (Courtesy of the Annie Halenbake Ross Library.)

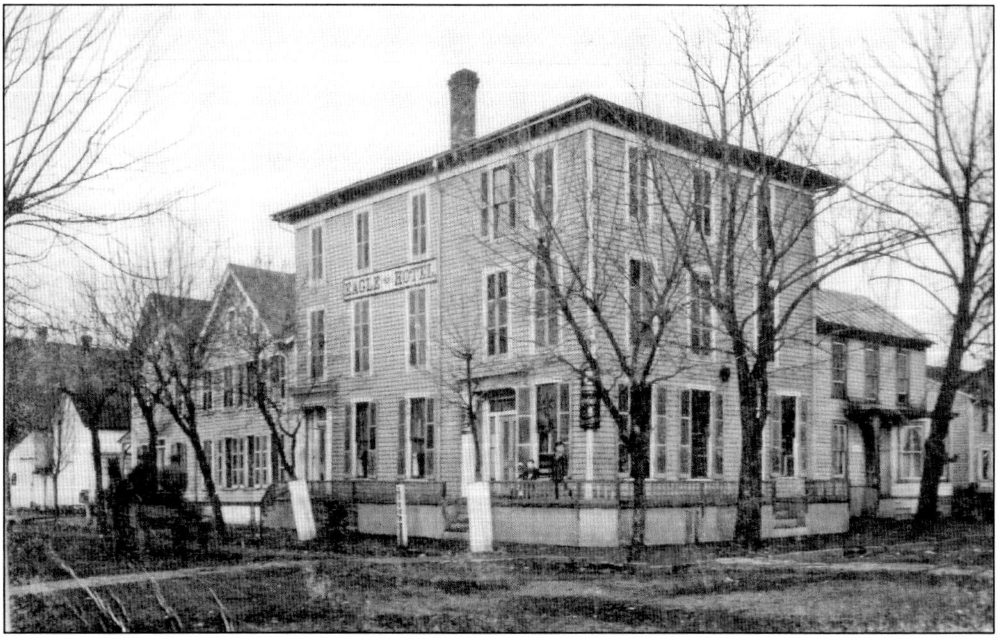


The Eagle Hotel was built in 1855 by Jacob Smith. It is a frame building located at the corner of Bald Eagle and Vesper Streets. The first landlord was Jacob Smith. The hotel contained 25 sleeping rooms with accommodations for 50 guests. (Courtesy of the Annie Halenbake Ross Library.)

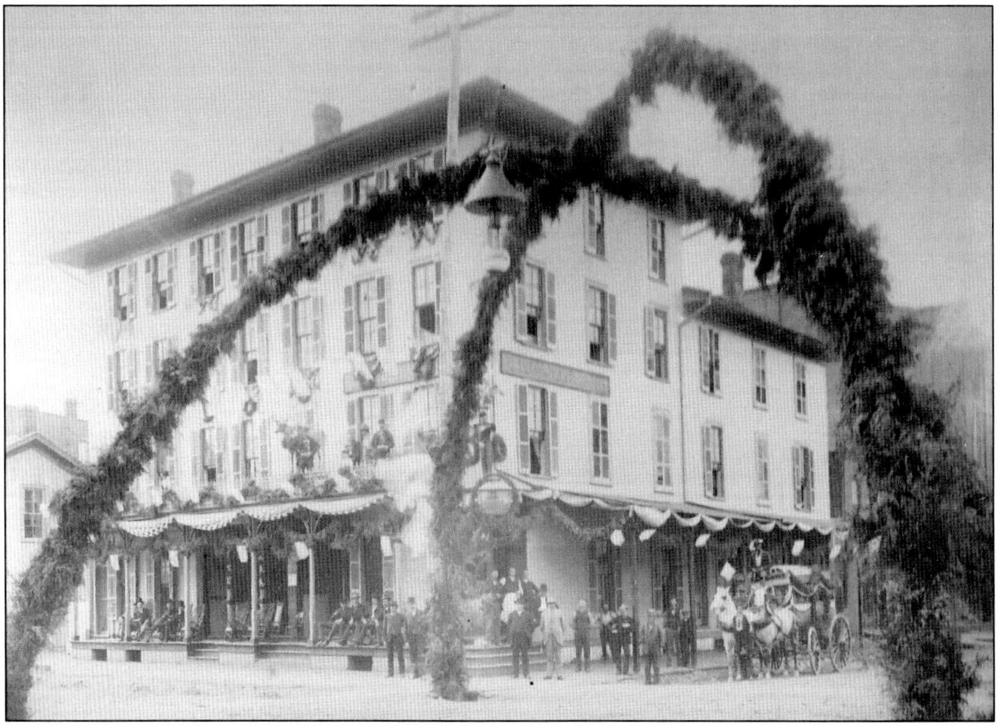

Jacob Smith built the U.S. Hotel, formerly the Girard House, in 1863. Peter Meitzler owned this three-story frame building on the corner of Grove and Church Streets. (Courtesy of the Annie Halenbake Ross Library.)

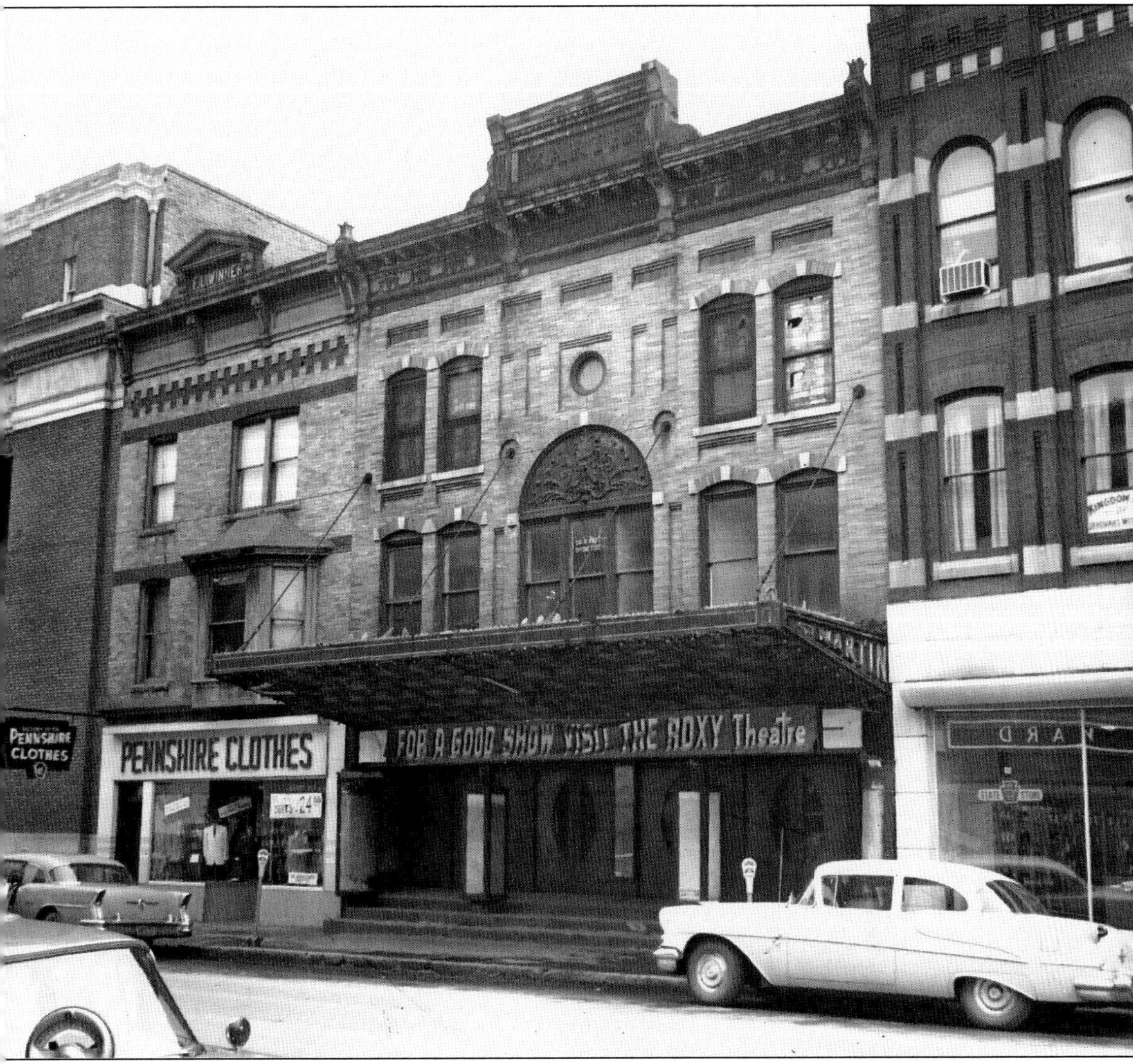


The Martin Theater was located on East Main Street near the present Masonic Temple. It was one of the city's early movie houses. It was preceded by the Lyric Theater. The theater, built in 1911 by the late Harry H. Martin Sr., was razed in 1960. (Courtesy of the Annie Halenbake Ross Library.)

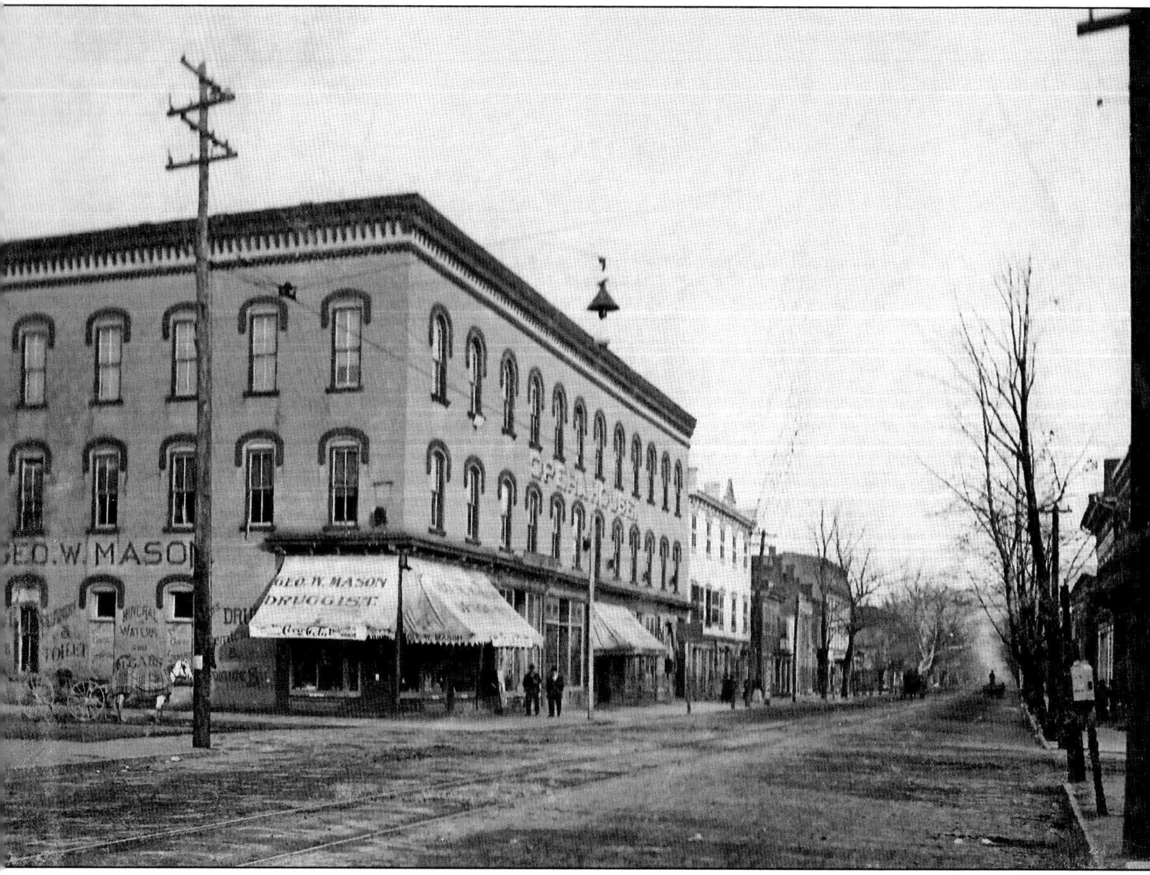


Built in 1868 at a cost of $100,000, the Opera House had retail storerooms on the first floor, an opera room on the second floor, and a meeting hall on the third floor. A set of gas jets forming the words "Opera House" were lighted on evenings when there was entertainment. In 1882, Mussina and Mason, owners of the Opera House, completed plans for an addition to the building. The improvements included a gallery furnished with benches, a balcony with folding chairs, two tiers of private boxes with draperies, and the orchestra with roomy opera chairs on the first floor. The seating capacity was 1,200. In addition, plans called for a new stage, dressing rooms, ventilators in the roof, steam from a private plant for heating, and electricity for lighting the auditorium and stage. (Courtesy of the Annie Halenbake Ross Library.)

## *Four*

# Golden Rule Days

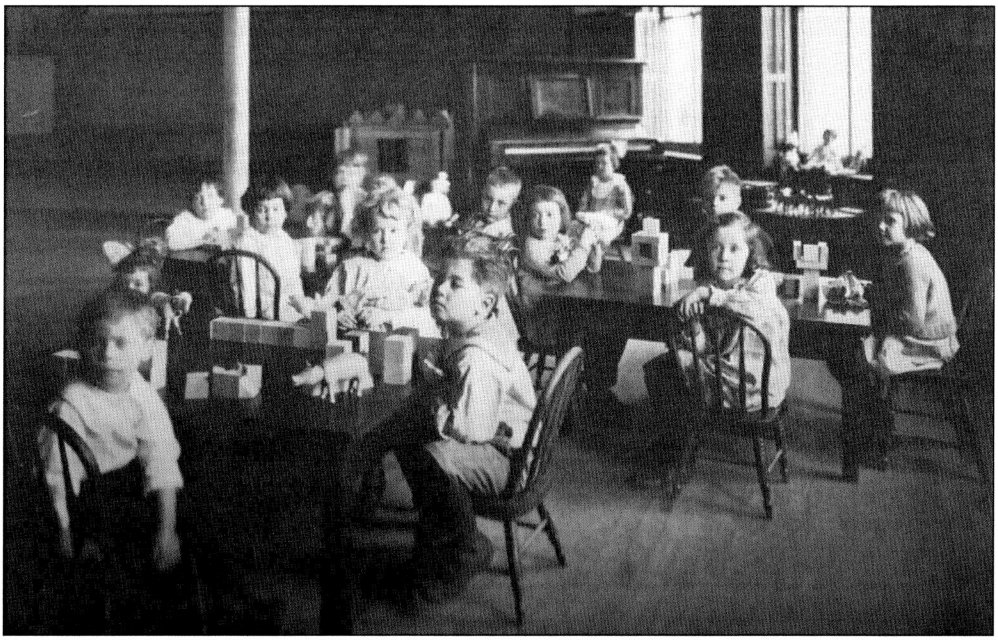

Education was very limited in the beginning years of Lock Haven. The first schoolhouse was located near the north end of the Castanea Bridge and offered only reading, writing, spelling, and arithmetic. In 1809, an act by the Pennsylvania Legislature required that each county provide free education for all children ages 5 to 12 if their parents could not afford to pay for it. In 1834, the Free School Act provided a free public school system in the commonwealth. In 1854, the county superintendent was responsible for issuing teacher certificates. Examinations were given and those who passed received a one-year teacher certificate. This picture, taken at the Central Normal School, shows a training classroom for future teachers. (Courtesy of the Annie Halenbake Ross Library.)

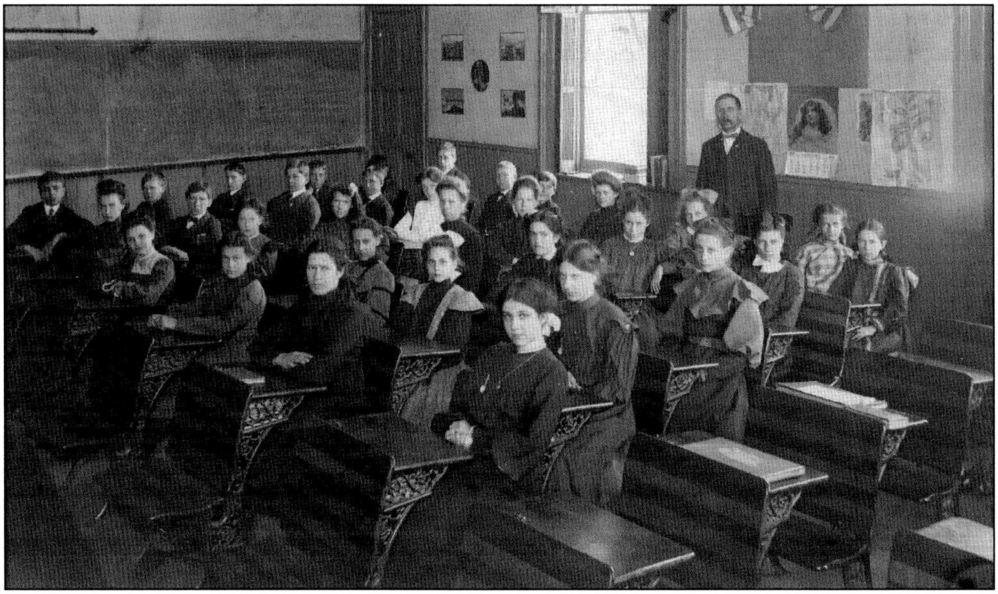

The Third Ward School building was also referred to as the West Ward School building. It was built in 1868 at West Church Street between Third and Fourth Streets. It cost $24,000 and was modeled after a school house in Franklin, Venango County. This class picture was taken in 1905. Included are Bruce Kreamer, William Hall, Bert Stevenson, Henry Bender, Lyol Bush, Marcus Hall, Blair Klepper, Helen Geary, Ned Wagner, Ed Miller, Florence Kaufman, Gertrude Ubil, Elizabeth Walters, Carrie McCloskey, Vera Gardner Marr, Lena Lose, Edith Warner, Nell Burrows, Florence Bickford, Florence Candor, Ruth Pursley, Agnes Hamilton, Viola Sohmer, and Edna Batchelder. (Courtesy of the Annie Halenbake Ross Library.)

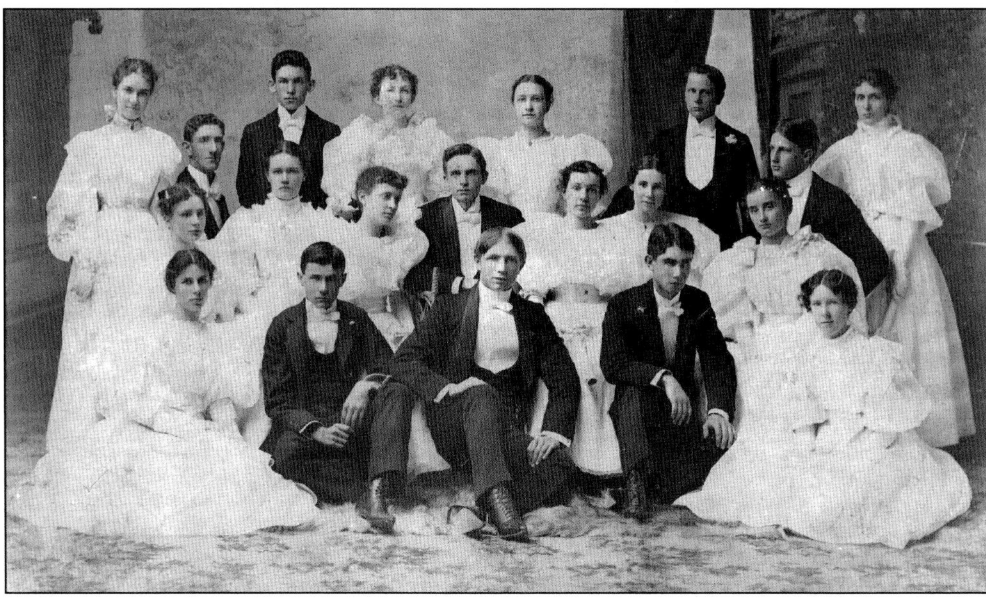

The first Lock Haven High School was built in 1868, opening its doors January 4, 1869. Professor A. N. Raub was the supervising principal, and there were three teachers on the high school faculty. The Lock Haven High School held its first commencement exercises in 1876 for a graduating class of two. Seen here is the class of 1896. (Courtesy of the Annie Halenbake Ross Library.)

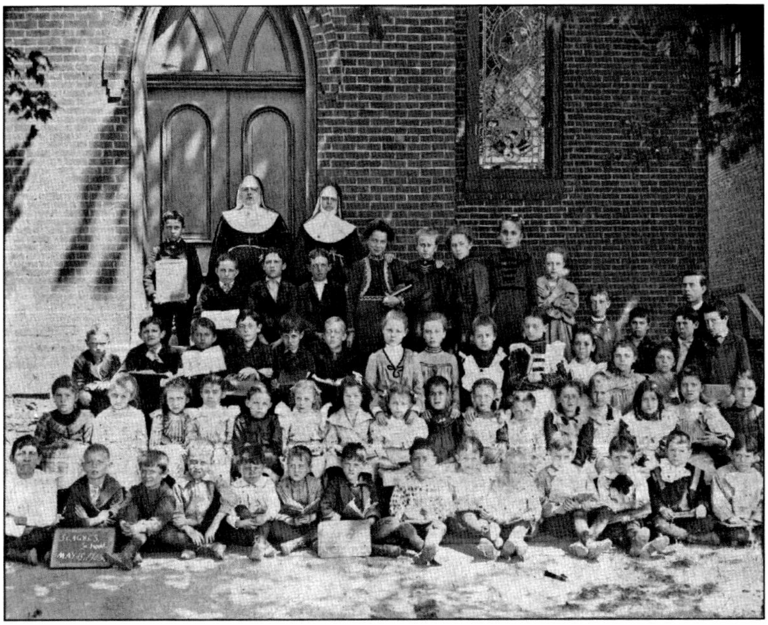

This school picture was taken in about 1902 at the Immaculate Conception parochial school. The children posed at the entrance of the school with two of the teaching sisters, Sister Frances and Sister Stanislaus. (Courtesy of the Annie Halenbake Ross Library.)

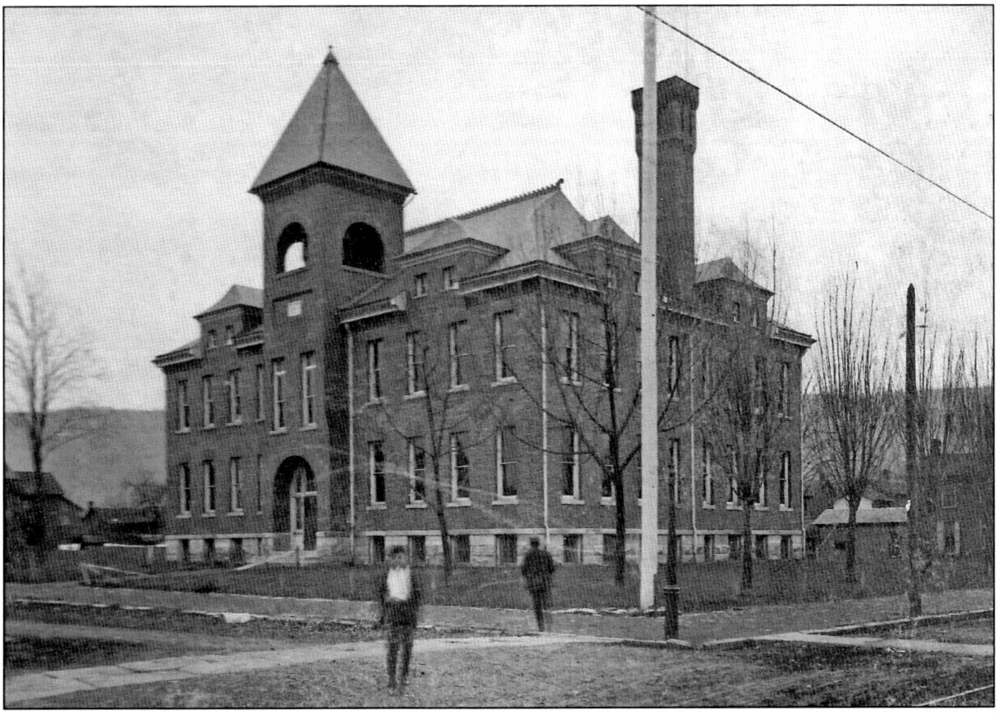

The First Ward School building was located at East Church Street between Henderson and Washington Streets. The First Ward School was conducted in the old courthouse from 1869 to 1893. The new building was constructed in 1893. (Courtesy of the Annie Halenbake Ross Library.)

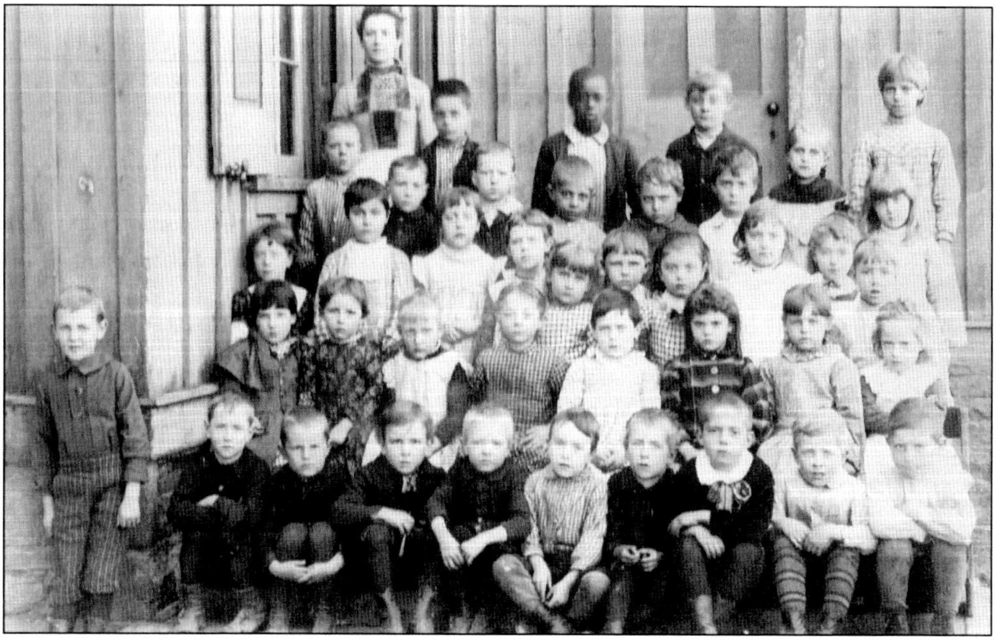

In 1889, these children started school. Mrs. John M. Dauer, 362 East Bald Eagle Street, then Miss Minnie Henry, guided these children through their first year of school at Penn in 1889. Dauer taught the first grade for 32 years and was considered one of the best teachers in the system. (Courtesy of the Annie Halenbake Ross Library.)

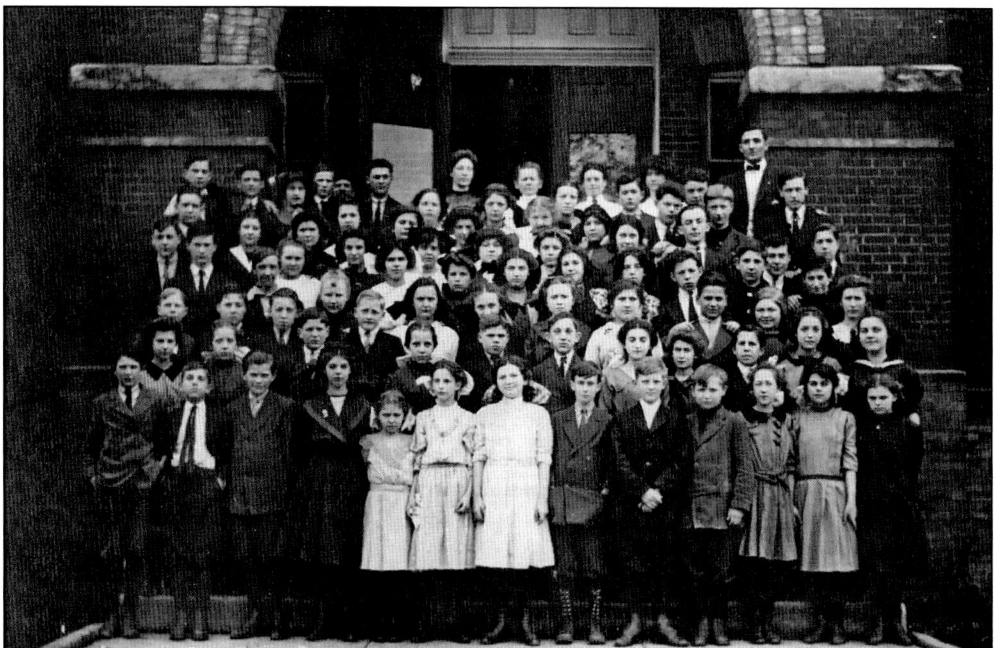

This is the Central Grammar School class photograph for 1913. Classes were held at the Second Ward School while the junior high school building was under construction. The principal was Chester M. Houseknect. (Courtesy of the Annie Halenbake Ross Library.)

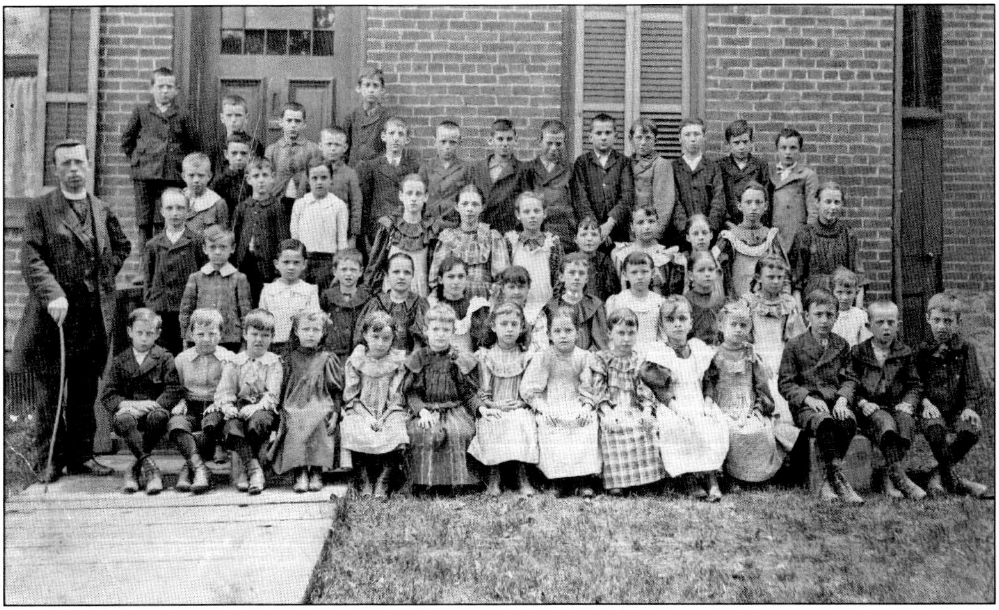

St. Agnes School students in the early 1900s pose for a class photograph with their priest. German-speaking members of the Immaculate Conception Parish formed St. Agnes Church in 1857. In 1892, St. Agnes School was built on Liberty and Walnut Streets and that building served students until 1930, when a new building was constructed. St. Agnes was the first school to operate the federally funded hot lunch program. (Courtesy of the Annie Halenbake Ross Library.)

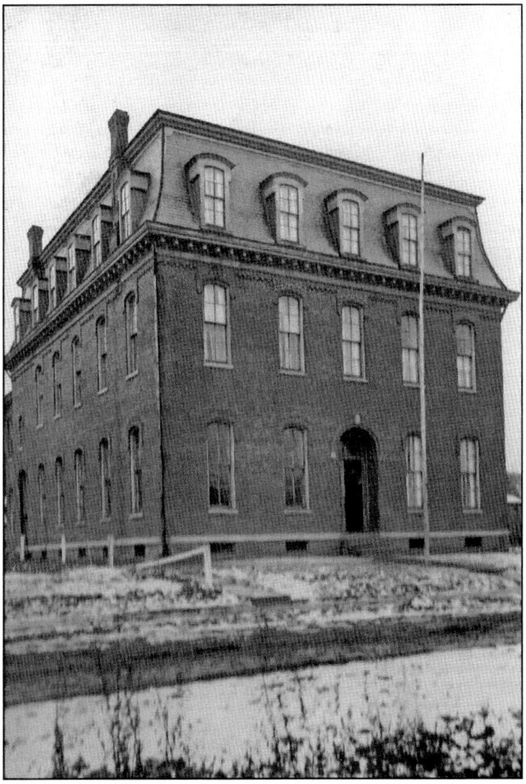

The Immaculate Conception Parochial School is shown here in 1900. The school was used until it was torn down in 1961 and replaced with the present school on Water Street. The Sisters of Mercy, Sisters of the Immaculate Heart of Mary, and Dominican Sisters served the school over the years. (Courtesy of the Annie Halenbake Ross Library.)

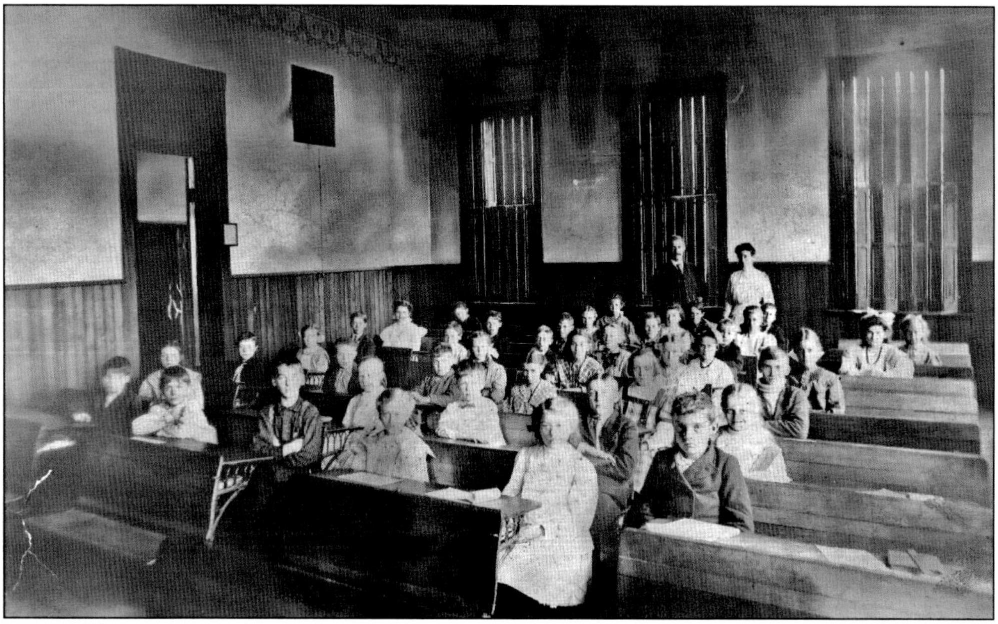

Pictured here are the third and fourth grade classes at the First Ward School located on East Church Street between Henderson and Washington Streets. Originally classes were conducted at the old courthouse from 1869 to 1893. (Courtesy of the Annie Halenbake Ross Library.)

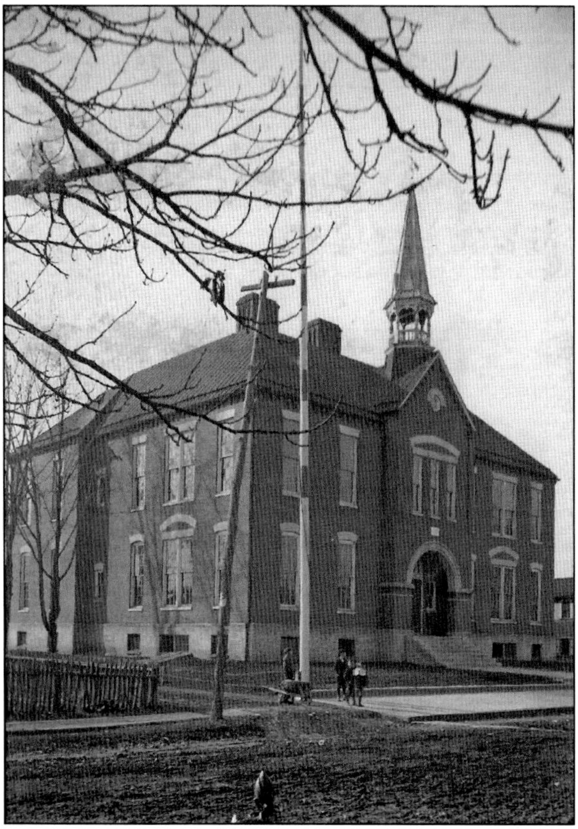

The Second Ward School building was located at East Bald Eagle Street between Vesper and Grove Streets. During the spring of 1892, an old white schoolhouse was razed to make way for the present building. This 1854 frame building was the first constructed in Lock Haven for school purposes and was the only graded school in Pennsylvania outside of Philadelphia. Today this building is used as the administrative offices for Keystone Central School District. (Courtesy of the Annie Halenbake Ross Library.)

The Fourth Ward School building, built in 1882, was located at South Fairview Street. It was later known as the Lincoln School. The building included nine rooms. An elementary education consisted of eight grades and graduation from grammar school often meant the end of formal education for many. James Stoughton was the first principal. The school's location made it an ideal place as a training school for student teachers. (Courtesy of the Annie Halenbake Ross Library.)

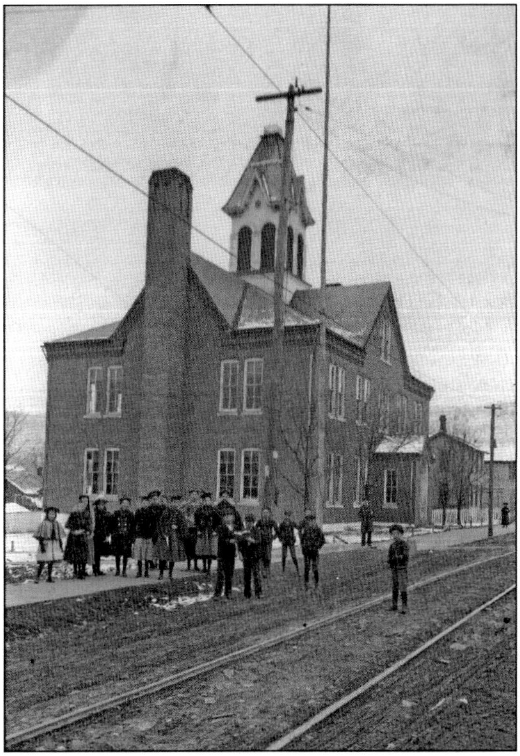

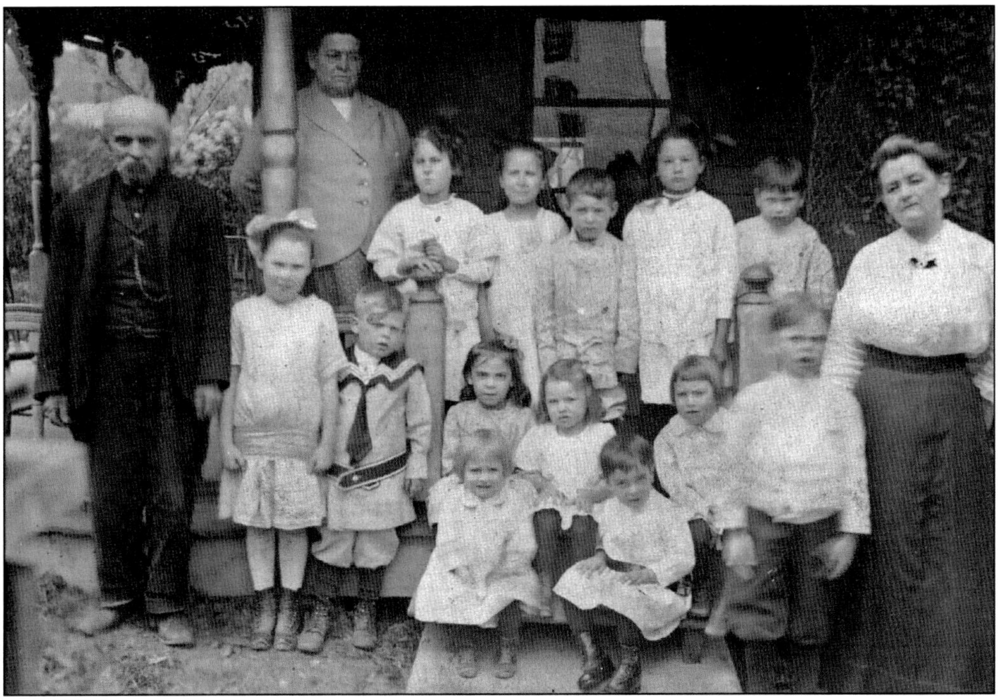

This early Children's Home in 1909 was maintained at Third and Hampton Streets. It was the forerunner to child welfare services. Most of the children living here were orphaned by the death of their parents. (Courtesy of the Annie Halenbake Ross Library.)

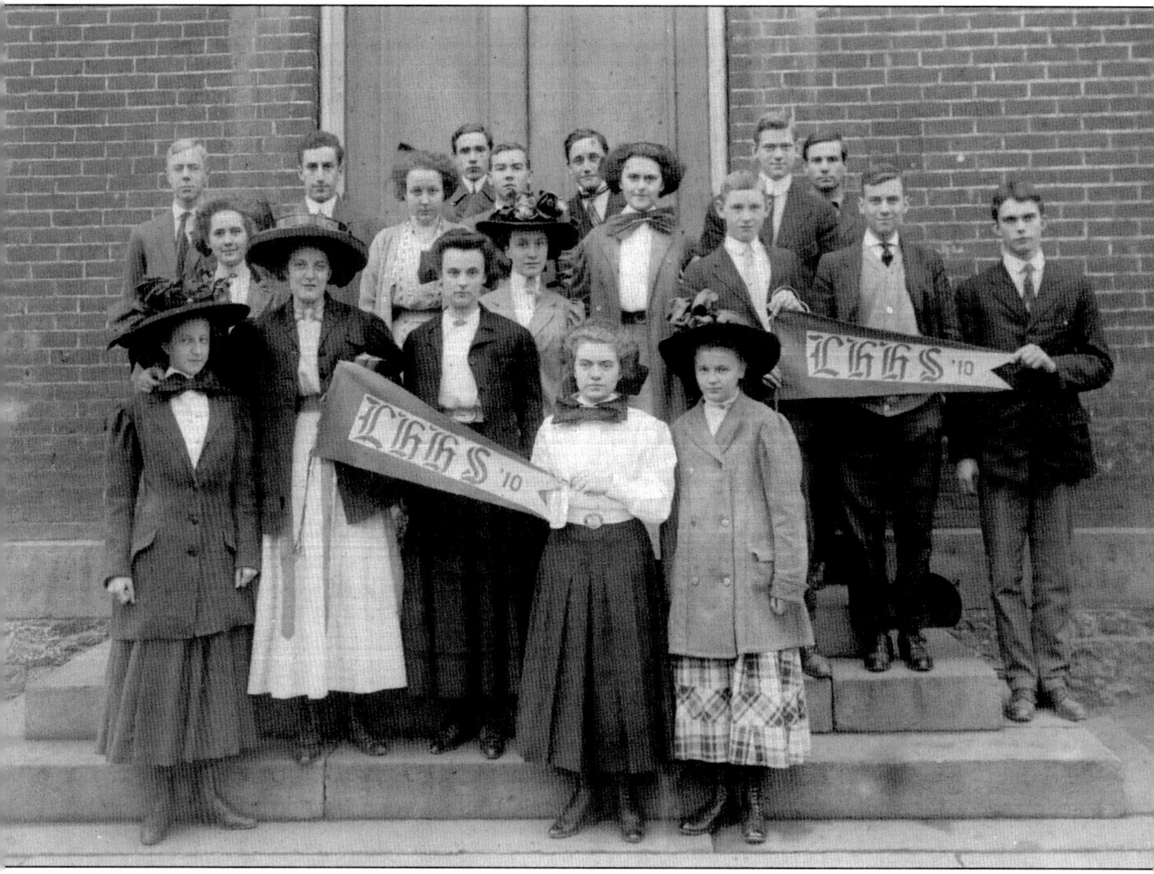


In 1910, the graduating class of Lock Haven High School stands outside the school for their class photograph. The students are, from left to right, (first row) Eleanor Seltzer, Ethel Probst, Gladys Lyon, Lilian Harvey Pletcher, and Edith Lawrence; (second row) Anna Klepper, Ruby Kress, Annabel Breesler, Anna Waite, Robert Myers, Charles Scheid, and Hayes Shaffer; (third row) New Wagner, Joel Claster, Clarence Wilson, Early Quinlan, Sharon McCloskey, Harry Swope, and Frank Baird. (Courtesy of the Annie Halenbake Ross Library.)

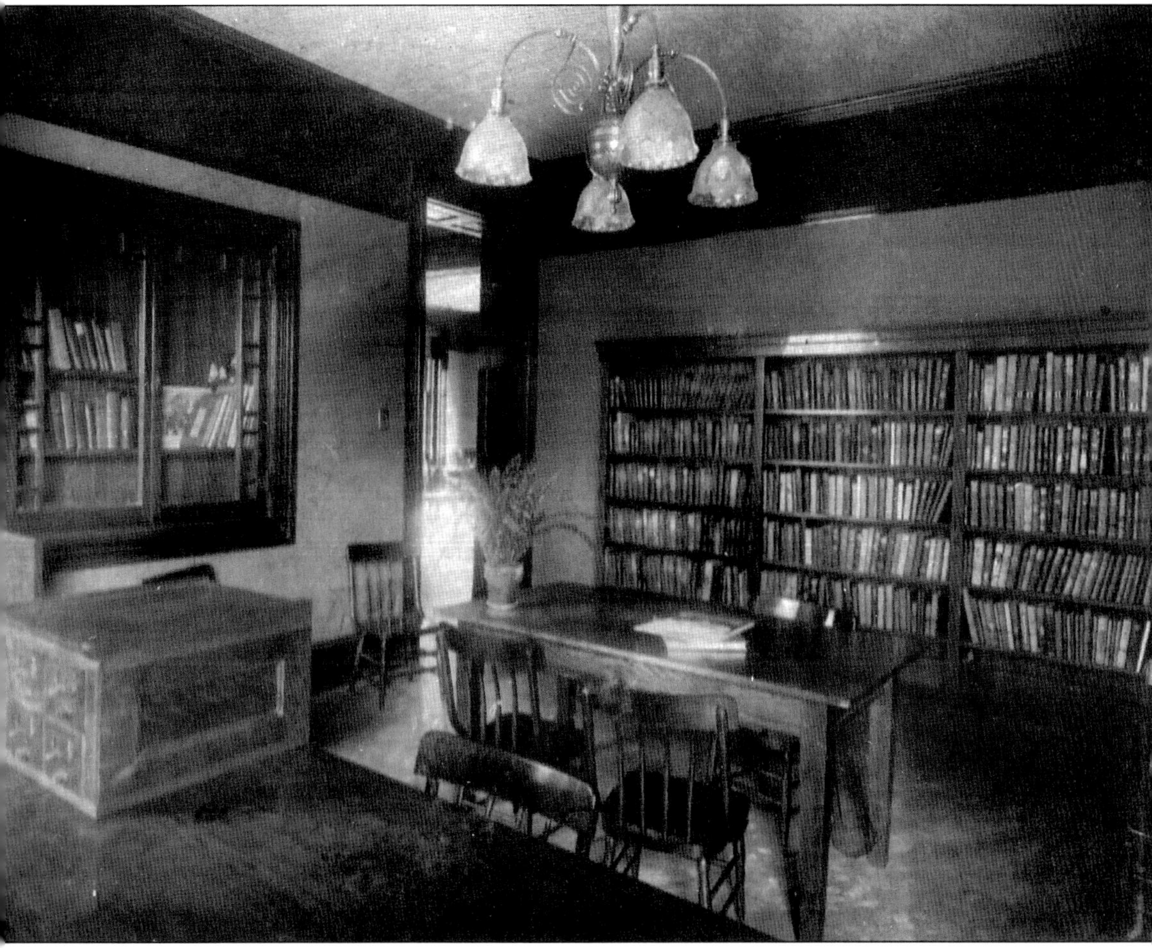

The Lock Haven Library Company was founded in 1869 and was housed in a small room on East Water Street. It was supported by a bequest from Philip M. Price, a tax on dogs, and membership dues of $1.50 per year. When Annie Halenbake Ross died in 1907, she left her home at 232 East Main Street to the city for use as a public library. The Annie Halenbake Ross Library opened on Thanksgiving Day, November 24, 1910. Pictured here is the Pennsylvania Room of the library in 1915. (Courtesy of the Annie Halenbake Ross Library.)

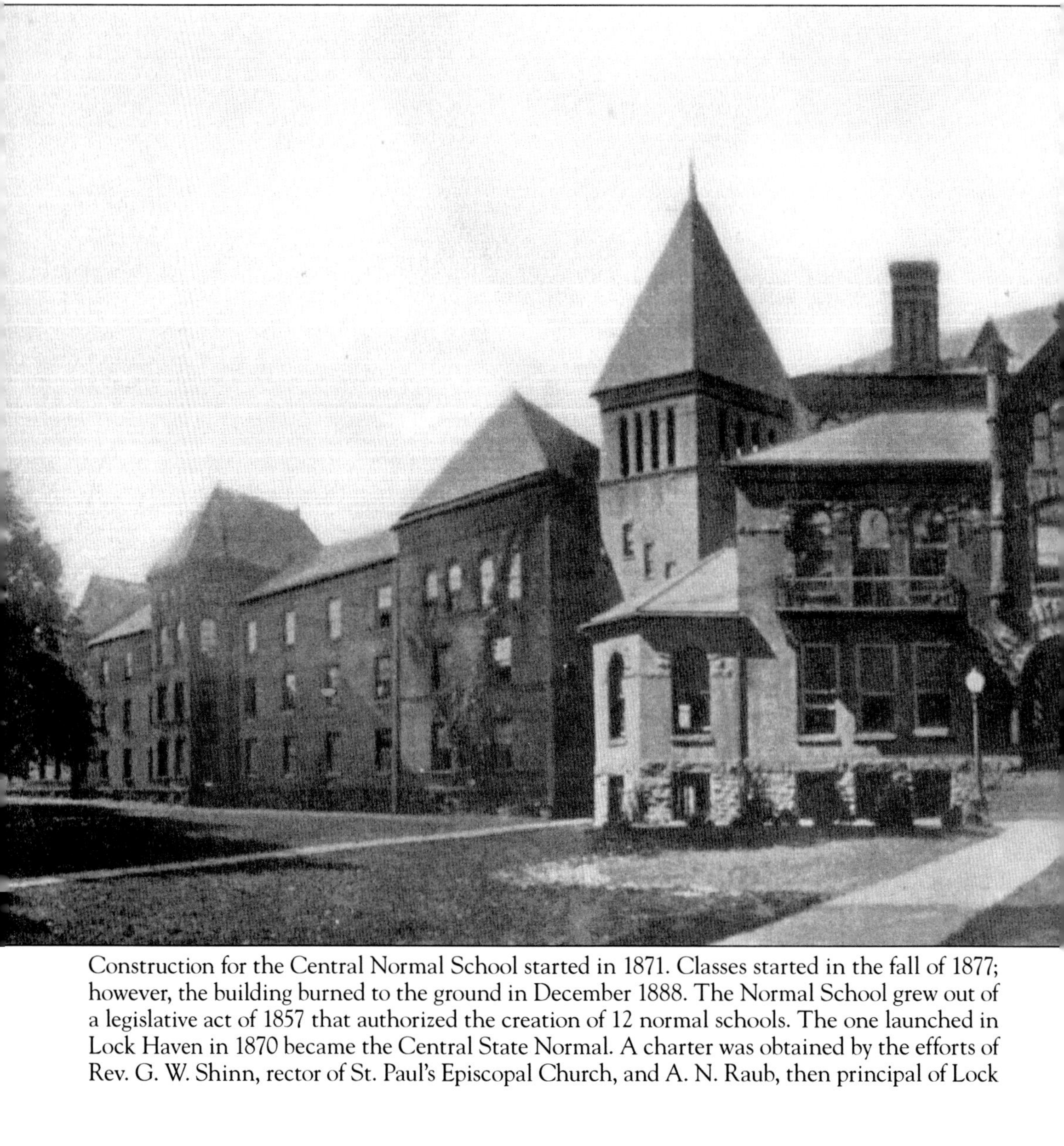

Construction for the Central Normal School started in 1871. Classes started in the fall of 1877; however, the building burned to the ground in December 1888. The Normal School grew out of a legislative act of 1857 that authorized the creation of 12 normal schools. The one launched in Lock Haven in 1870 became the Central State Normal. A charter was obtained by the efforts of Rev. G. W. Shinn, rector of St. Paul's Episcopal Church, and A. N. Raub, then principal of Lock

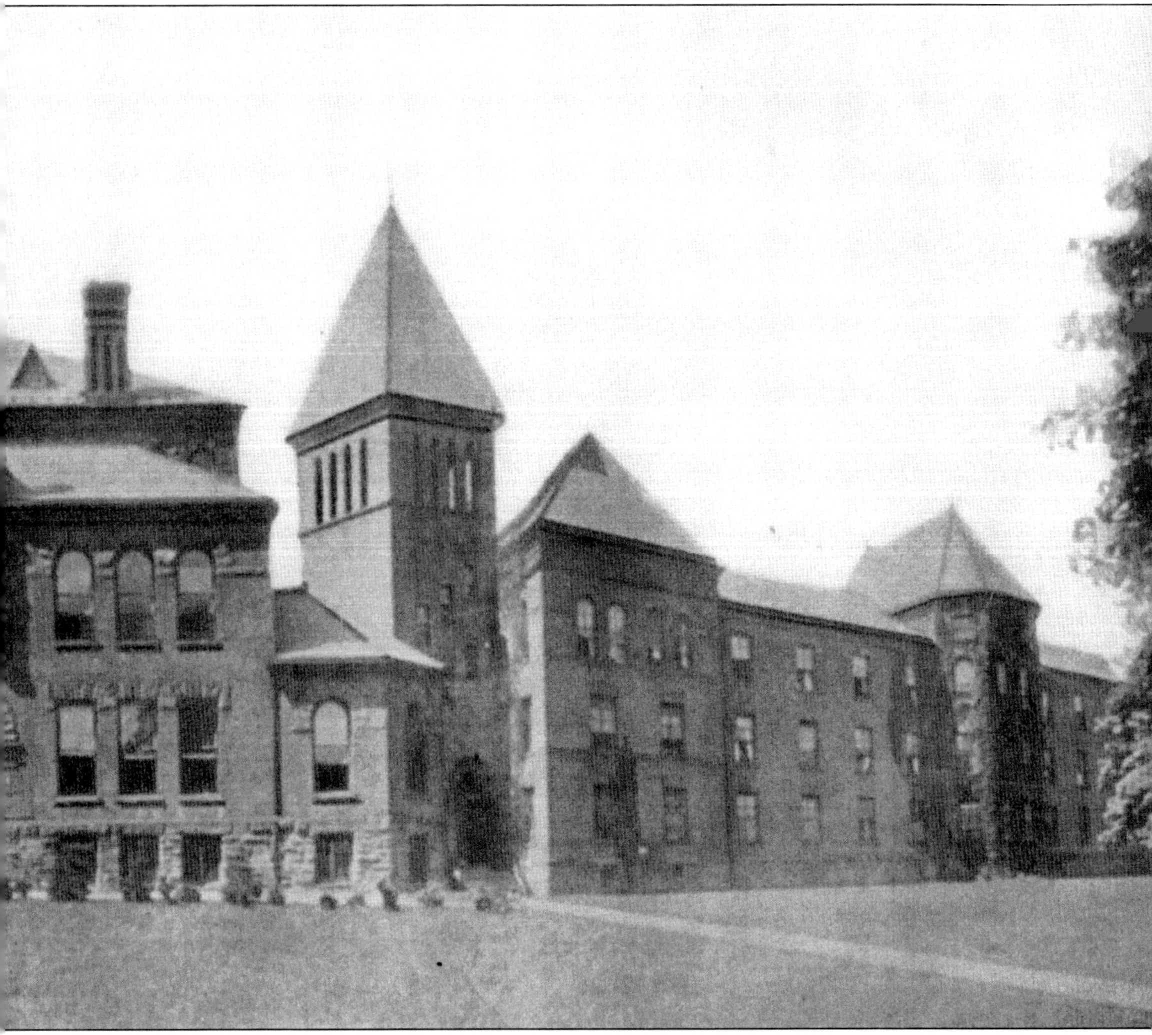

Haven High School. Philip Price, a Quaker and real estate developer in Lock Haven, donated 16 acres of land. The cornerstone of the building was laid in 1873, and four years later it was recognized as a state institution. After the 1888 fire destroyed the first building on top of the hill, a new building was constructed at the foot of the hill. (Courtesy of the Annie Halenbake Ross Library.)

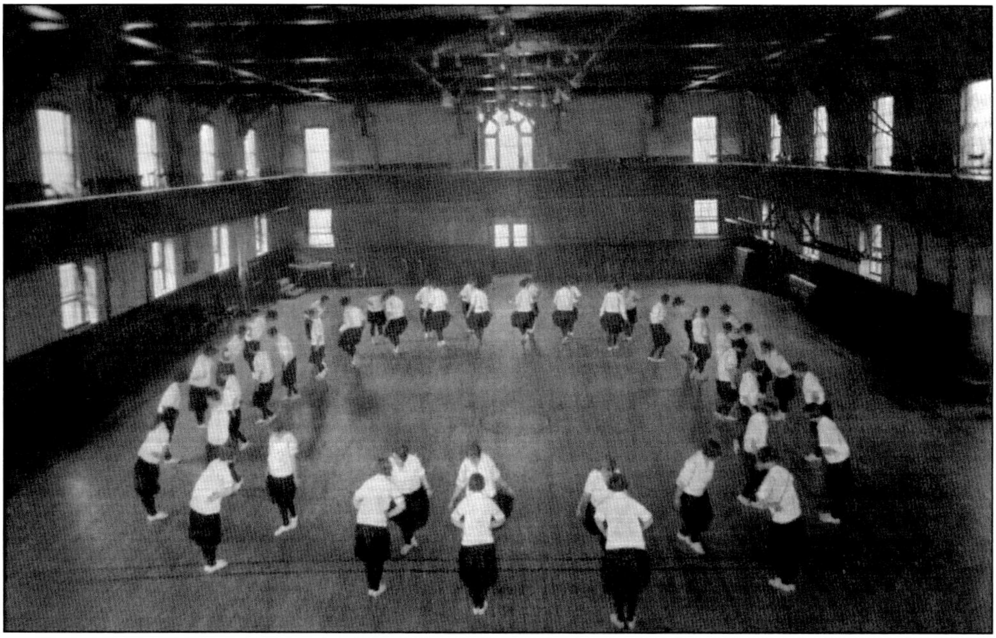

Rogers Gymnasium was the Normal School's first gymnasium. Work was completed in 1896 at a cost of $14,000. Classes in "physical culture" were under the direction of F. G. Brosius during the fall term of 1896. (Courtesy of the Annie Halenbake Ross Library.)

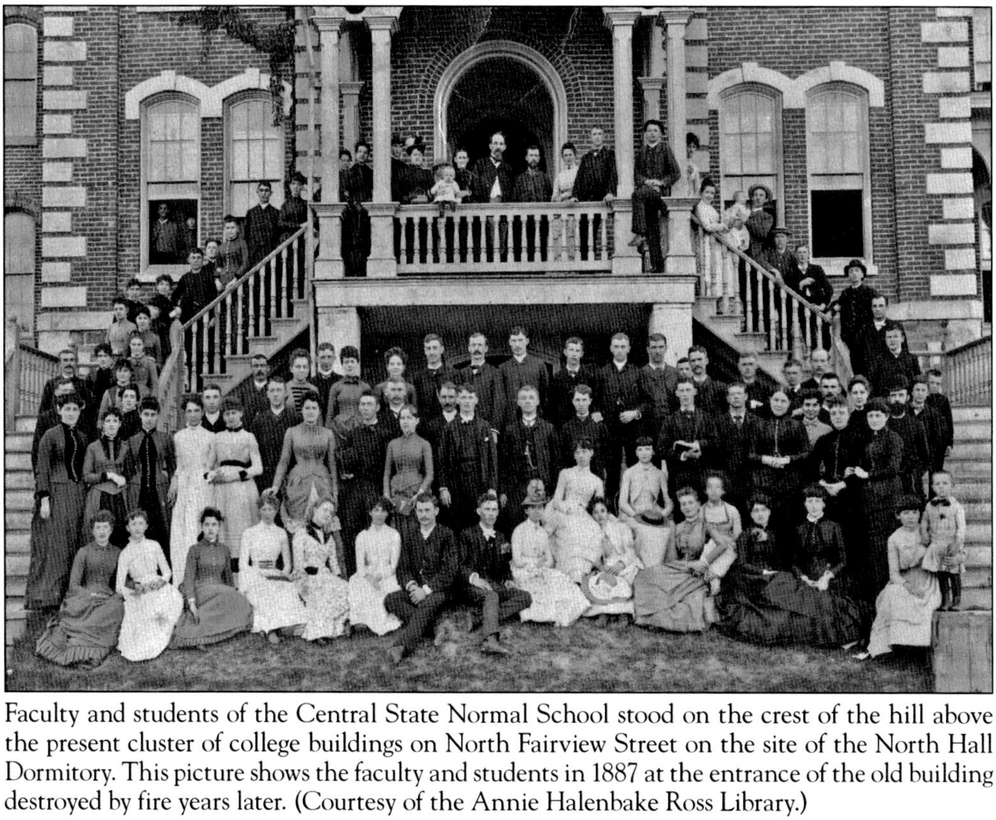

Faculty and students of the Central State Normal School stood on the crest of the hill above the present cluster of college buildings on North Fairview Street on the site of the North Hall Dormitory. This picture shows the faculty and students in 1887 at the entrance of the old building destroyed by fire years later. (Courtesy of the Annie Halenbake Ross Library.)

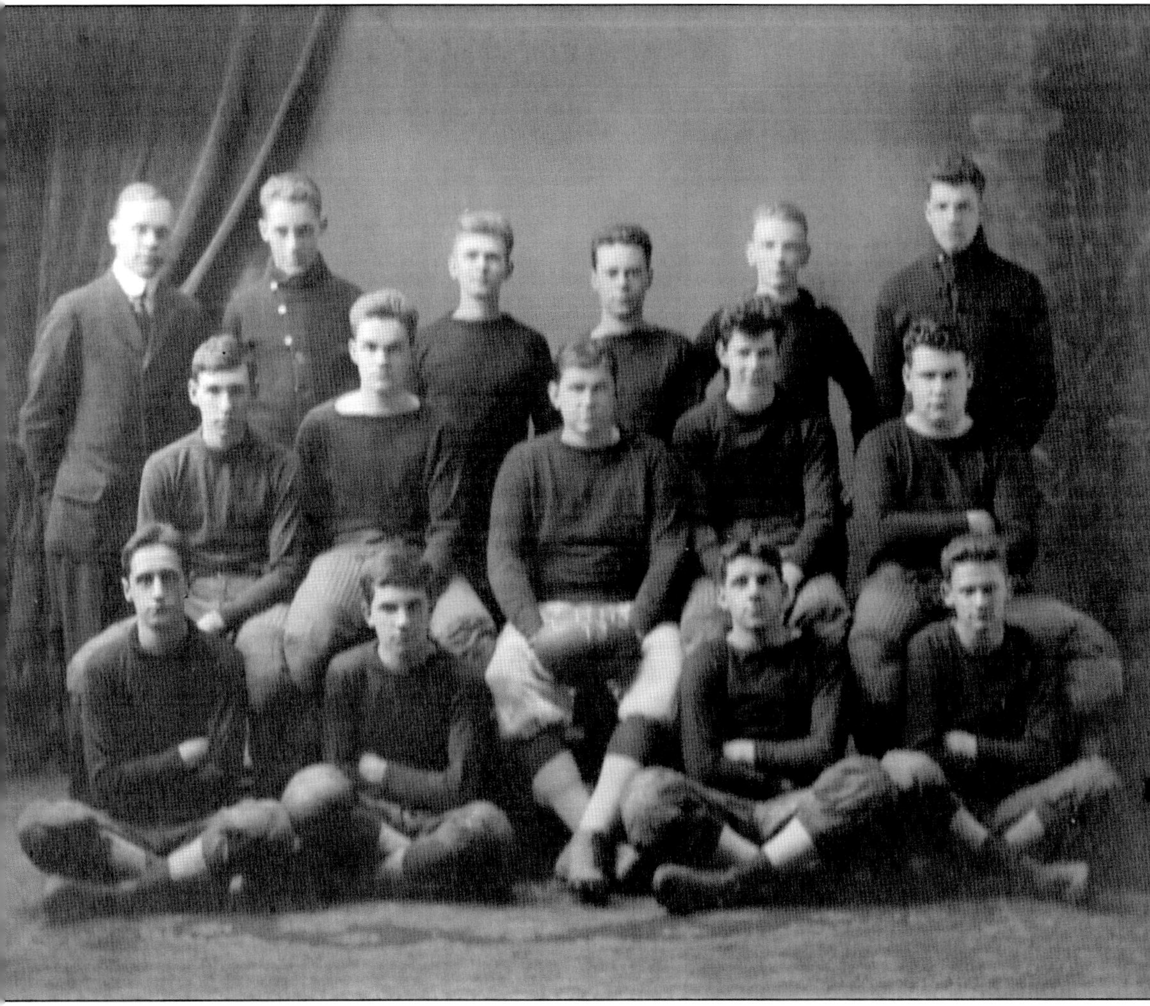

The Lock Haven High School football team of 1913 was coached by George B. Stevenson, seen at the left of the back row. George had just graduated from Dickenson Law School. He also served as postmaster and mayor of Lock Haven. He retired in 1962 after 24 years in the senate of Pennsylvania. Seen here are (first row) Lester Keller, Wynn Fredericks, John C. English, and Lewis Rathgeber; (second row) Ernie Houck, Hiram Rothrock, Lester Henry, Francis D. Smith, and Paul Simon; (third row) Carl Hecht, Paul K. Kepper, Thomas J. Hamberger, James P. Dennehy, and Lamont Smith. (Courtesy of the Annie Halenbake Ross Library.)

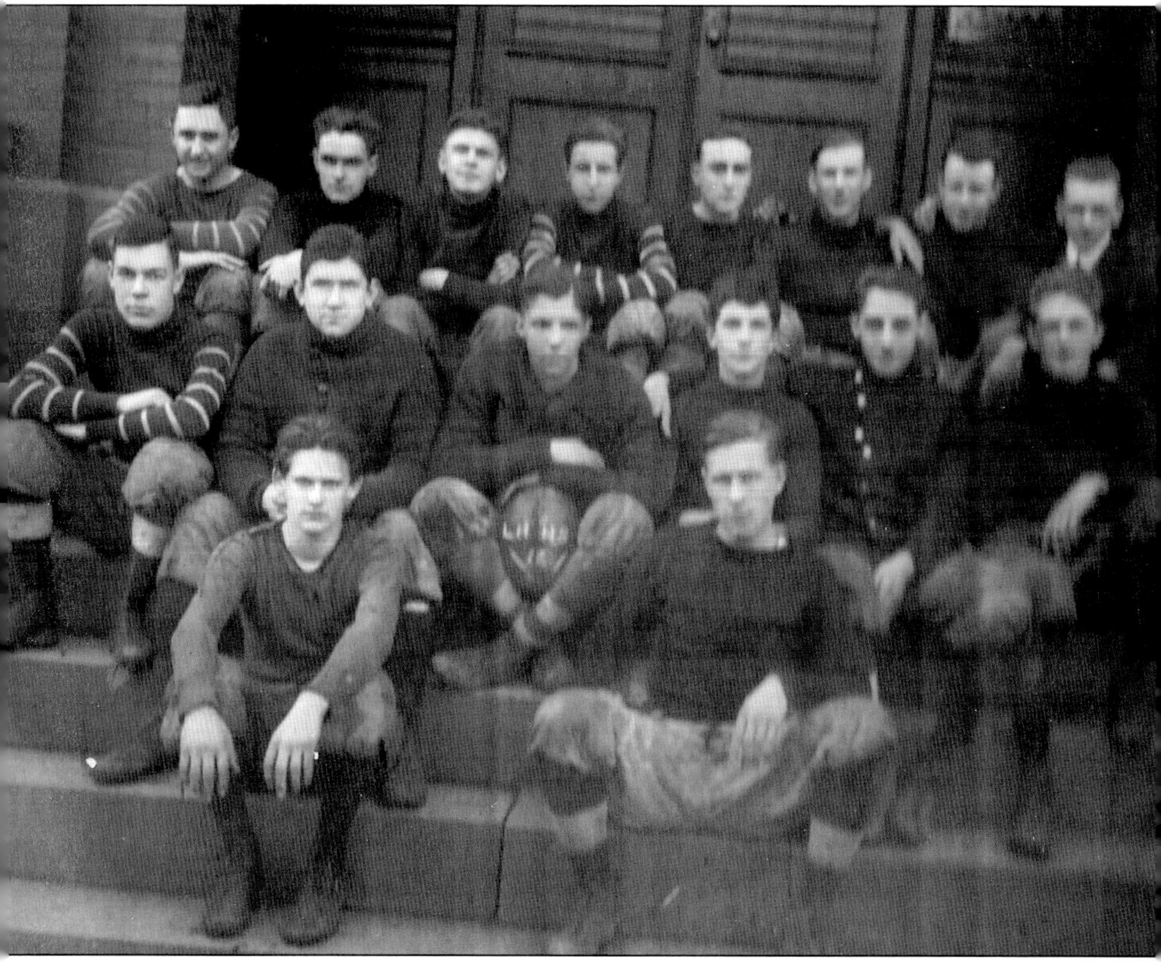

This football team wore the Lock Haven High School purple and white colors. The team was photographed on the front steps of the old high school building. Pictured are, from left to right, (first row) Lew Rathgerber and Harold Oberheim; (second row) Norman Fox, Lester Henry, Sal Patterson, team captain Wynn Fredericks, Carl Hecht, and Paul Kintzing; (third row) Morris Perr, Hiram Rothrack, Paul K. Klepper, Richard A. Smeltzer, Clair Bauman, Hiram Myers, Philip Cummings, and Jim Dennehy. (Courtesy of the Annie Halenbake Ross Library.)

# *Five*

# Communities of Faith

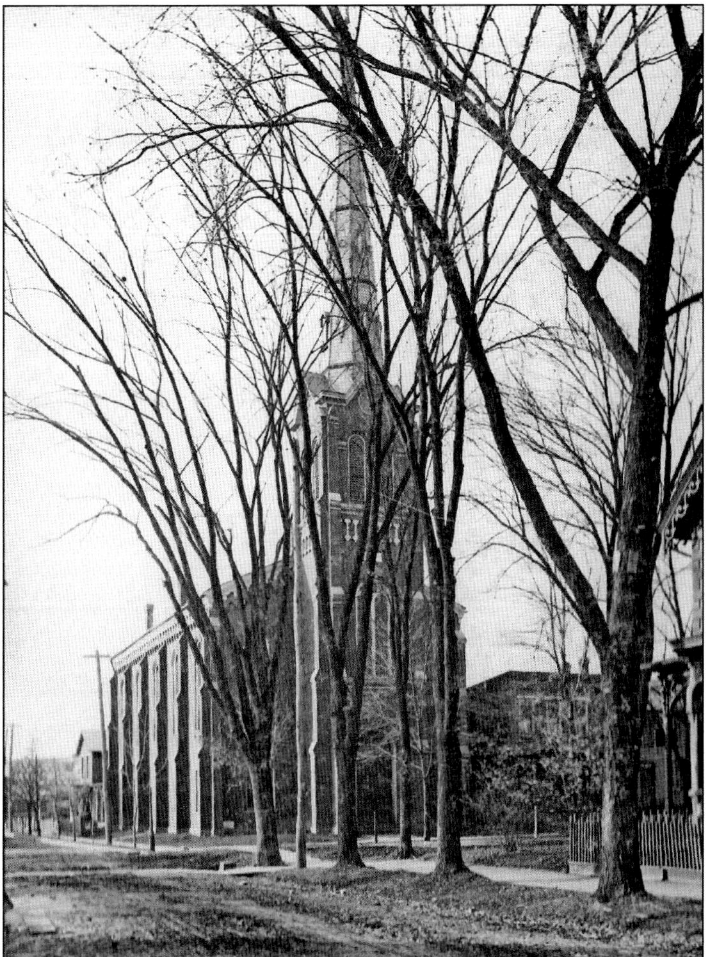

Along with the growth of Lock Haven came the rise of churches. Many faiths sent missionaries to preach the gospel. Notices of services were posted on trees, and services were held along the river, in homes, and meetinghouses. As congregations grew, beautiful churches were built throughout the city. The English Lutheran Church met in Bergen's Hall on Main Street and then in Odd Fellow's Hall. The cornerstone for this church was laid in 1869 at the southwest corner of West Church and First Streets. In 1910, the name of the church was changed to St. John's English Lutheran Church. (Courtesy of the Annie Halenbake Ross Library.)

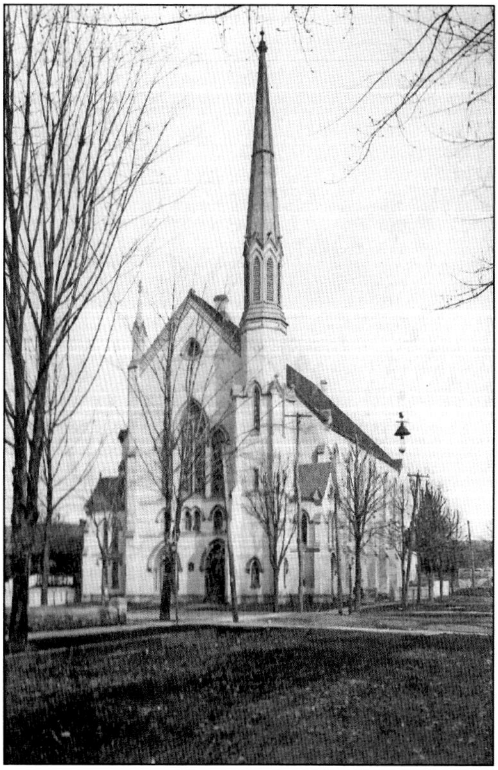

Methodists in Lock Haven met for church services in Peter Poorman's red house below the dam. Services were then held in the first schoolhouse and also in the academy building. The Trinity Methodist Church was located at the corner of Second and West Main Streets, where the church tower was 133 feet high. The building was completed in 1872 at a cost of $32,000. (Courtesy of the Annie Halenbake Ross Library.)

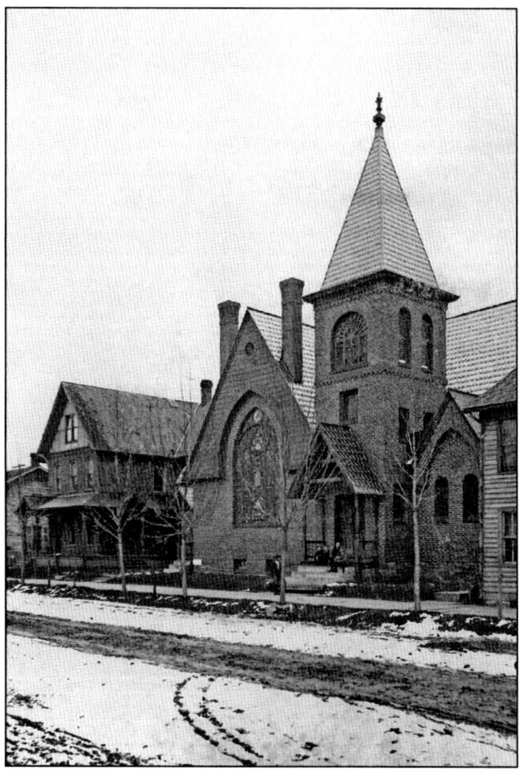

The East Main Street United Methodist Church was located at this site in 1880. The original structure had previously been used as a tavern. The church was located in that building until 1884. A new church was built in 1893, and as the parish grew, a kitchen, fellowship room, and educational room were added to the building. (Courtesy of the Annie Halenbake Ross Library.)

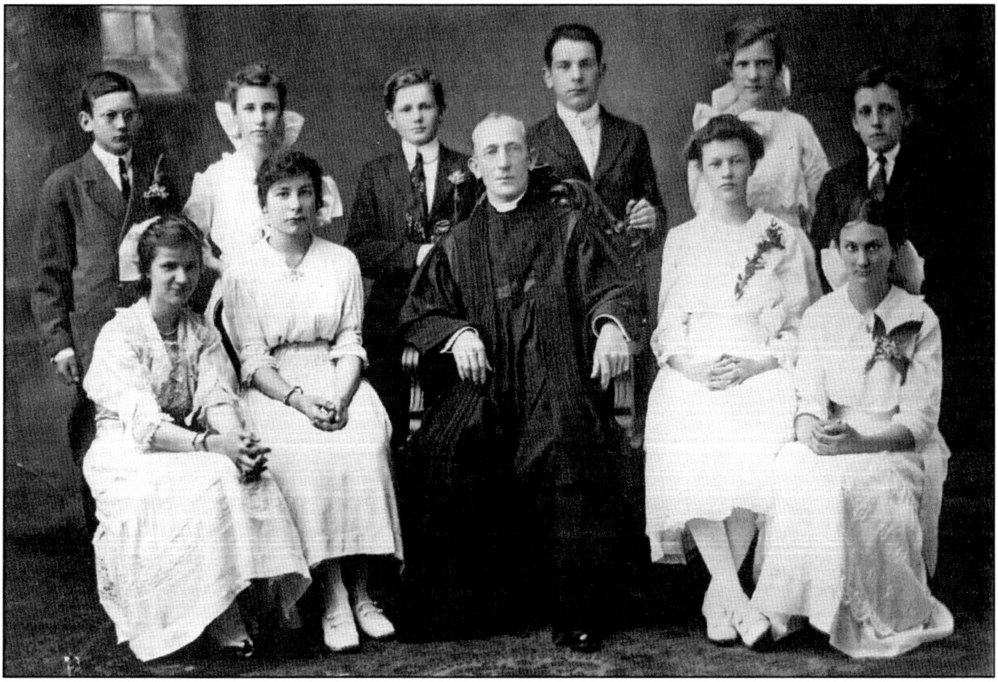

The confirmation class of the First Lutheran Church sits with Rev. John F. Bruch. From left to right are (first row) Erma Dietz, Florence Randecker, Rev. John F. Bruch, Elizabeth Hanna, and Helen Fritz; (second row) Hans Fritz, Marie Pfenninger, Homer Lucas, Carl Randecker, Helen Fabel, and Paul Bruch. (Courtesy of the Annie Halenbake Ross Library.)

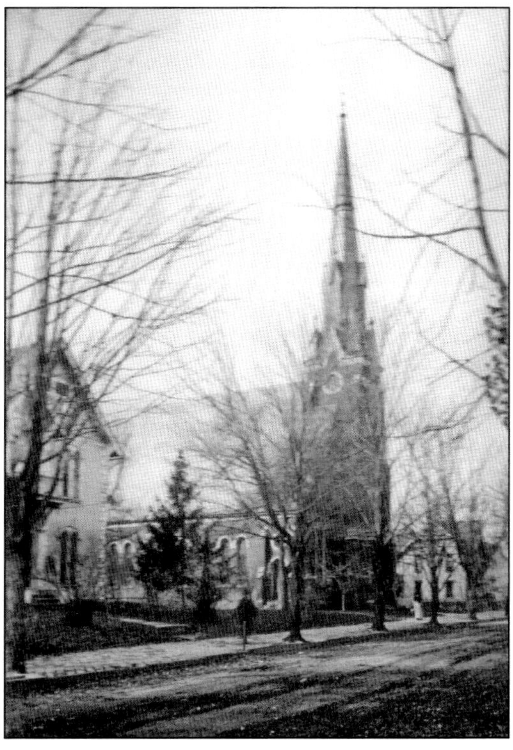

The Great Island Presbyterian Church is the oldest church in Lock Haven. It was organized in 1792 at a log house built on Bellefonte Avenue on land donated by Mrs. John McCormick. In 1850, a church building was constructed below the canal on Water Street but later sold to the German Lutheran Church. In 1865, a chapel was built at 12 West Water Street, and the church was built in 1872 at a cost of $42,000. (Courtesy of the Clinton County Historical Society.)

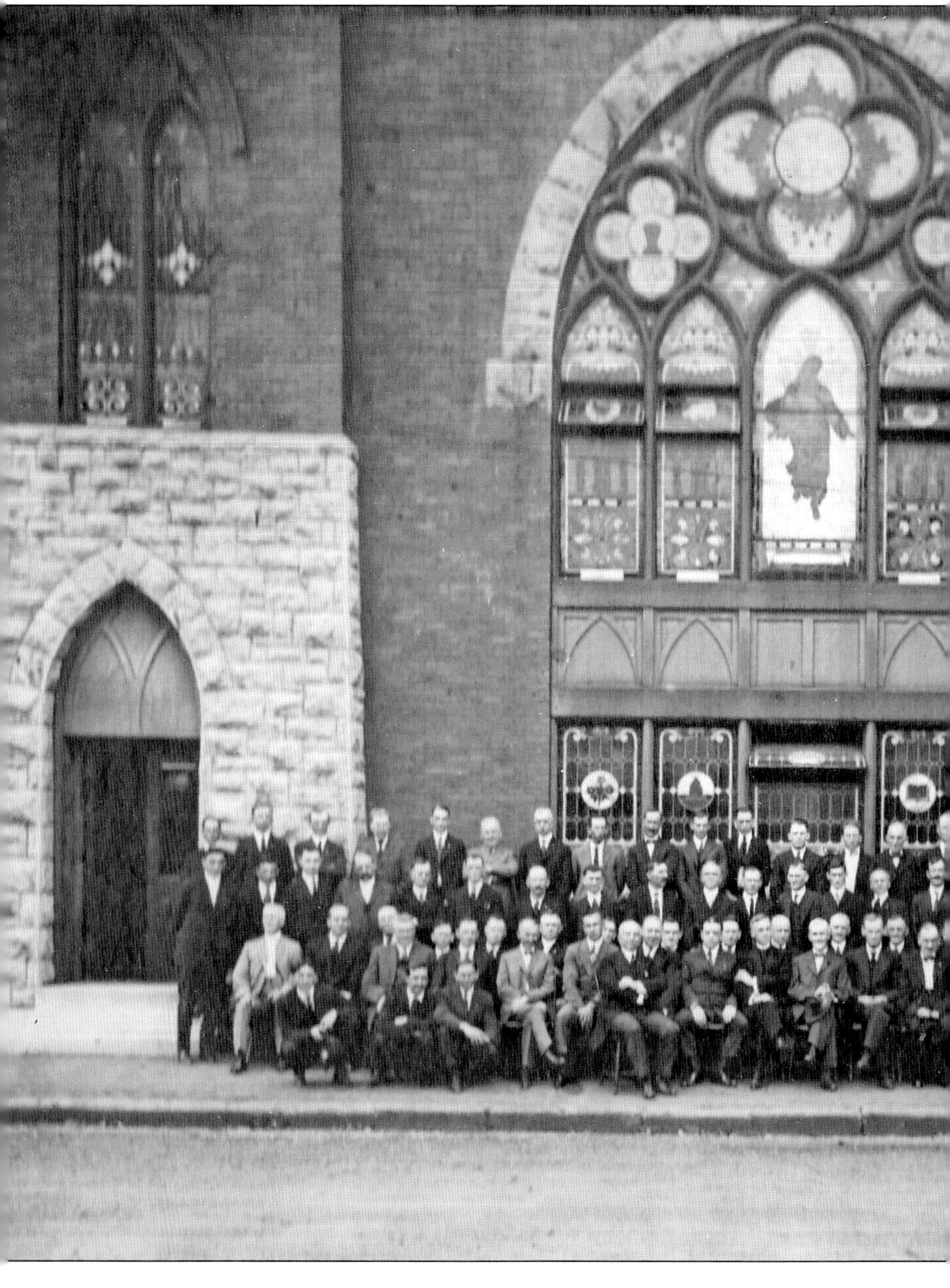

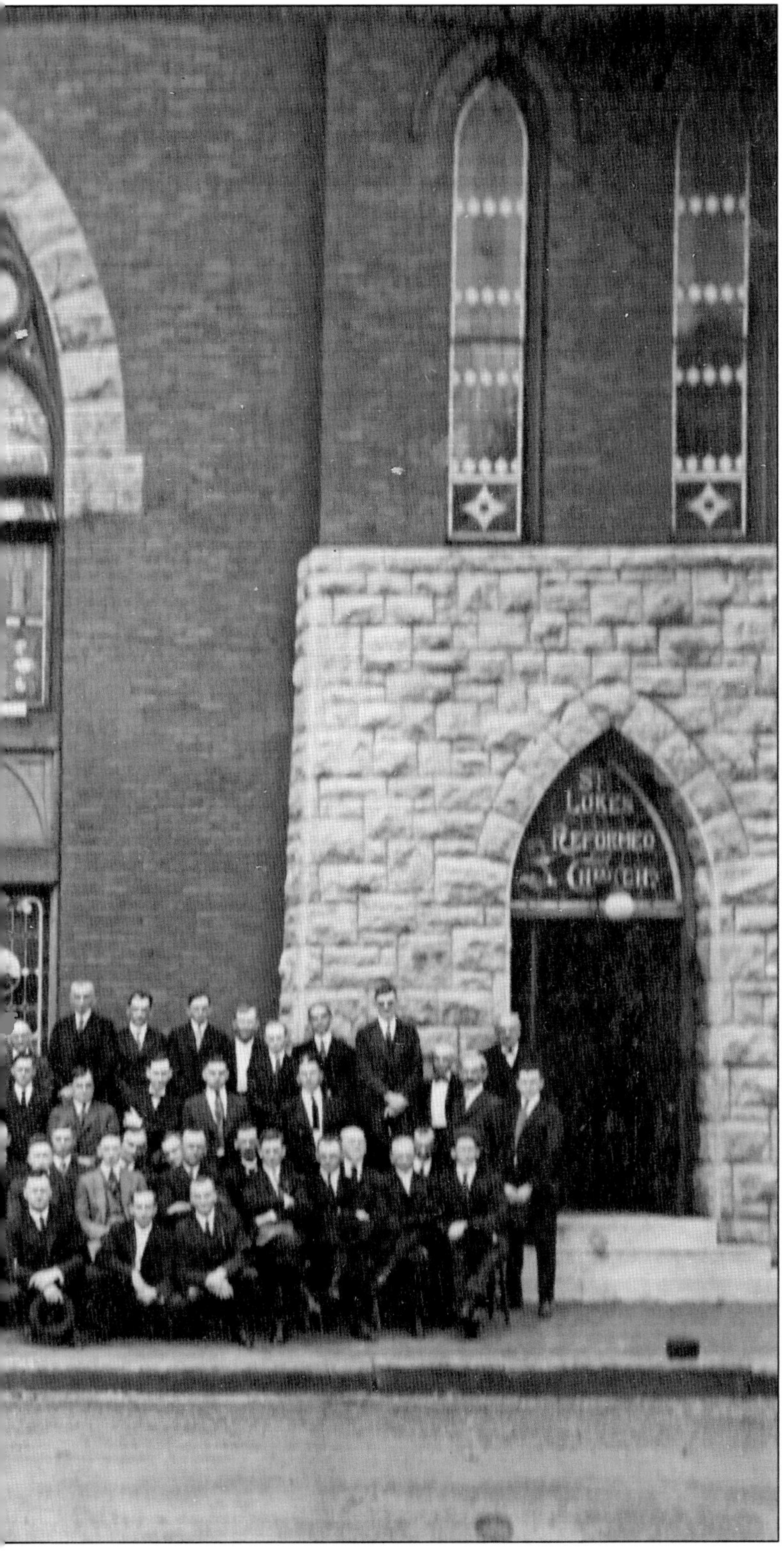

From 1825 to 1851, German Reformed families gathered together in their homes. By 1874, the Reformed group was holding services in the Second Presbyterian Church as the Church of the Resurrection. In 1878, the congregation purchased the Second Presbyterian Church. A massive twin-towered church was built facing Main Street. A fire later destroyed the building; however, the "Christ Ascending" stained glass window was salvaged from the fire. Ninety-four members of the Men's Bible Class of St. Luke's Reformed Church pose on Rally Day in 1921. (Courtesy of the Clinton County Historical Society.)

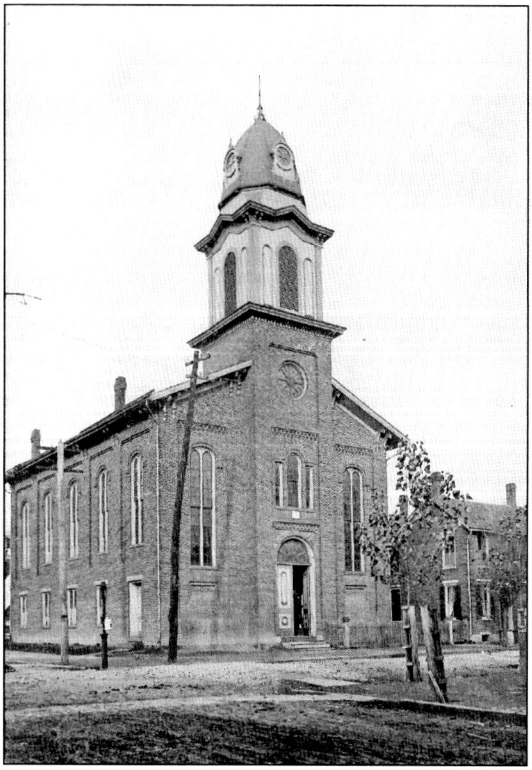

In 1860, the First Baptist Church in Lock Haven was built on the corner of Vesper and Church Streets. It was not until 1887, under the direction of Reverend Dr. R. W. Perkins, that the church membership grew. Perkins was an active member of the community, supporting the growth of the library, hospital, and Lock Haven Chorus. A parsonage was added in 1910. (Courtesy of the Clinton County Historical Society.)

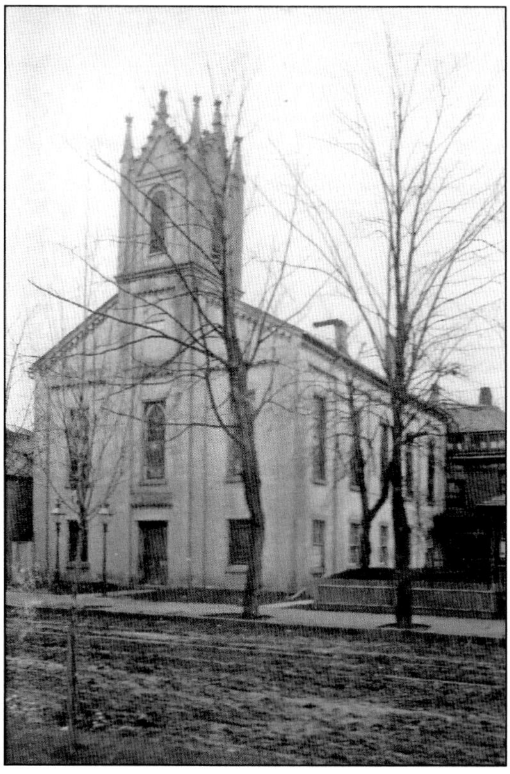

St. Luke's Reformed Church was located at 30 West Main Street. Services for this congregation were originally held in the rooms of the YMCA. The church congregation began renting the building of Second Presbyterian, a church that was disbanded. In August 1878, the church building was purchased for $2,200, which was considered low for its proximity to the center of town. By 1883, under the direction of Rev. George W. Gerhard, the congregation had grown to 200 members. Gerhard was responsible for considerable growth of the congregation, as well as improvements to the church building. (Courtesy of the Clinton County Historical Society.)

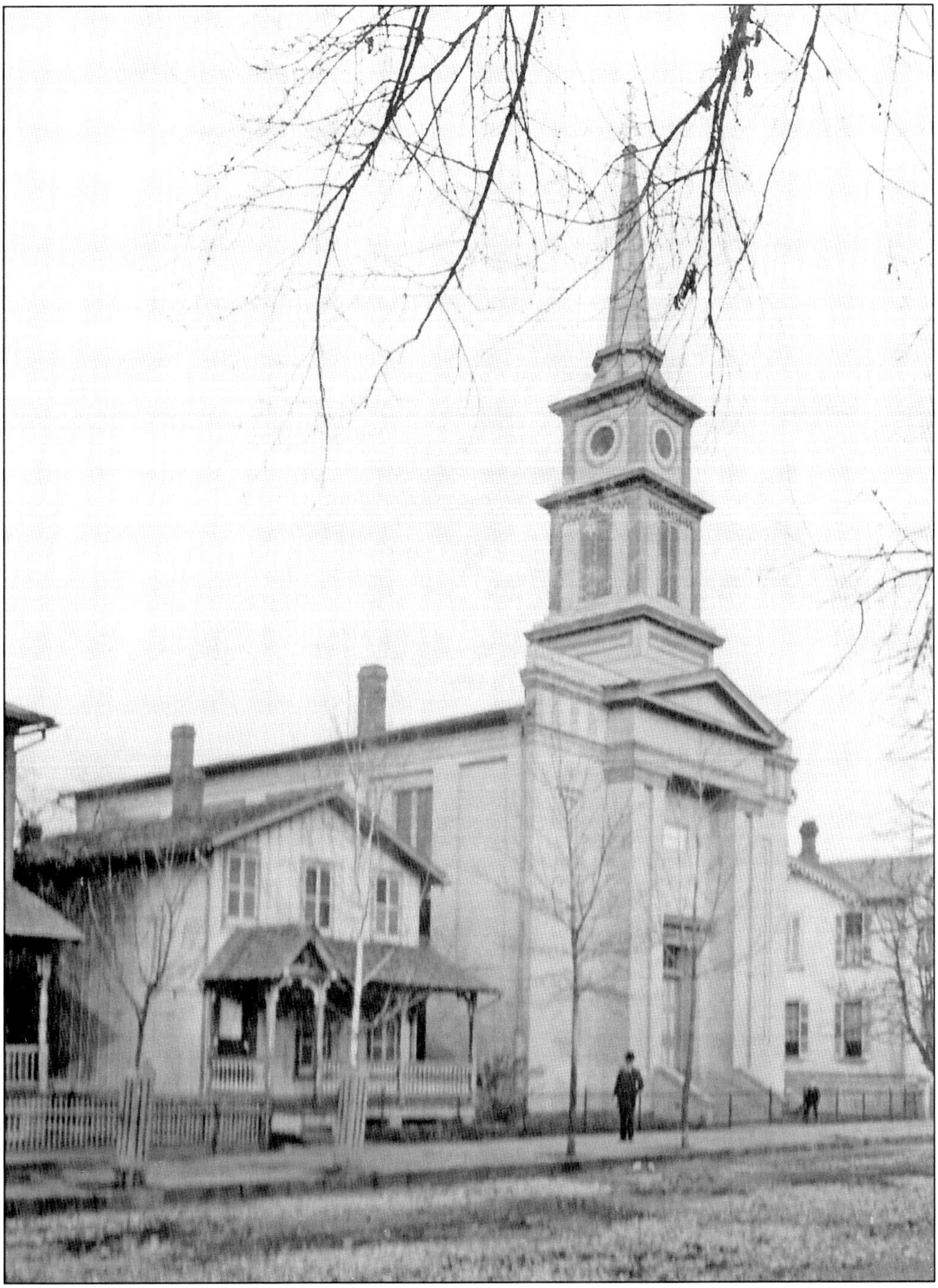

Members of the First Church of Christ began meeting in 1869. The Church of Christ was incorporated in 1860. The congregation first worshipped at a building on the corner of East Church and Fallon Alley, which they purchased for $6,000. A new building was constructed in 1923 and dedicated in June of that year. The cost of the building was $70,000. Additions to the church in 1969 included the educational building, library, and office complex. (Courtesy of the Clinton County Historical Society.)

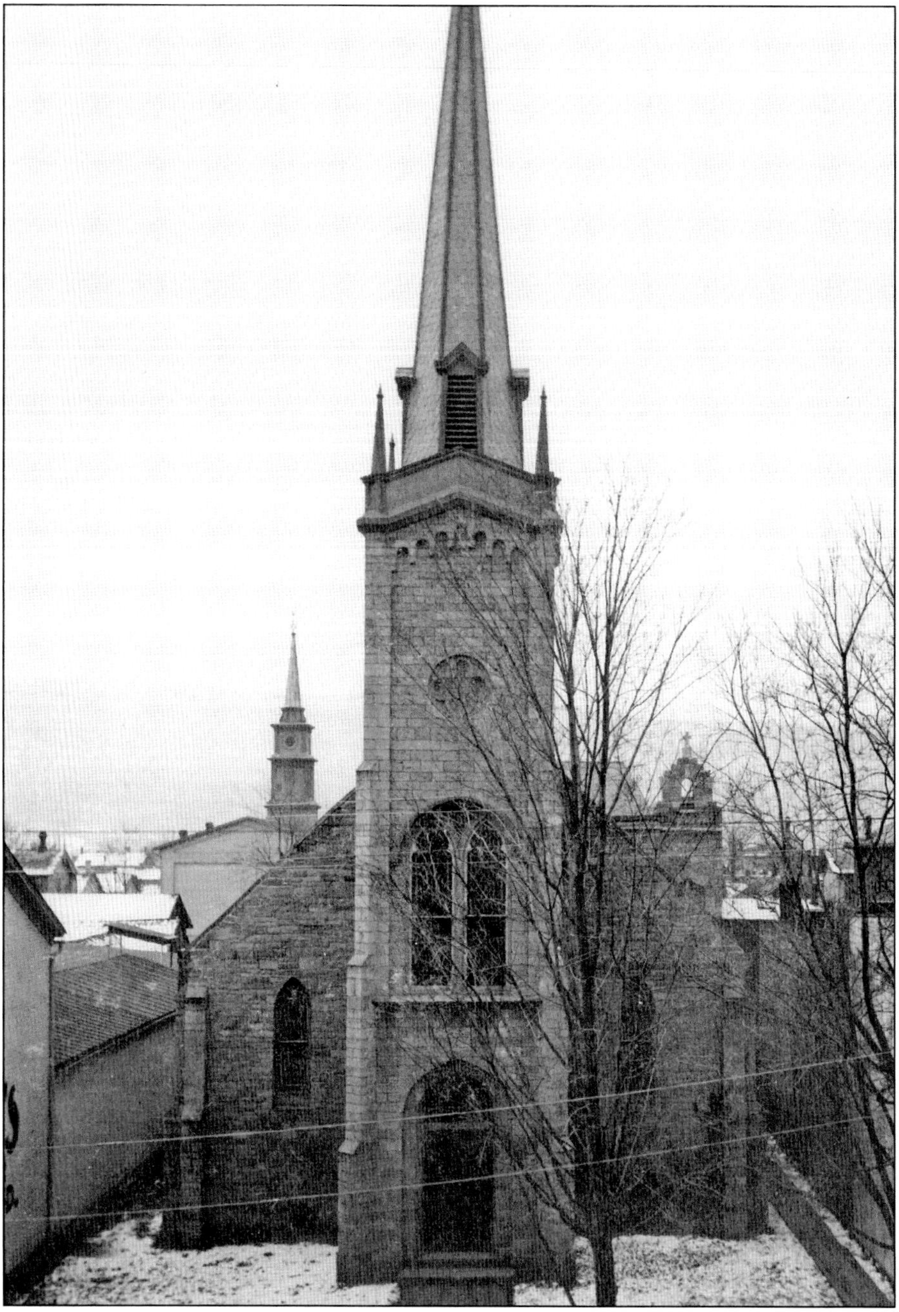

In June 1775, a missionary of the Church of England, the Reverend Mr. Page, conducted church services in Lock Haven. In 1850, Bishop Onderdonk and others traveled along the valleys of the Susquehanna and Bald Eagle baptizing children. In 1852, Rev. George Herbert Walsh of Bellefonte and Rev. Richard Channing Moore of Williamsport held services in Lock Haven by posting notices on trees. In September 1855, a meeting was called at the Clinton Hotel by the Rev. D. S. Miller of Philadelphia to organize an Episcopal church. The St. Paul's Parish was incorporated on August 12, 1856. The original church building began in 1856. (Courtesy of the Clinton County Historical Society.)

A fire during the 1936 flood destroyed St. Paul's Episcopal Church and parish house; all that remained were the damaged stone walls. The church was rebuilt in 1937 at a cost of $32,000. During the rebuilding, the congregation met at Odd Fellows Hall, which was the location that the congregation used during the building of the church in 1856. (Courtesy of the Clinton County Historical Society.)

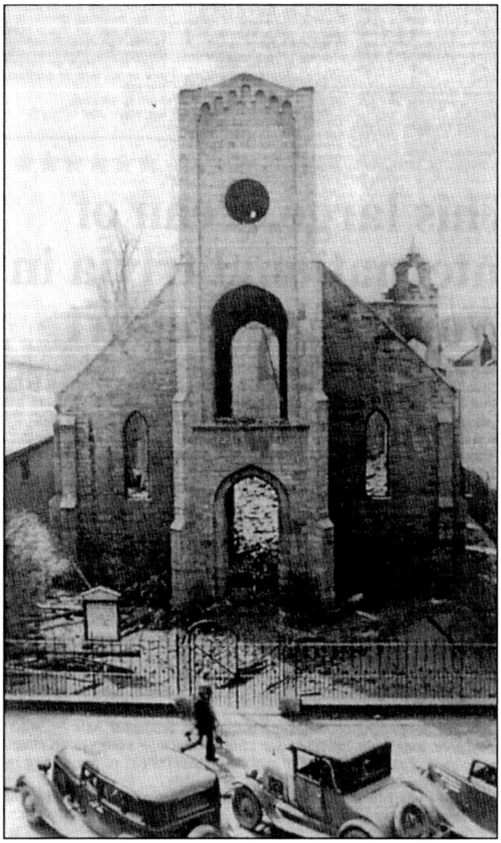

The first place of worship for Catholics of Lock Haven in 1852 was in a black wood frame building on lots 124 to 134 East Bald Eagle St. Church services were conducted there for nine years by Rev. John C. Gilligan, who had been a pastor of St. John's Church in Bellefonte. Two years later, in 1854, the property on East Bald Eagle Street was sold. On August 19, 1857, the cornerstone for St. Mary's Catholic Church was laid on a lot at Third and West Water Streets. The church name was changed to Church of the Immaculate Conception. The land was purchased from Christopher Fallon and John Fallon and their wives for the sum of $1. (Courtesy of the Clinton County Historical Society.)

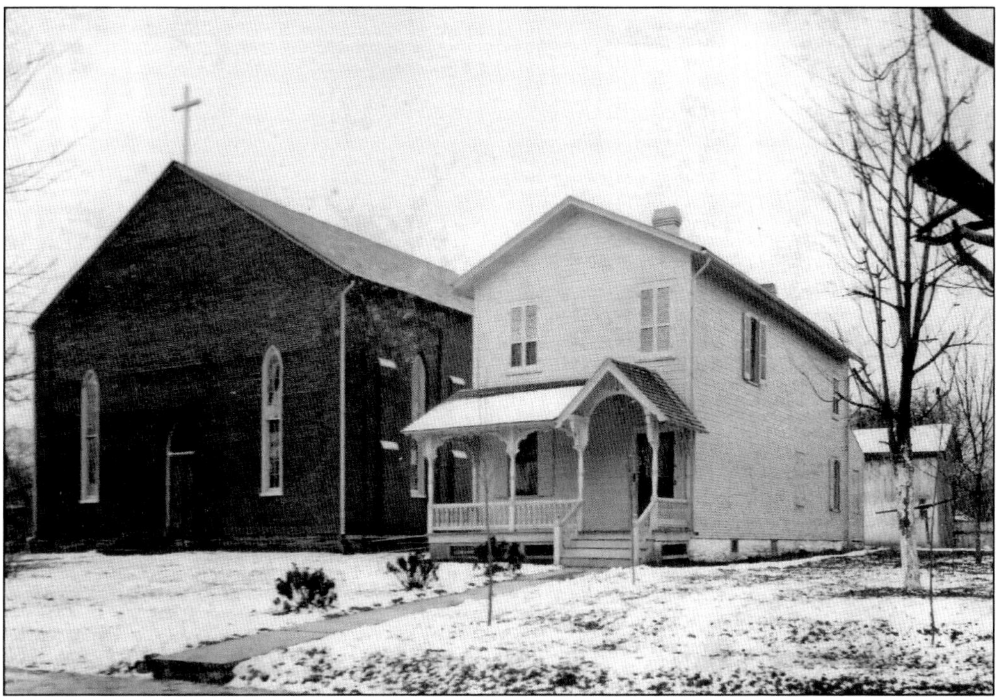

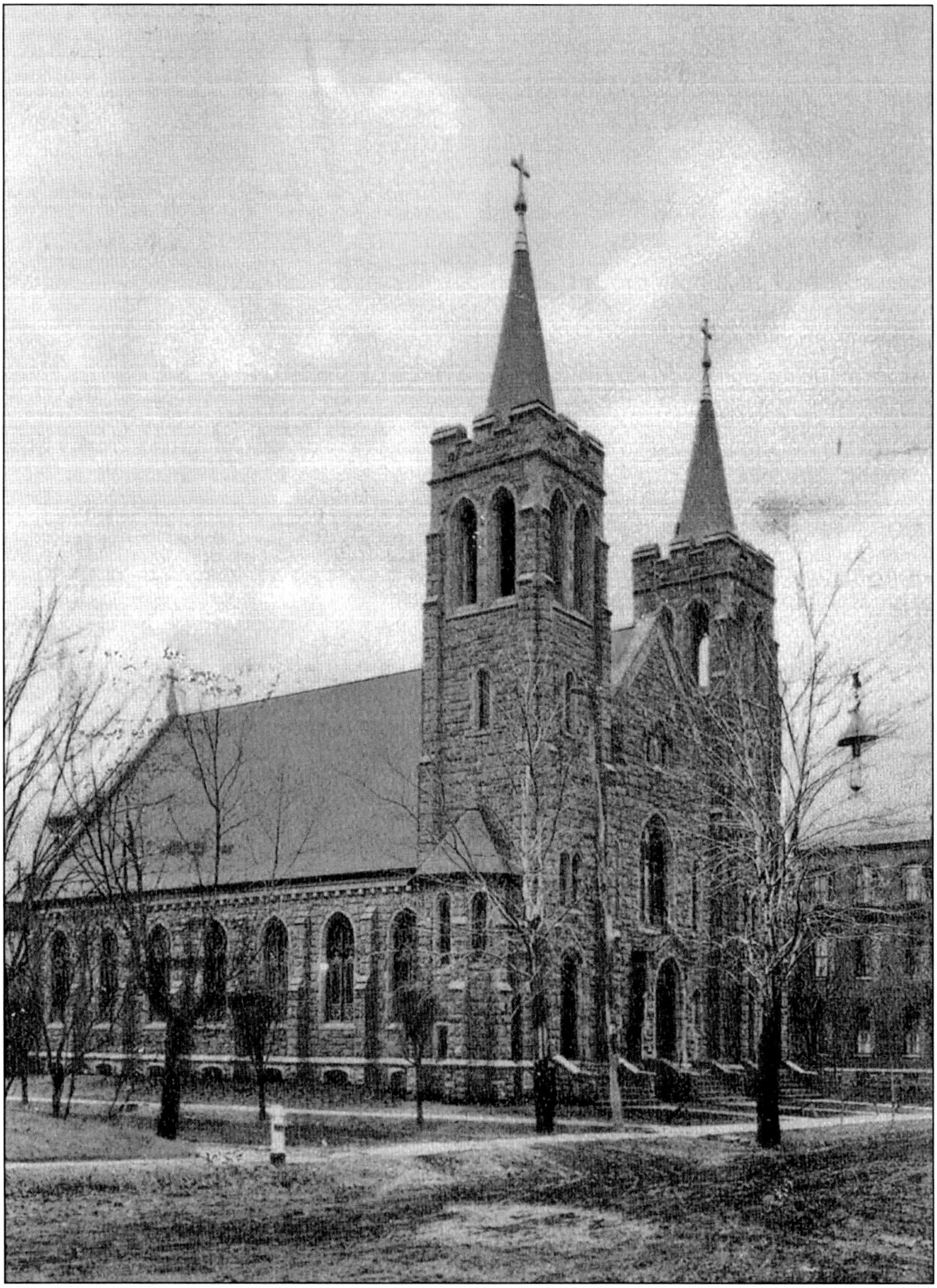

The Church of the Immaculate Conception is located at Third and West Water Streets. A new brownstone church was built on the site replacing the 1857 building and consecrated in 1905. A parochial school was built in 1876 adjoining the property. The school prospered under the direction of the Sisters of Mercy and in later years by the Sisters of the Immaculate Heart of Mary and the Dominican Sisters. The school was relocated across the street and continues to serve the community today. (Courtesy of the Clinton County Historical Society.)

*Six*

# Life Along the River

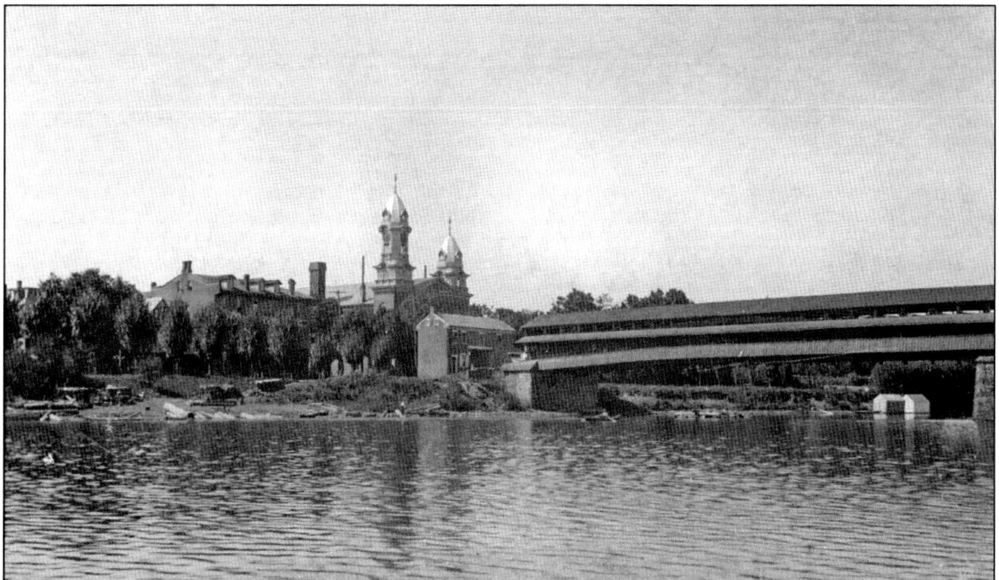

The West Branch of the Susquehanna River has always played a vital role in the stability of Lock Haven. The river was a source of transportation, a means of earning a living in the lumber era, and a source of recreation. The Jay Street Bridge was completed in 1852. It was about 800 feet long with a brick two-story Toll House located on the Lock Haven side of the river immediately at the end of the bridge. Passengers entering the bridge passed beneath the arch, which united two wings of the building. Fees were collected for a number of years. The bridge was originally constructed in 1877, and after its destruction was replaced by a steel structure resting on three piers and two abutments. (Courtesy of the Clinton County Historical Society.)

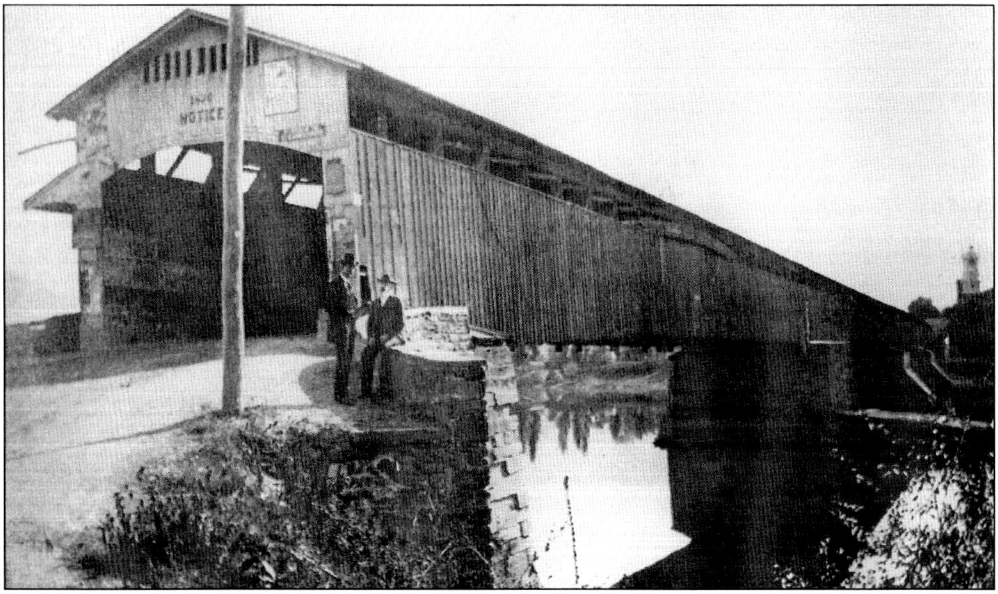

Between 3:00 p.m. on May 30, 1889, and 4:00 a.m. on June 1, 1889, the rainfall from a storm that swept across central Pennsylvania amounted to more than 7 inches, causing creeks and small streams to swell. At Lock Haven, the West Branch of the Susquehanna River reached 30.5 feet above the low water mark. The only bridge standing between Lock Haven and Sunbury was the old covered bridge at Jay Street. The lumber industry suffered the heaviest loss as thousands of logs and boards were swept away, and many mills were destroyed. (Courtesy of the Clinton County Historical Society.)

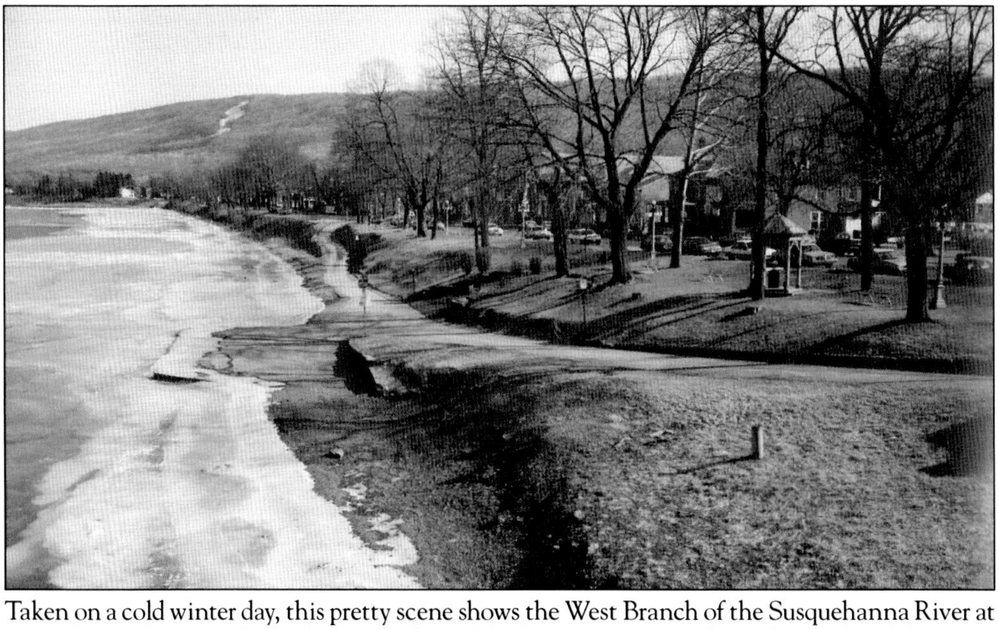

Taken on a cold winter day, this pretty scene shows the West Branch of the Susquehanna River at Water Street, just past the Jay Street Bridge. This picture was snapped in February 1992, just prior to the flood protection project. This is now the site of the J. Doyle Corman Amphitheater. From the beginning, the flood protection project was met with both opposition and support as the costs and benefits of the project were debated. (Courtesy of the Clinton County Historical Society.)

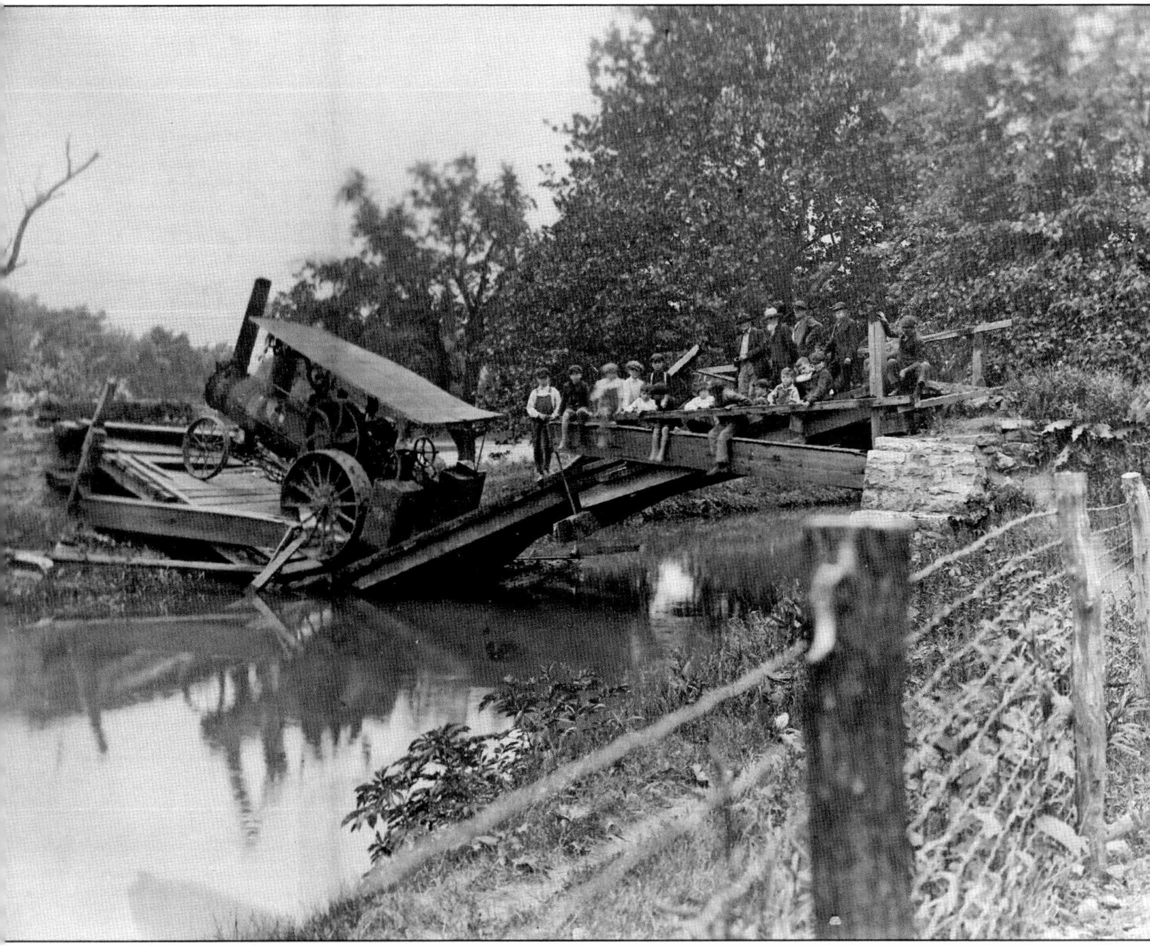

The old canal bridge in this picture spanned the crosscut between Lock Haven and Flemington. This picture shows what happened to the bridge when a threshing machine tried to cross it sometime in the 1930s on the way to the field on the other side of the canal. Local children, many barefoot, sit and stand precariously along the damaged bridge for this picture. (Courtesy of the Clinton County Historical Society.)

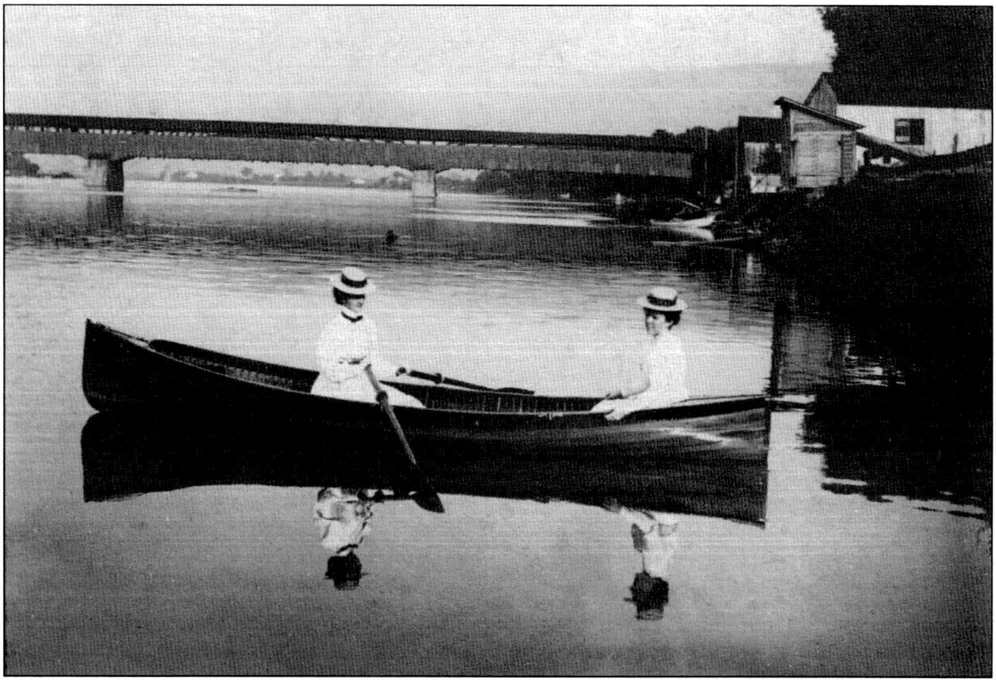

The West Branch of the Susquehanna River has served as a means of recreation and transportation for residents and visitors alike. Before bridges, residents crossed the river by boat. In 1838, a ferry was started from East Water Street to Lock Haven. J. P. Huling, owner of the Washington House, managed the Lock Haven end, and Judge Hanna managed the Lockport side. There were many ferries in the area including the Sour Ferry and the Quiggle Ferry. Below, George Kreamer, one of Lock Haven's mayors, makes his way across the West Branch of the Susquehanna River. (Both, courtesy of the Anne Halenbake Ross Library.)

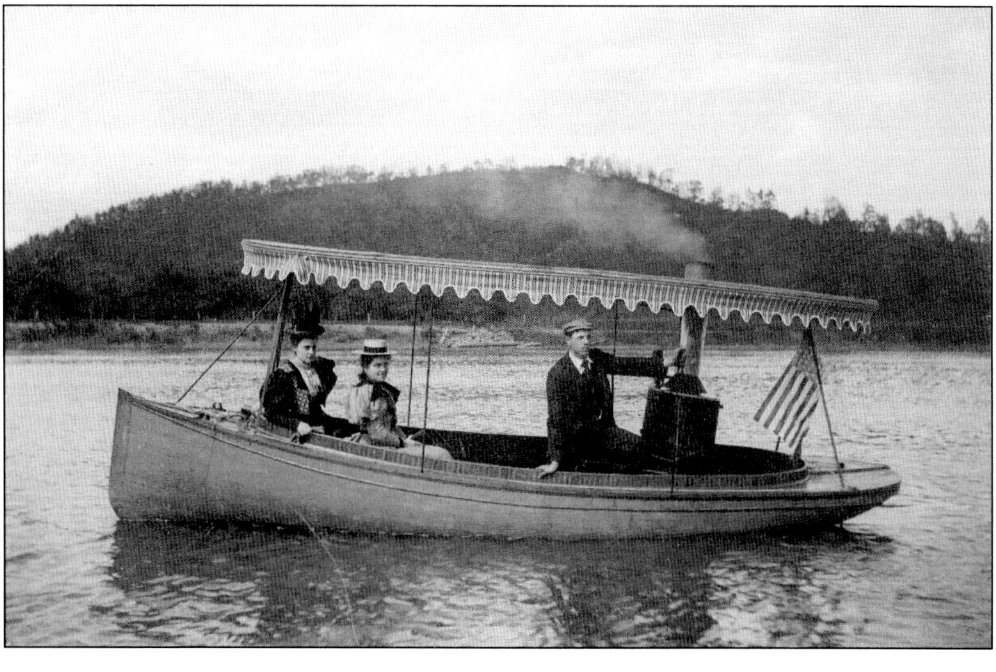

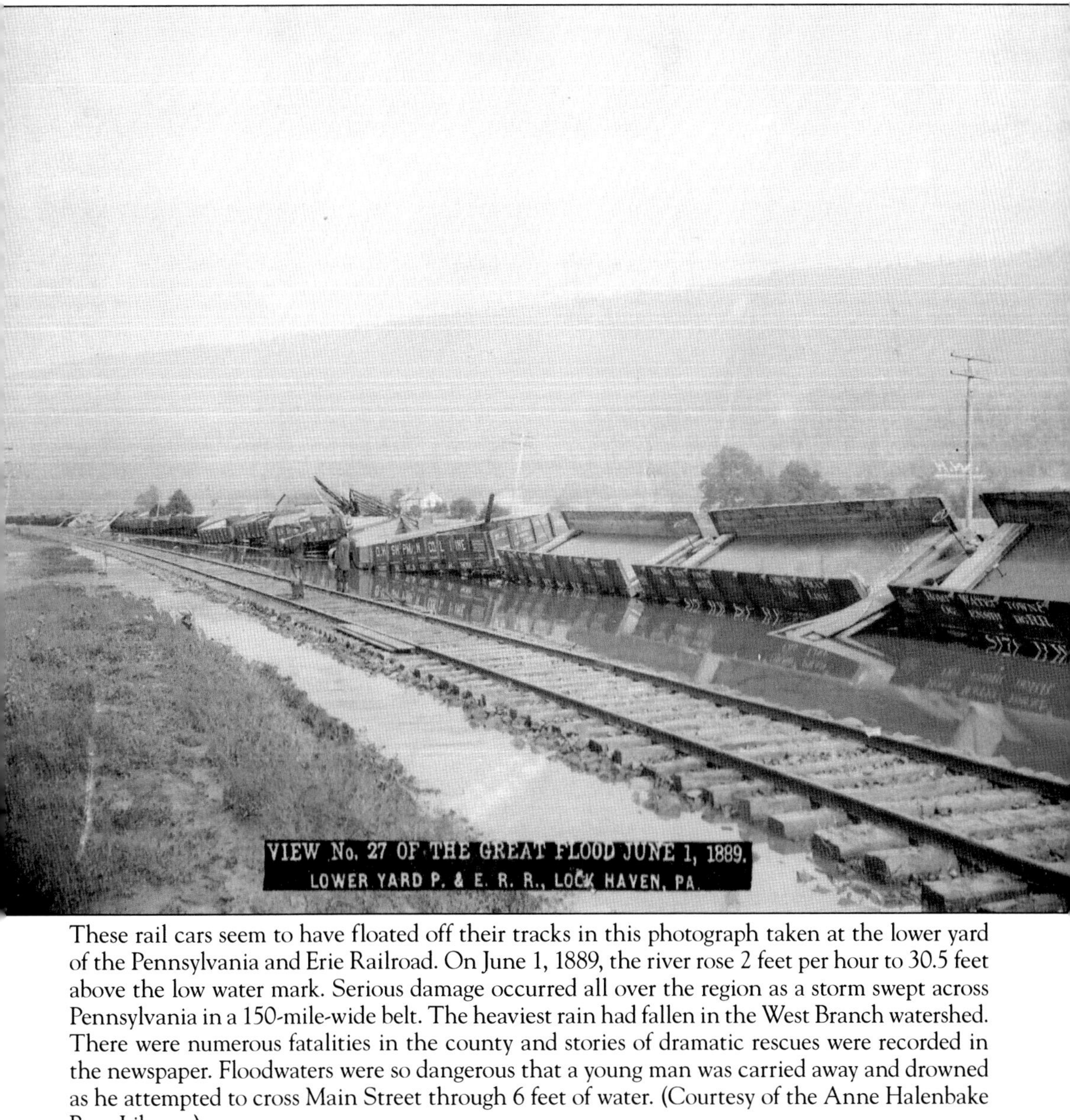


These rail cars seem to have floated off their tracks in this photograph taken at the lower yard of the Pennsylvania and Erie Railroad. On June 1, 1889, the river rose 2 feet per hour to 30.5 feet above the low water mark. Serious damage occurred all over the region as a storm swept across Pennsylvania in a 150-mile-wide belt. The heaviest rain had fallen in the West Branch watershed. There were numerous fatalities in the county and stories of dramatic rescues were recorded in the newspaper. Floodwaters were so dangerous that a young man was carried away and drowned as he attempted to cross Main Street through 6 feet of water. (Courtesy of the Anne Halenbake Ross Library.)

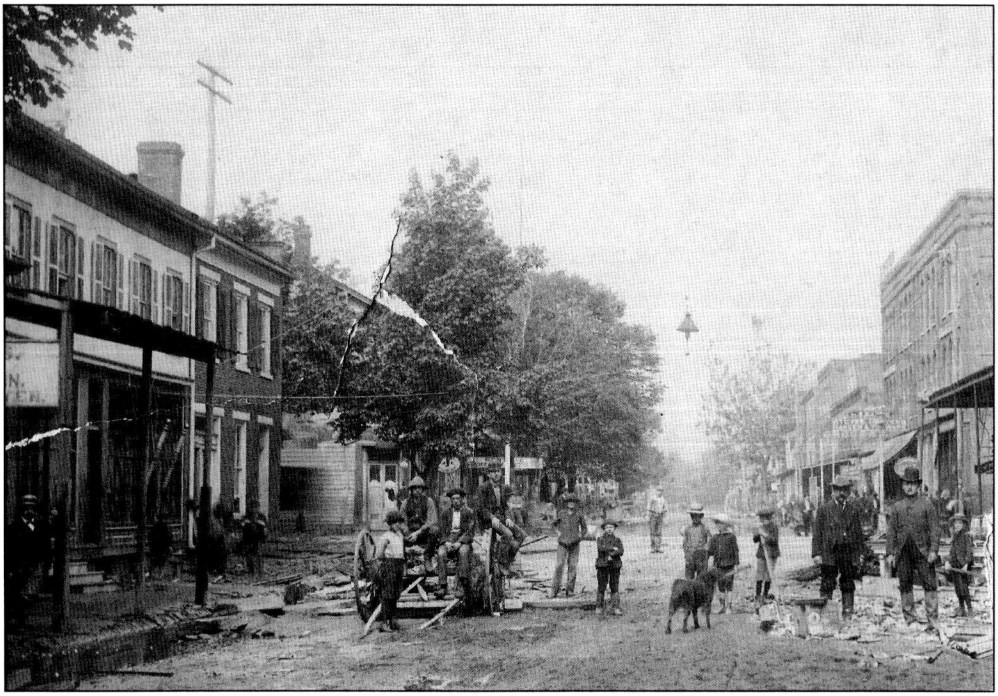

Cleanup after the 1889 flood was horrific. As the floodwaters receded, the city was left with layers of mud. This flood damaged Lock Haven's log boom and canal boat system, putting an end to the lumber era. Houses, furnishings, and all were caught up in the floodwaters. Backyards and main thoroughfares were littered with debris. Almost every community along the West Branch of the Susquehanna River was affected by the flooding. Hundreds of livestock, including cows, pigs, and horses, were drowned, while some animals found refuge in the courthouse. It was reported that a horse made its way from a stable and walked up the courthouse steps to the second floor. (Both, courtesy of the Clinton County Historical Society.)

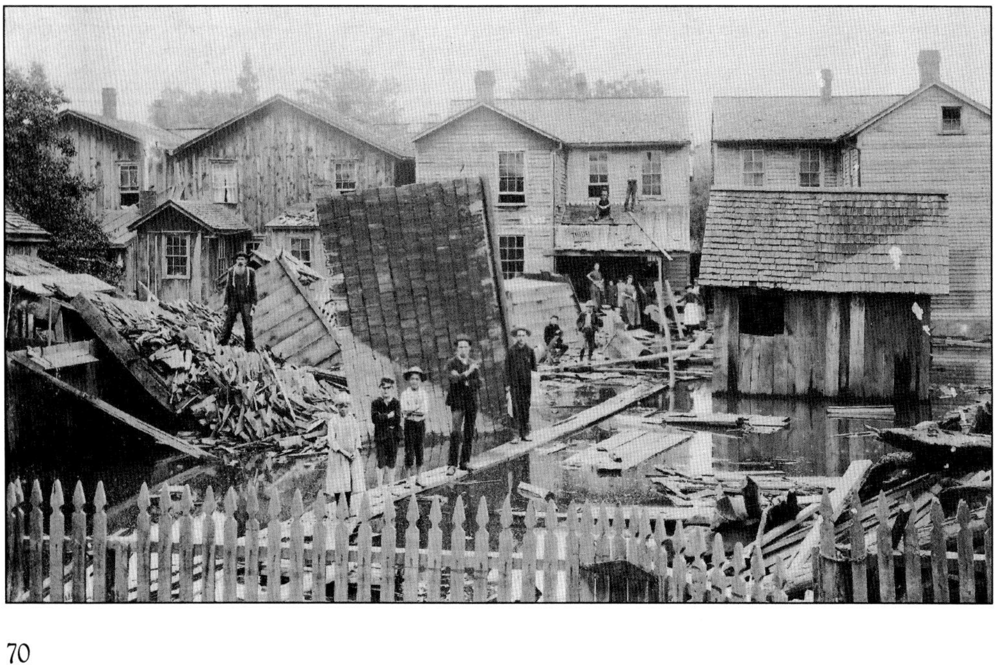

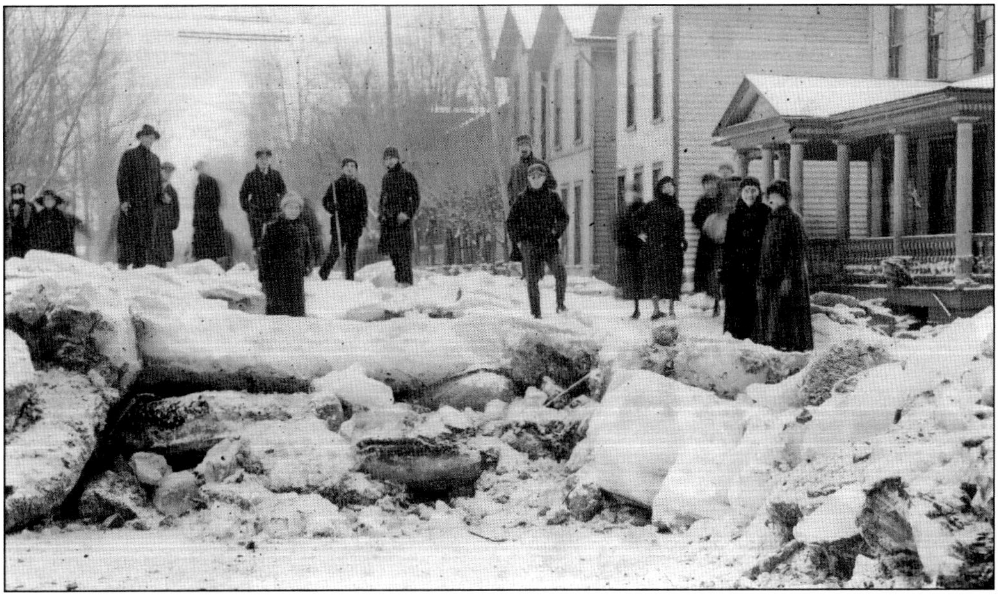

In February 1918, Lock Haven suffered an "ice flood." Property damage in the city was severe. The river rose too high, and an ice jam in the river and floodwaters from the West Branch and Bald Eagle Creek backed up and flooded Lock Haven. In some parts of town the frigid water, with floating cakes of ice, rose to 12 feet. Electricity was shut off and heating units were extinguished. Huge blocks of ice crushed windows, broke fences, and destroyed homes. Surrounding communities responded with aid, supplies, and volunteers to clear the streets. (Both, courtesy of the Clinton County Historical Society.)

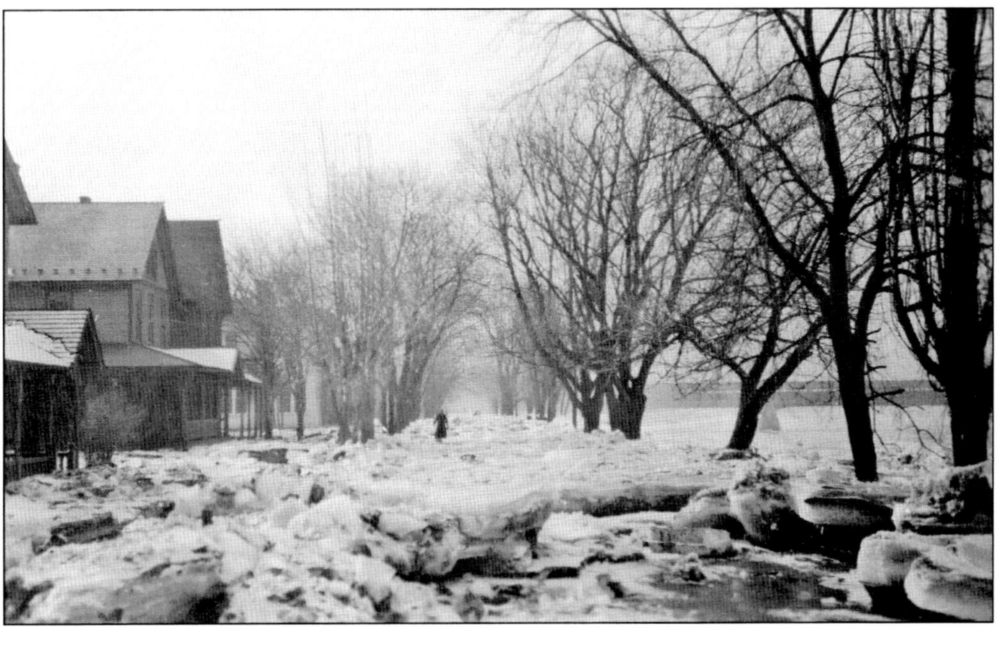

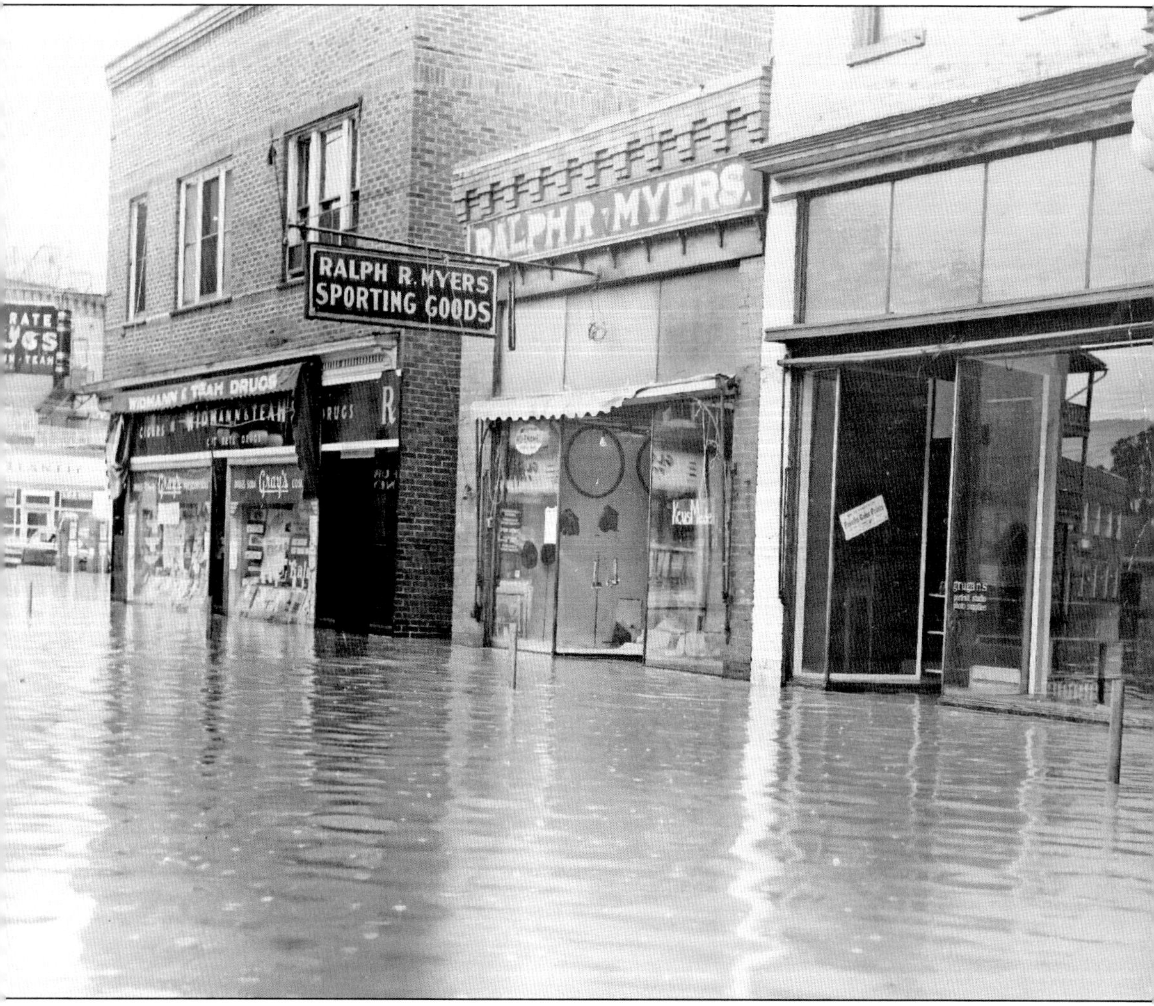


On March 17, 1936, the St. Patrick's Day flood caused extensive damage to the city and surrounding communities. Extreme cold and snow followed by rain and rising temperatures caused extensive damage. (Courtesy of the Clinton County Historical Society.)

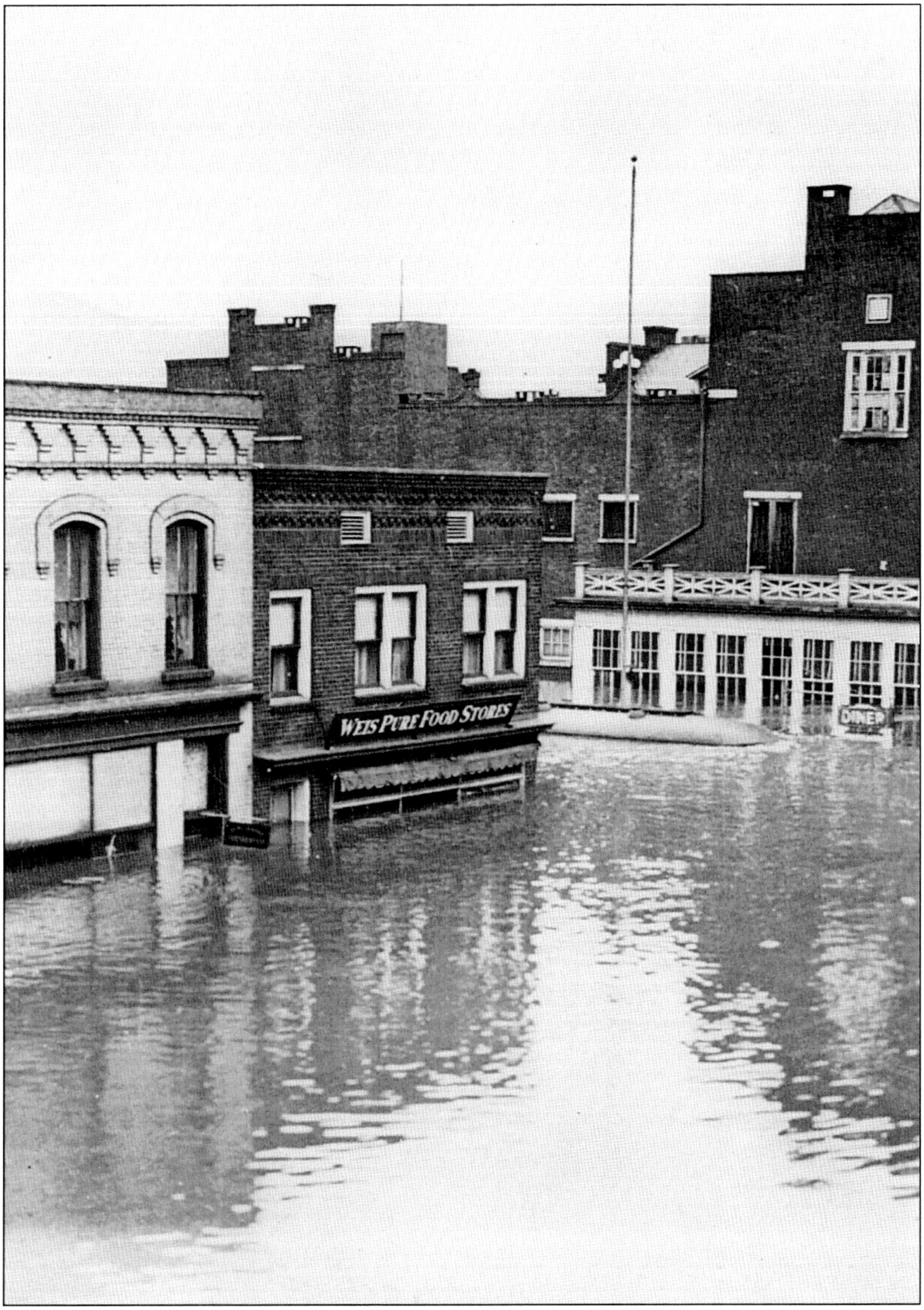


Under the direction of the Red Cross and Lock Haven Disaster Committee, hundreds of volunteers helped to clean up the city. During the week after the flood, more than 25,000 meals were served to victims. (Courtesy of the Clinton County Historical Society.)

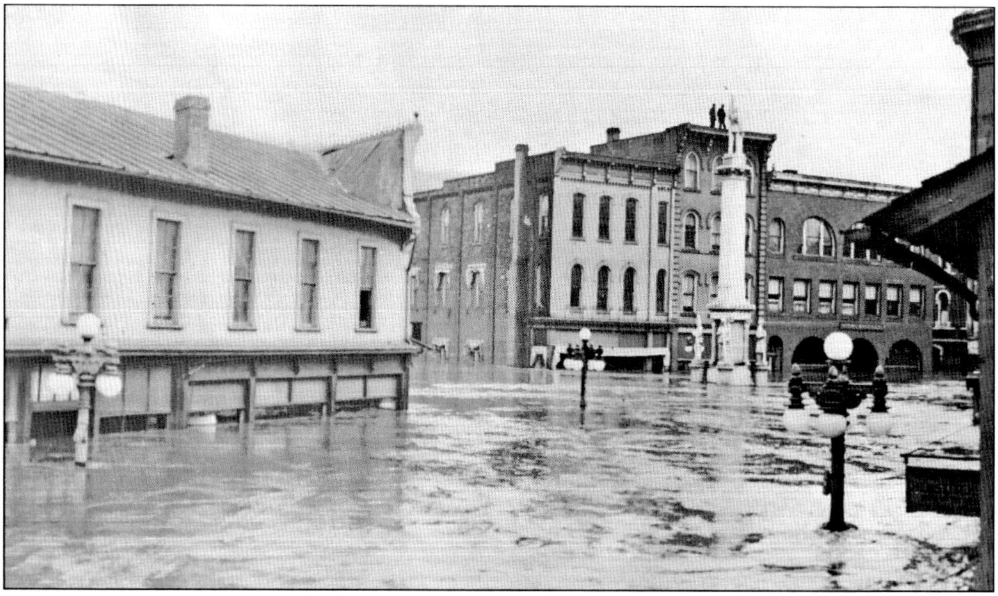

The Lock Haven Disaster Committee dispatched volunteers in all types of boats to the flooded areas to assist residents to safety. Views of town along Main Street and Bellefonte Avenue show floodwaters reaching the second floors of buildings. The city was cut off from transportation and communication, and surrounding communities again offered aid, including safe drinking water. The city reported no deaths directly associated with the flooding. When the waters receded, the damage was again devastating as 12 homes had been destroyed and another 70 were severely damaged. (Both, courtesy of the Clinton County Historical Society.)

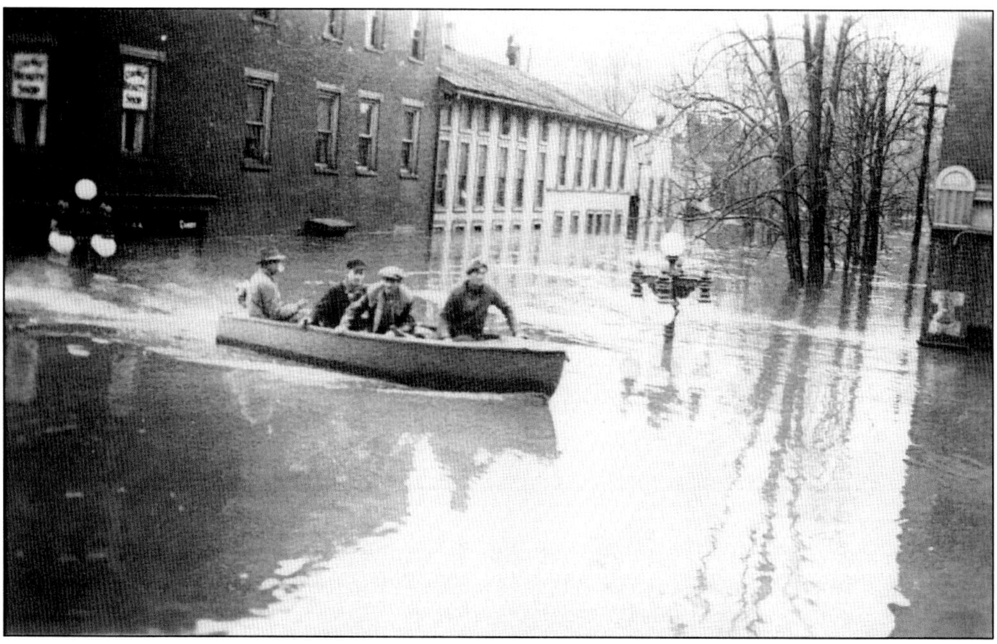

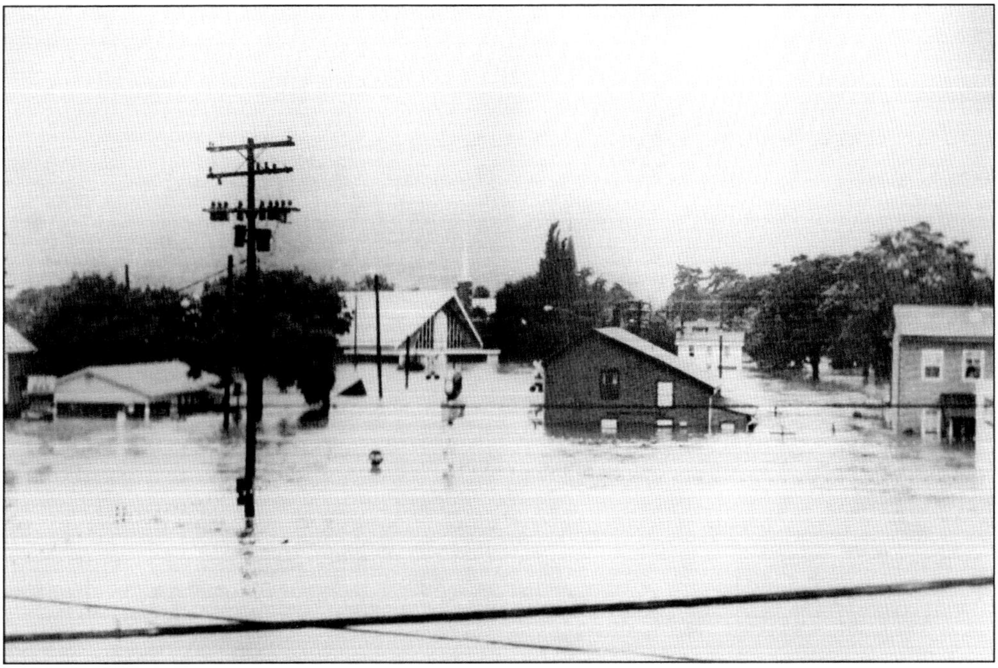

The tropical storm Agnes flood caused more than $88 million in damage when it struck the Susquehanna Valley in 1972. Damage estimates were highly tentative but would be over $5 million. Families were without utilities and phone service. Twelve bridges were swept away. The Lock Haven State College offered housing for more than 1,000 evacuees. The National Guard and Red Cross worked together to gather and distribute clothing, food, personal items, and cleaning supplies. (Courtesy of the Clinton County Historical Society.)

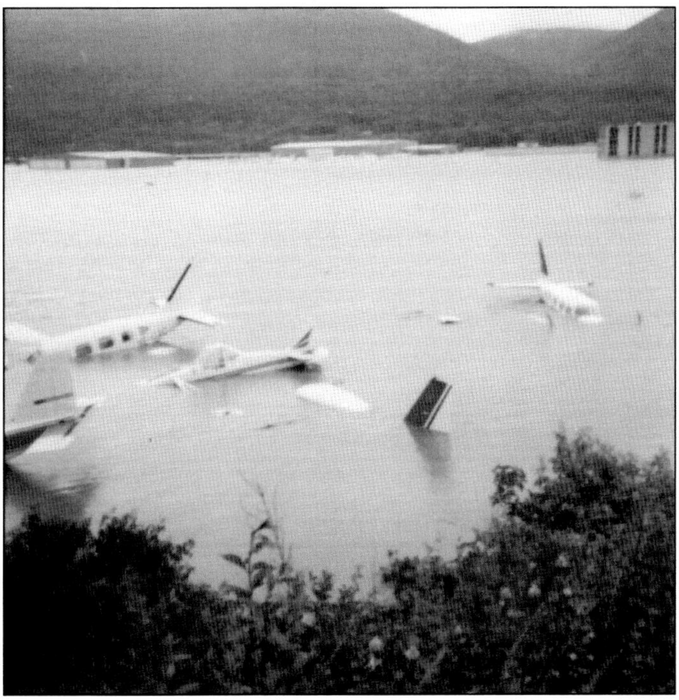

During the 1972 flood, Piper Aircraft Company lost more than $1 million; workers at Hammermill Paper Company temporarily cancelled their strike to pitch in and clean up the factory. The National Guard and the Red Cross pushed together to distribute food, clothing, and cleaning items. By the end, more than $50,000 worth of goods was distributed. A temporary chapter of the Red Cross was set up in the Lock Haven State College in the Rogers Gymnasium. (Courtesy of the Clinton County Historical Society.)

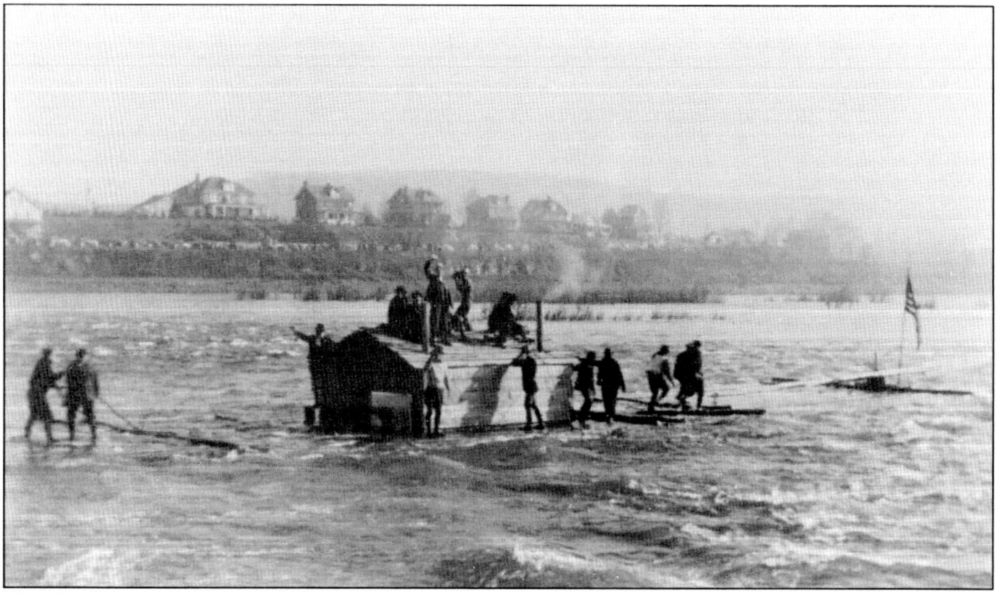

The last commercial rafts were seen around 1911. An authentic raft was built at Cherry Tree and was launched from McGee's Landing on March 14, 1938. The trip down river to Harrisburg was publicized as a tribute to the past. Six old-time river men and 30 passengers were aboard. At least 5,000 people watched the take-off with hundreds of people lining the banks and the highways along the river. The Hon. George B. Stevenson, mayor of Lock Haven, and his party met the raft at Queens Run, and a banquet was given in their honor at the Fallon Hotel. The City of Williamsport also hosted celebrations. However, the trip ended in tragedy—as the raft approached the railroad bridge at Muncy, it went out of control and crashed, throwing all of the passengers and crew into the water. Seven people drowned. The remaining group continued their journey, ending at Fort Hunter, above Harrisburg, on March 24, 1938. (Both, courtesy of the Clinton County Historical Society.)

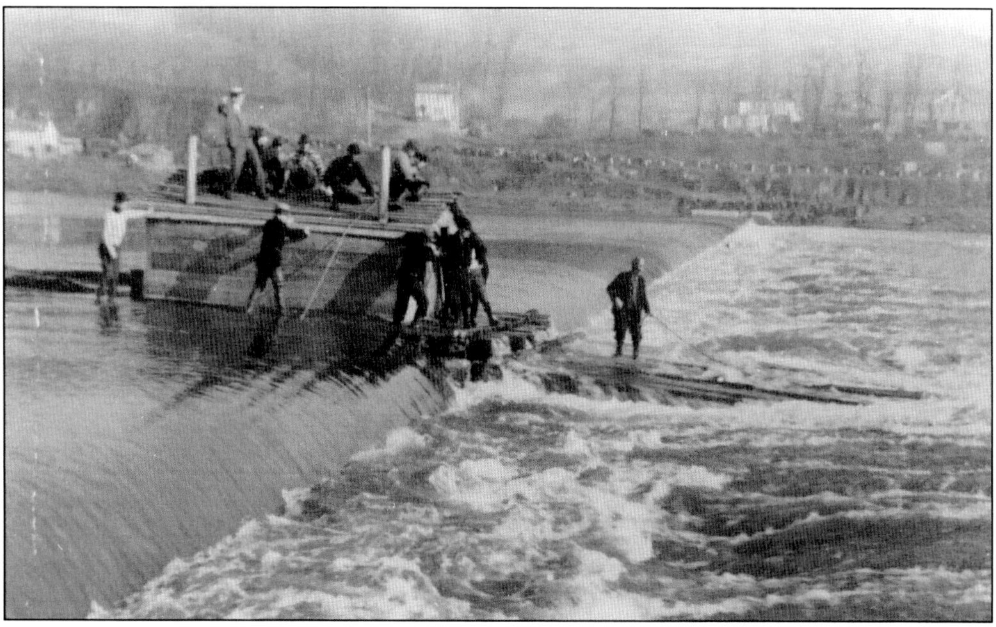

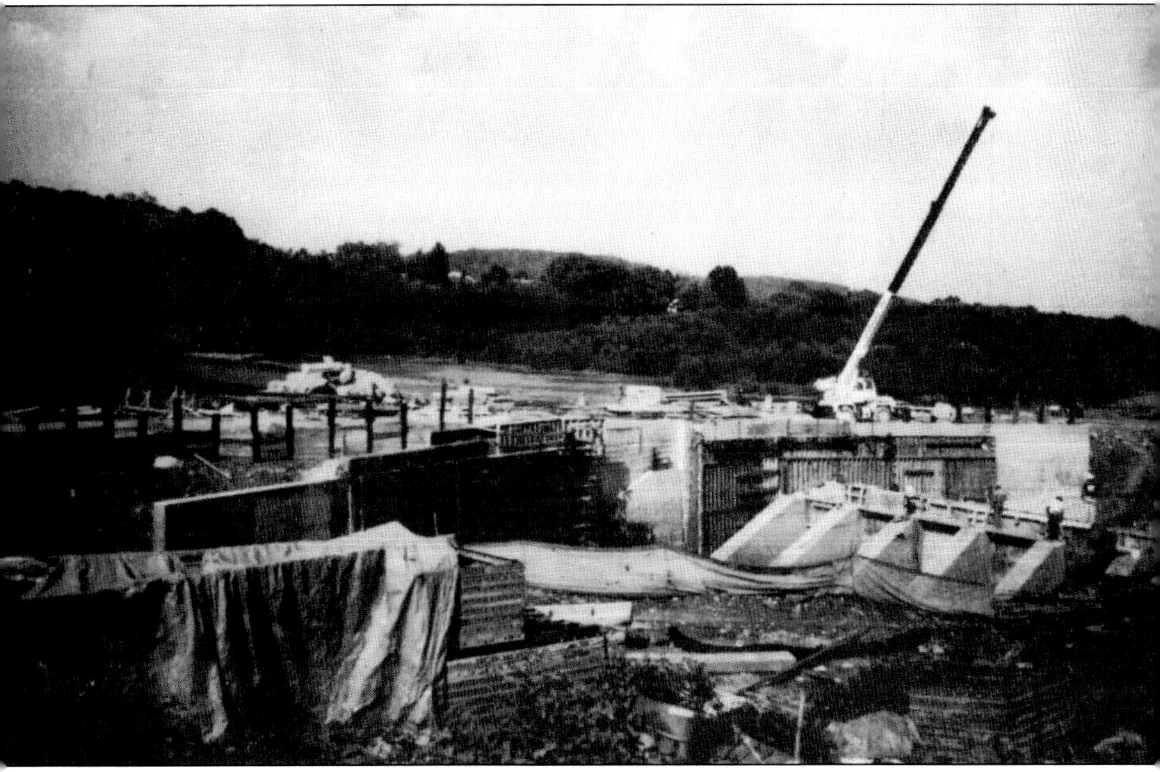

Lock Haven has suffered through 19 devastating floods in 147 years. Today, residents benefit from the $85 million flood protection project. A granite monument sits at the corner of Water and Jay Streets, dedicated to the people of Lock Haven to secure protection from the Susquehanna River and to promote economic stability for future growth. Improvements include a 2.25-mile walkway with benches, trash receptacles, and lighting. The walkway also includes a recreational pavilion with a bathhouse and beach. The J. Doyle Corman Amphitheater and floating stage offer a beautiful setting for the summer concert series. (Courtesy of the Clinton County Historical Society.)

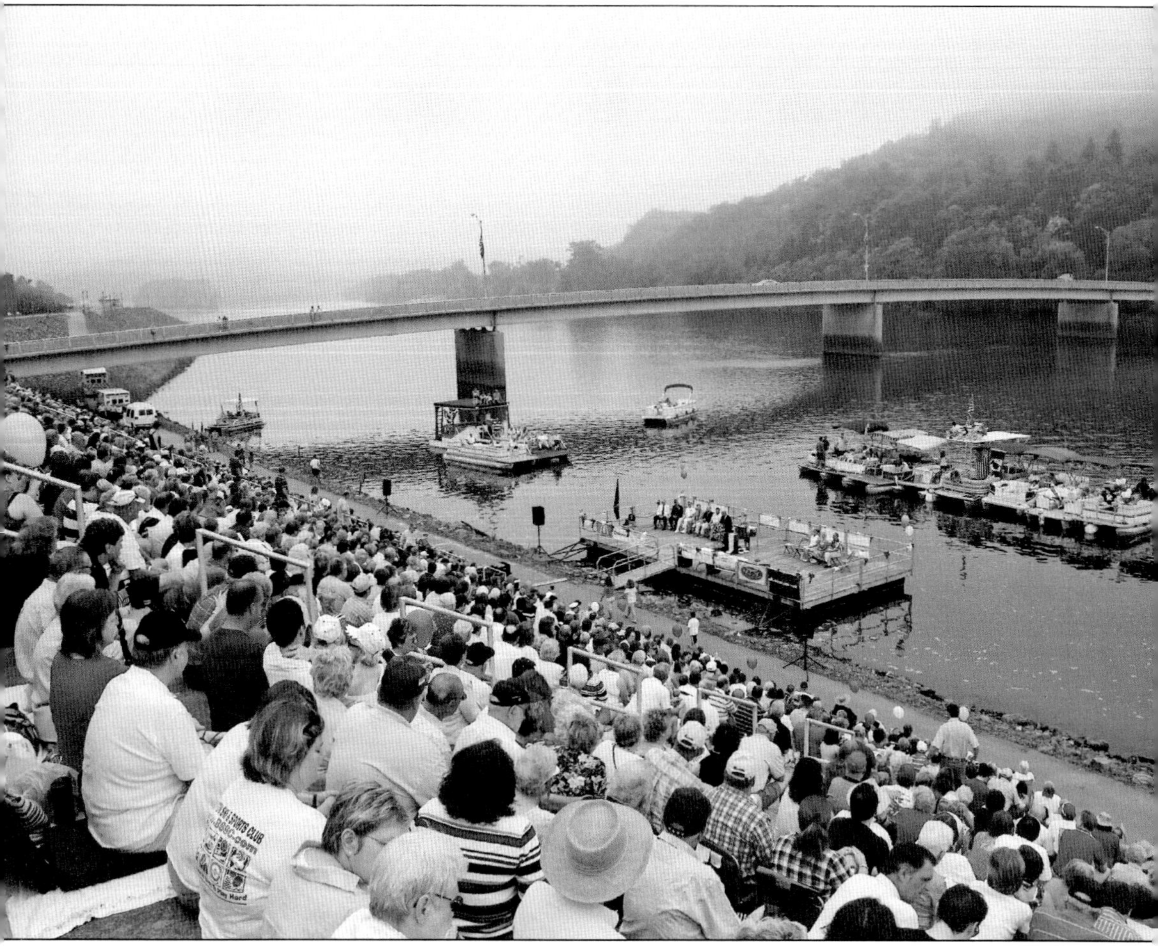

Today the amphitheater and walkway along the river are used extensively. The amphitheater hosts numerous outdoor events, including fireworks, concerts, and boat races. The City of Lock Haven's summer concert series offers music on the river each Sunday evening from June to September. Seen here, the city celebrates the 2009 Hometown Hero Banner Program. Hundreds of residents filled the amphitheater for a tribute to military veterans. (Courtesy of Downtown Lock Haven Inc.)

# *Seven*

# Serving the Community

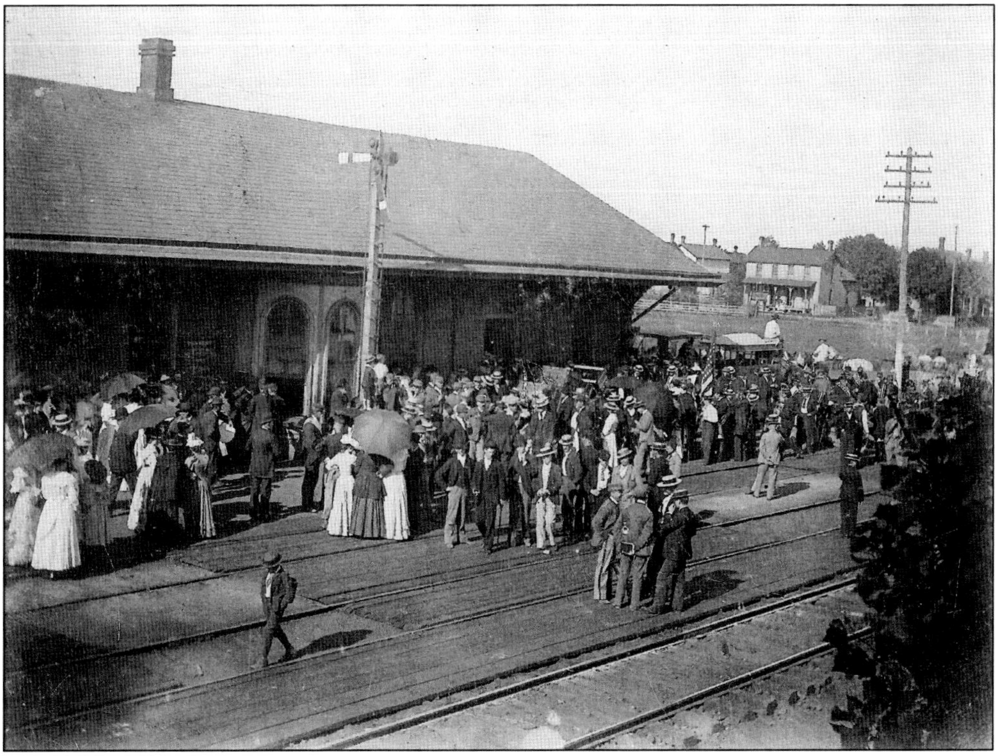

Friends and family wait at the Lock Haven train station for a homecoming. Lock Haven has a long history of military and public service. When the call for help was sounded from the time of the Civil War to present day, the community continually responded. And the support of veterans and their families was evident in parades and homecoming celebrations. Military units marched down Main Street as the community crowded the streets. Businesses decorated their store fronts with banners and patriotic bunting. (Courtesy of the Clinton County Historical Society.)

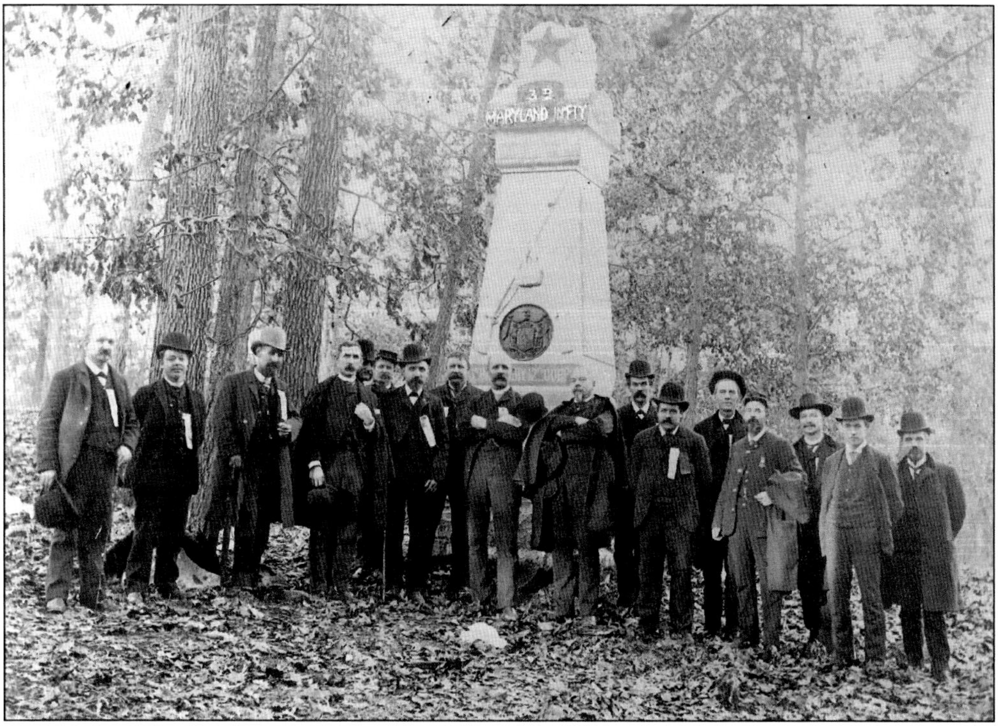


During the early months of the Civil War, appeals for help were so effective that the number of volunteers far exceeded the quota set for the county. Within two weeks after the attack on Fort Sumter, at least five companies awaited marching orders. The man third from the left, Edward J. Israel, a Civil War veteran, stands in front of this Gettysburg monument of the Company B, 3rd Regiment of the Maryland Infantry. Israel incurred a head would during the battle known as Cedar Mountain. (Courtesy of the Clinton County Historical Society.)

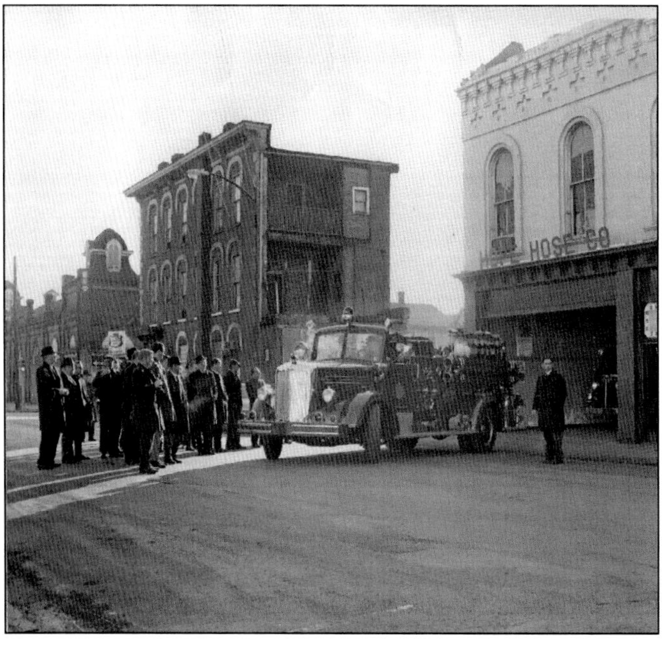


The Hope Hose Fire Engine leaves the building on Grove Street prior to the building being razed in 1970. The fire engine would travel over to the new station at 124 East Church St. with Fire Company members. On May 16, 1970, the new home of the Hope Hose Fire Company was dedicated. Past president Paul Mack presided over the ceremony. At that time the Hon. J. Arlington Young was mayor. The total cost of the new building was $128,530. (Courtesy of the Hope Hose Fire Company.)

The enthusiasm of the men answering the first request for volunteers during the Civil War was matched by the readiness of those who remained at home to take up the added responsibilities caused by the war. A fund was raised in Clinton County to pay the expenses of the volunteers waiting to serve their country. People who could not give cash gave food, clothing, and horses. In a short time, $4,000 and a large amount of resources was collected. A "volunteer tax relief" of one mill on the dollar of the assessed value of all property in the county was levied by the county commissioners to finance the care of the needy families of volunteers. (Courtesy of the Clinton County Historical Society.)

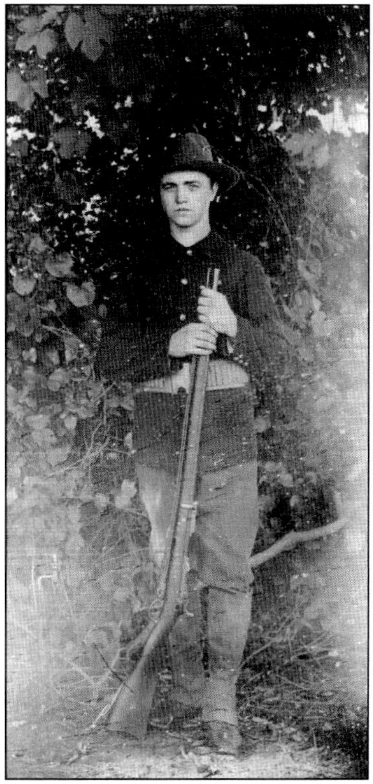

After the end of the Civil War, organizations were formed for veterans to network and maintain connections with each other. Many of the veterans wished to keep in contact with each other, using their shared experiences as a basis for fellowship. Groups of men began joining together, first for camaraderie and later for political power. Emerging most powerful among the various organizations was the Grand Army of the Republic, founded on the principles of "Fraternity, Charity, and Loyalty" in 1866. (Courtesy of the Clinton County Historical Society.)

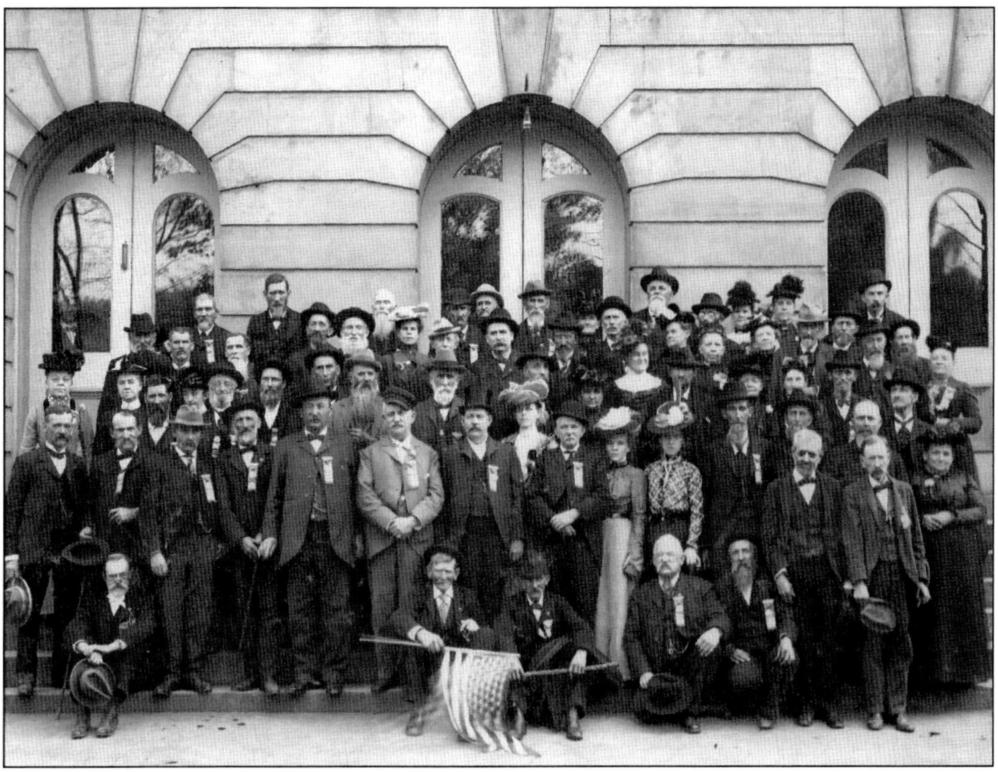

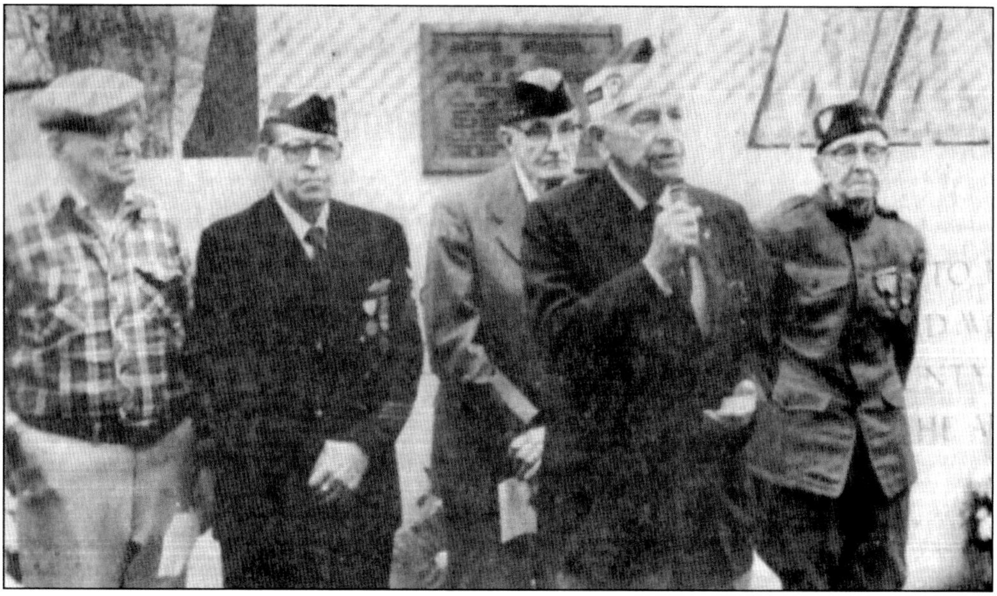

At this Veterans Day ceremony in 1984, Walter Grimm, one of the 13 remaining World War I veterans in the county, speaks about veterans. At the time, there were about 235,000 World War I veterans remaining. The country was losing 250 veterans per day. With Grimm are Eldon E. Spotts, a navy World War I veteran; Harry Pinge, a veteran of the Mexican War, World War I, and World War II; Vernie McRae, who served with the 162nd Infantry Division in World War I; and Bill Beschler, the parade's grand marshal and a member of the 6th Engineer Battalion, 3rd Infantry during World War I. The guest speaker for the service was commissioner James Bottorf. The event included a parade and ceremony. (Courtesy of the Bland J. Rossman Post 1630 VFW in Lock Haven.)

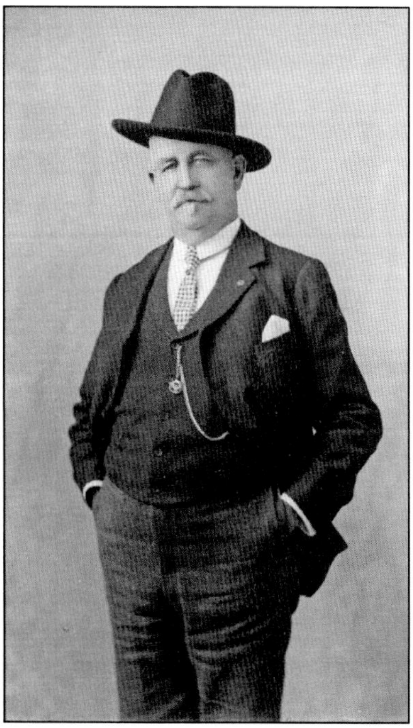

Born in 1846, Robert H. McGhee was known as the father of the Hope Hose Fire Company. McGhee served in the Union Army for three years during the Civil War. He was taken prisoner at Gettysburg but released after two days at the intervention of a command of New York troops. McGhee served as president of the Hope Hose Fire Company. He was also sergeant at arms of Lock Haven City Council for 30 years. Robert H. McGhee was called "Uncle Bob," father and organizer of Lock Haven Fire Department. (Courtesy of the Hope Hose Fire Company.)

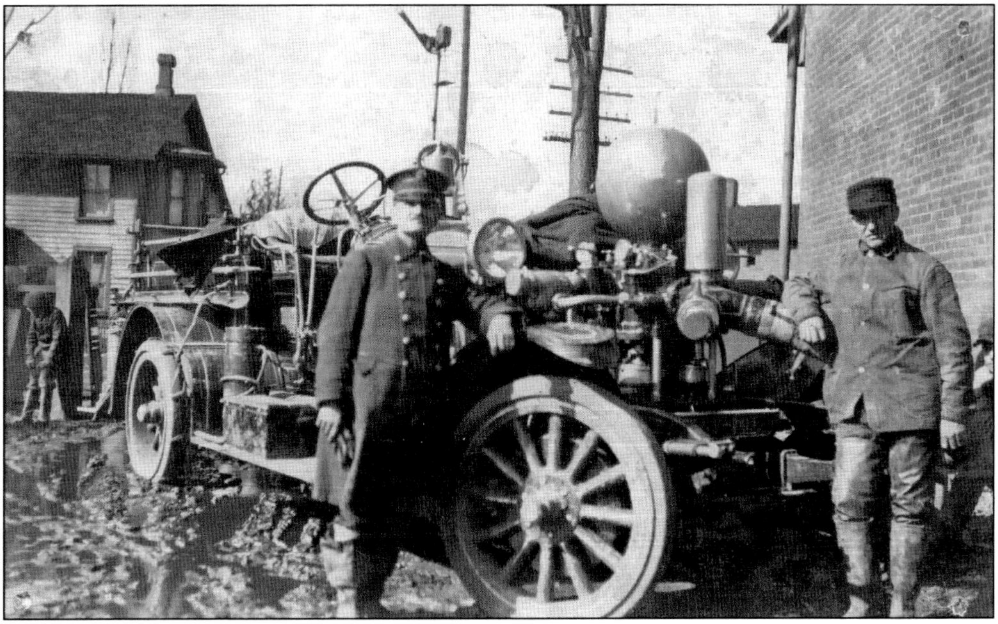

Philip Zindel stands to the left of this early fire engine. Early firefighting was not much more than a bucket and hose brigade. The pumper of the Good Will Company was critical for the fire company's work in the early 1830s. A steam fire engine was purchased in 1886, which was replaced by a Silsby steamer. The 1901 horse-drawn steam engine below was replaced with three engine companies equipped with a combination of trucks, pumpers, aerial ladders, and chemical tanks. (Both, courtesy of the Hope Hose Fire Company.)

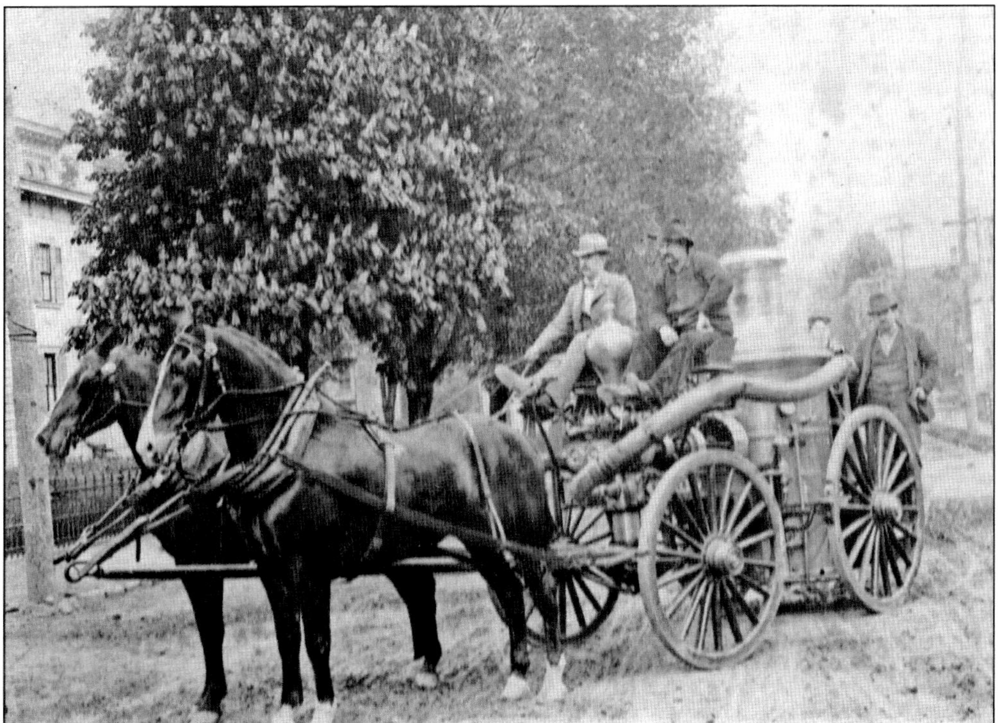

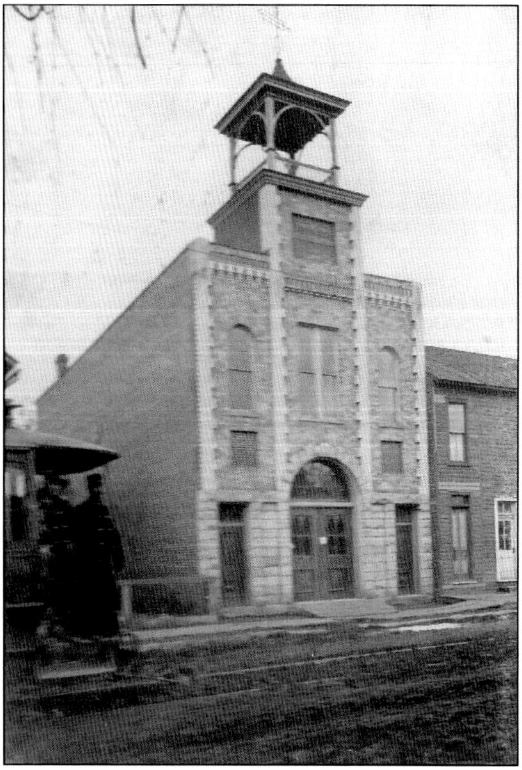

The Hope Hose Fire Company was first located on Grove Street. Members are pictured decorating the building when the troops arrived home from war. (Both, courtesy of the Hope Hose Fire Company.)

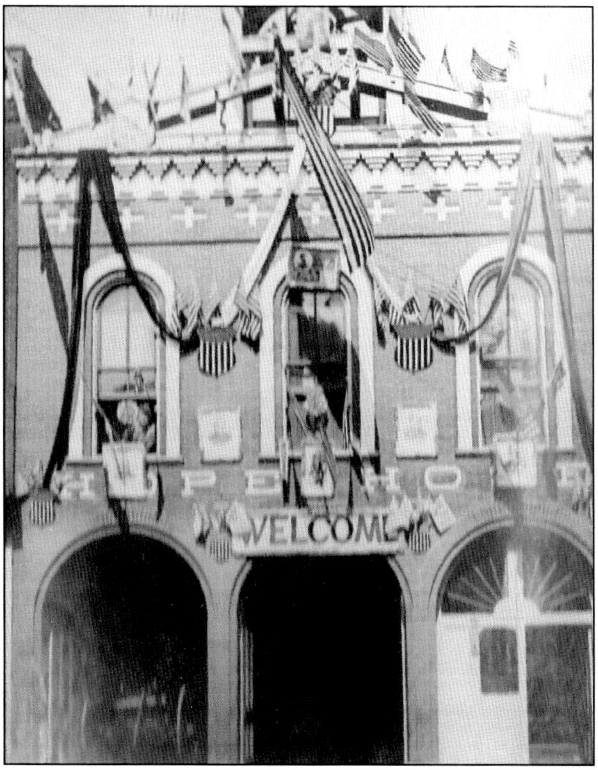

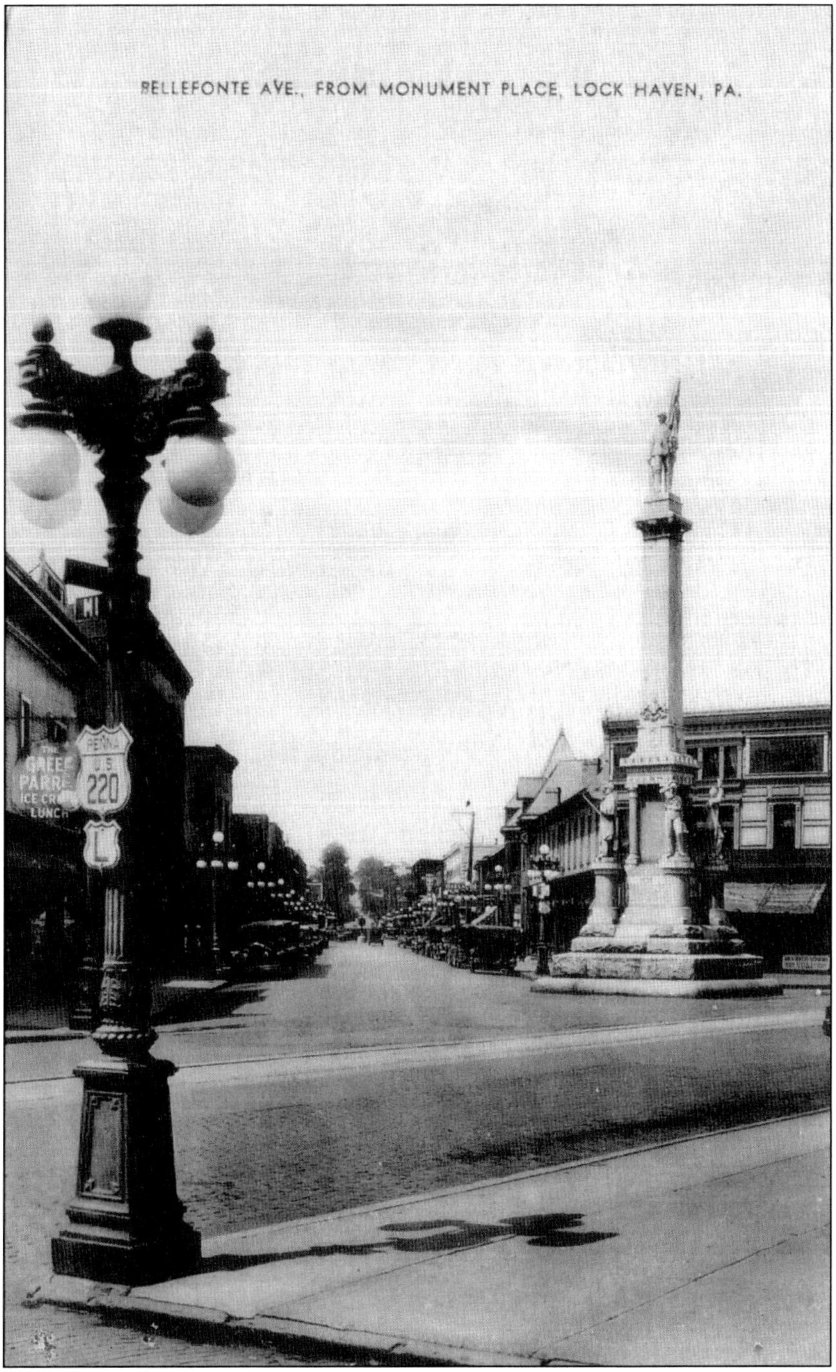


The *Soldiers' and Sailors' Monument*, which was located at Bellefonte and Main Streets, was moved as part of Lock Haven's redevelopment project in 1971. Its 107 parts were cleaned and polished and reconstructed at its new location at the intersection of Bellefonte Avenue and Church Street. Clinton Countians who lost their lives in the Civil War are memorialized in two monuments, one at Bellefonte Avenue and one in Linwood Cemetery in McElhattan. (Courtesy of the Annie Halenbake Ross Library.)

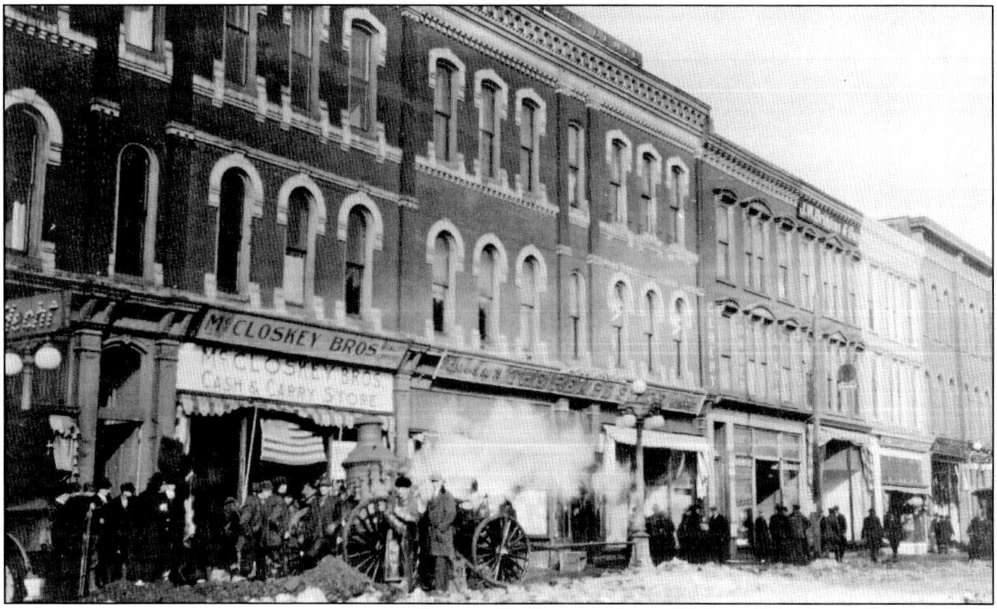


After a flood, the fire companies of the City of Lock Haven assisted this business in pumping water out of the building. (Courtesy of the Annie Halenbake Ross Library.)

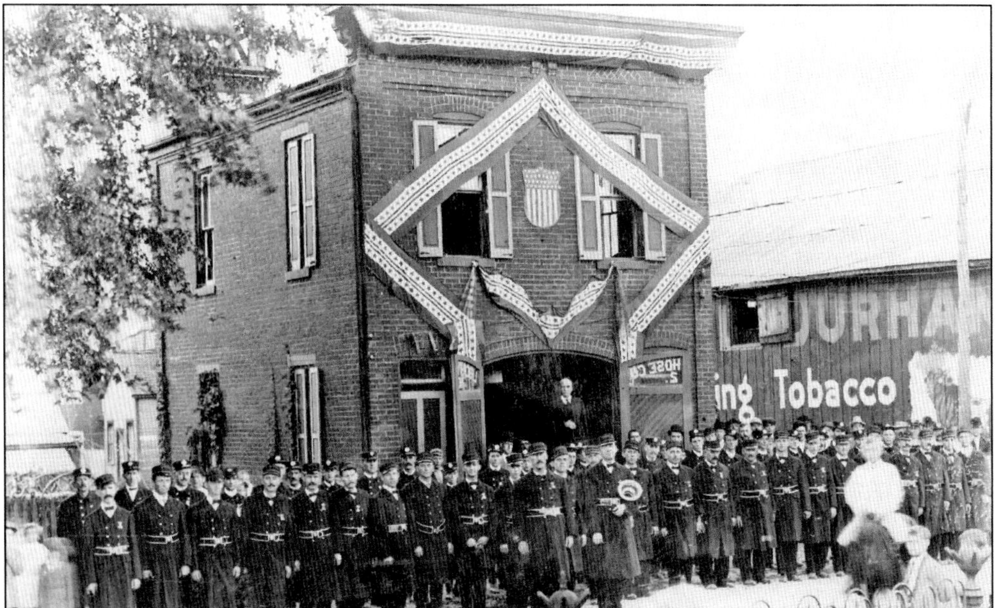


Hope Hose Fire Company was founded in 1881. This picture was taken in 1910 in front of the firehouse that was located on North Grove Street. (Courtesy of the Hope Hose Fire Company.)

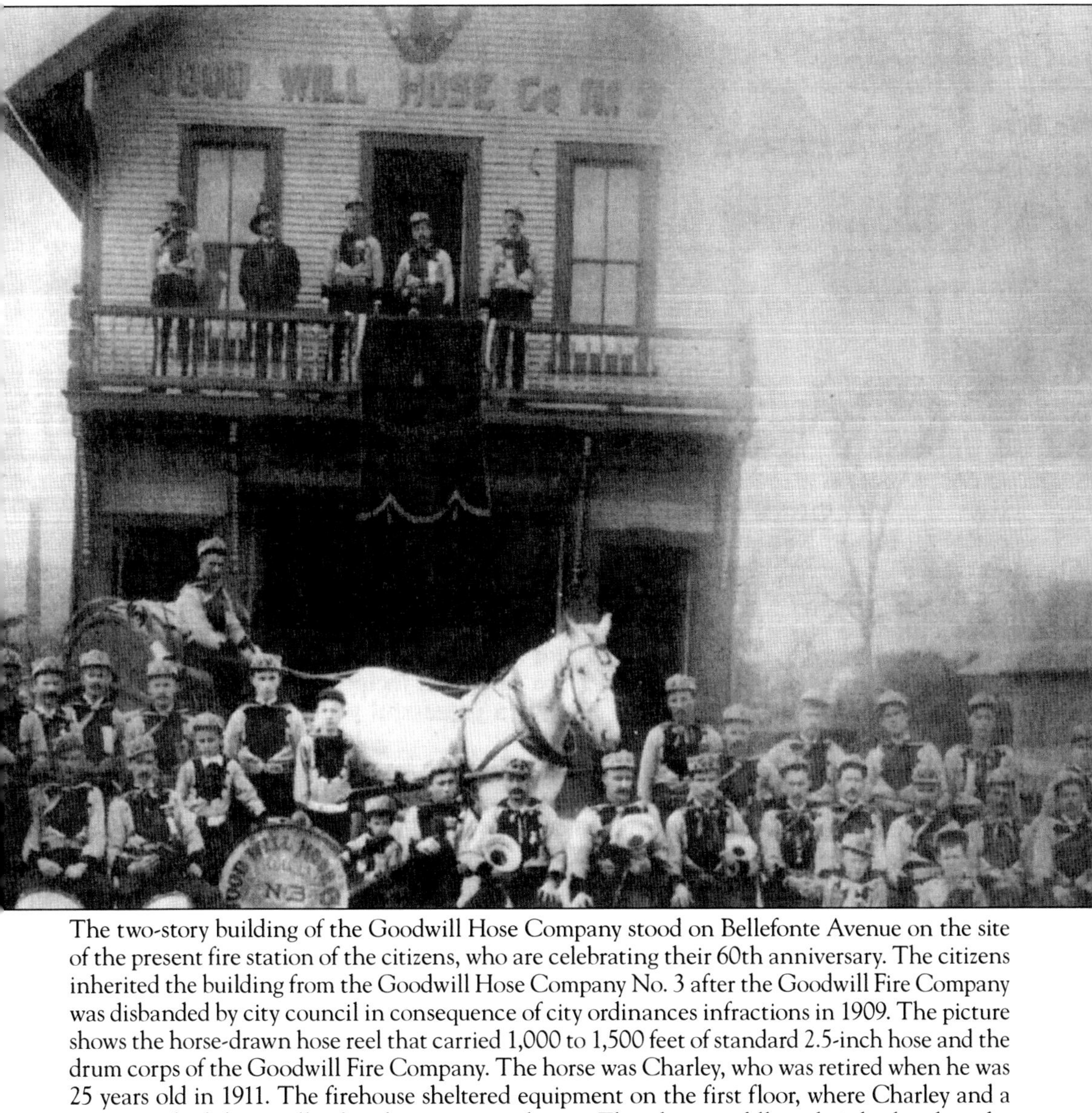


The two-story building of the Goodwill Hose Company stood on Bellefonte Avenue on the site of the present fire station of the citizens, who are celebrating their 60th anniversary. The citizens inherited the building from the Goodwill Hose Company No. 3 after the Goodwill Fire Company was disbanded by city council in consequence of city ordinances infractions in 1909. The picture shows the horse-drawn hose reel that carried 1,000 to 1,500 feet of standard 2.5-inch hose and the drum corps of the Goodwill Fire Company. The horse was Charley, who was retired when he was 25 years old in 1911. The firehouse sheltered equipment on the first floor, where Charley and a teammate had their stalls after the citizens took over. Their harness fell on their backs when the alarm sounded, and the driver released the mechanical device that held the harness above the wagon tongue of the firefighting apparatus. Upstairs there were sleeping quarters for the driver, a club room, and the library for the firemen. (Courtesy of the Hope Hose Fire Company.)

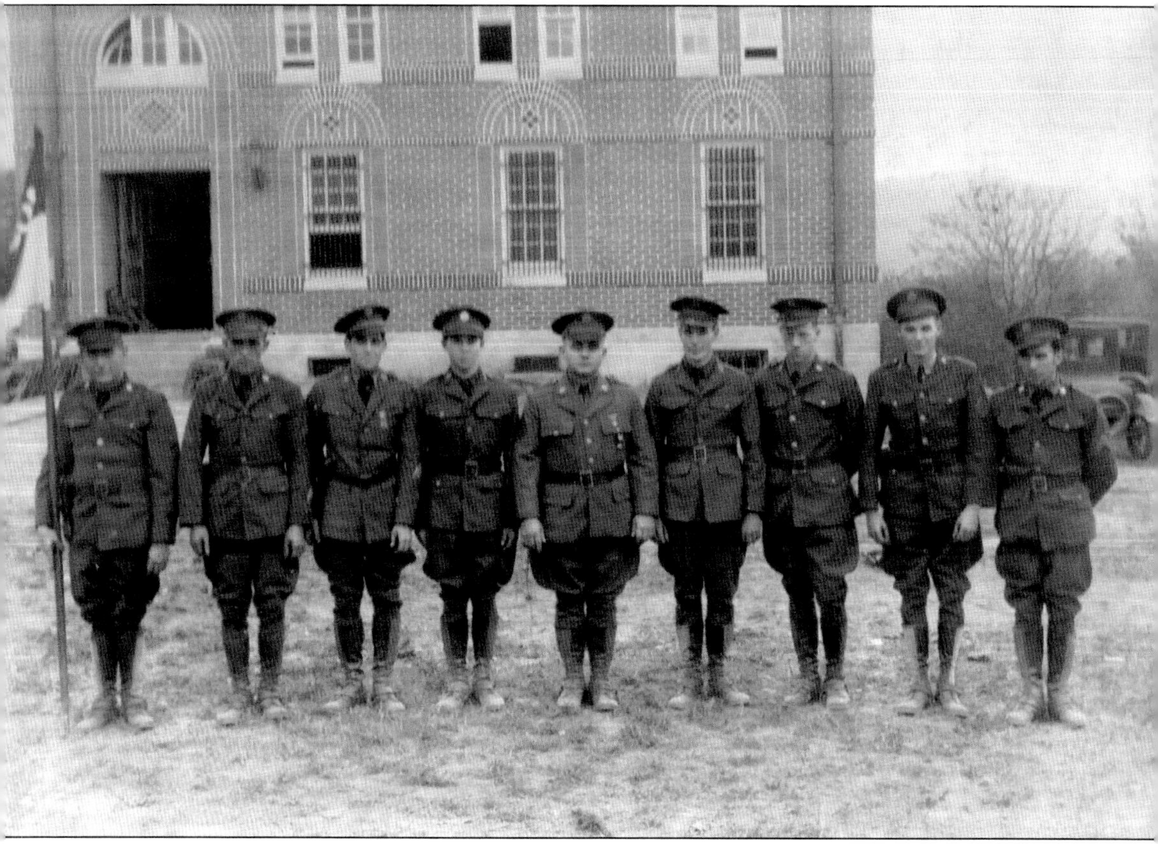

The non-commissioned officers of the Pennsylvania National Guard Troop F, 103rd Cavalry stand in front of the new building at the Fall 1928 dedication of the Lock Haven headquarters. Included in this picture are, from left to right, Stable Sgt. Edward F. Smith, Cpl. Gurn C. Weber, Sgt. Harry H. Pinge, Cpl. William Copenhaver, 1st Sgt. Foster S. McGhee, Sgt. William H. McCormick, Cpl. Hall F. Achenbach, Mess Sgt. Claude A. Martin, and Cpl. Lee L. Lucas. (Courtesy of the Bland J. Rossman Post 1630 VFW in Lock Haven.)

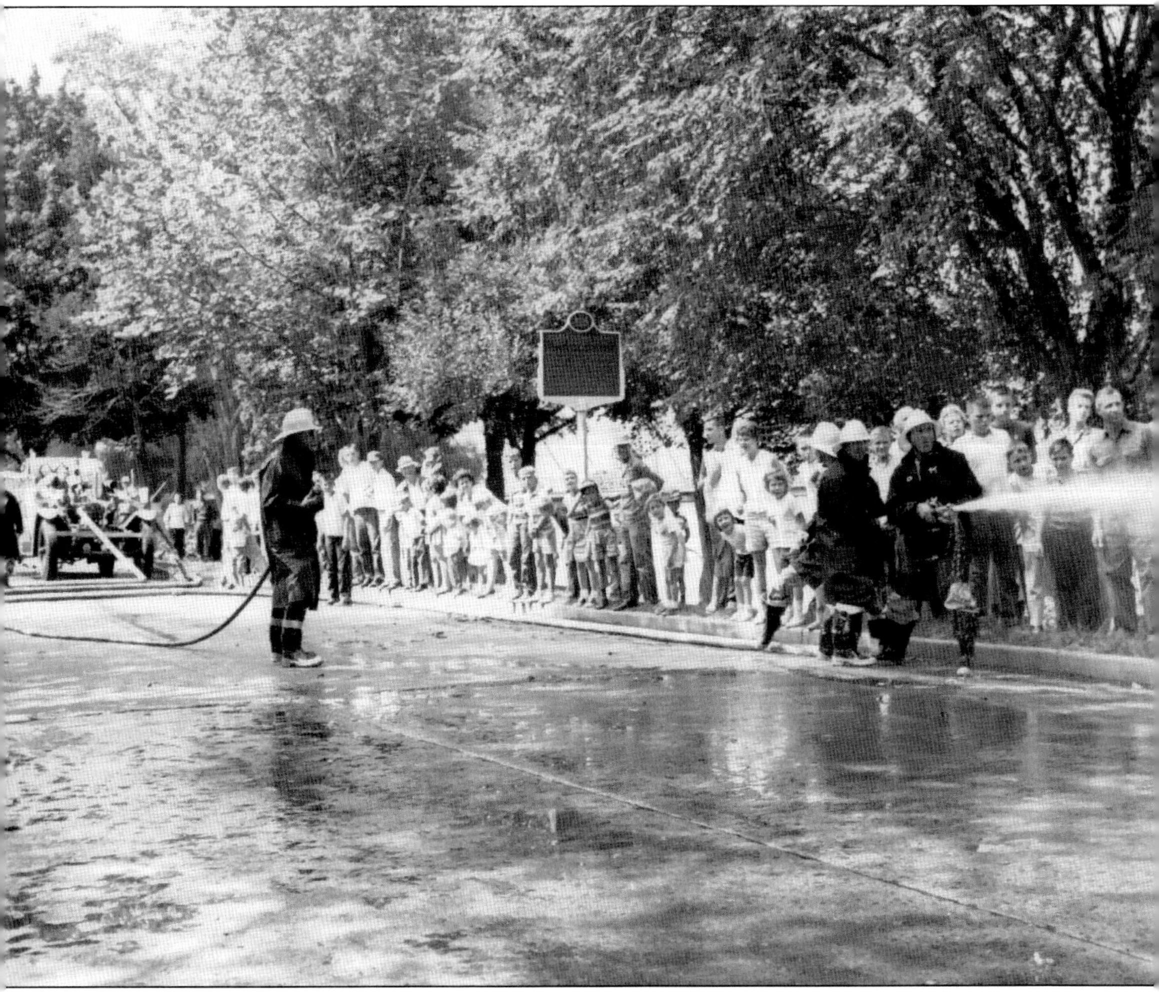

The City of Lock Haven was hosting the Central District Fireman's Convention and Parade during Labor Day weekend in 1960. The event included competitions. (Courtesy of the Hope Hose Fire Company.)

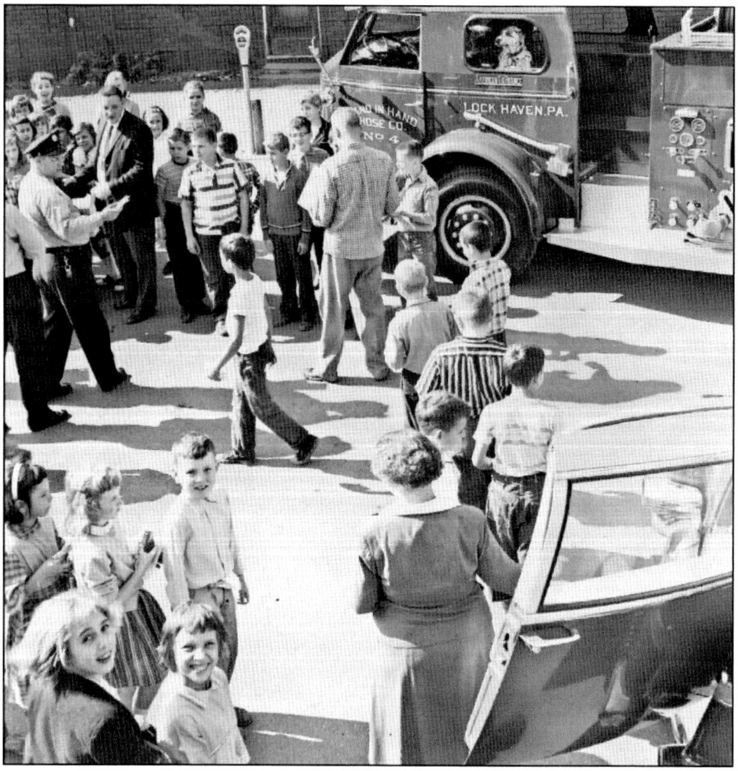


Even today Lock Haven's Hope Hose Fire Company offers fire prevention courses and presentations. Pictured here in October 1960, the children of the Penn School learn about fire prevention from fire company members. A very well-behaved dog looks on from the back seat of the fire engine. (Courtesy of the Hope Hose Fire Company.)

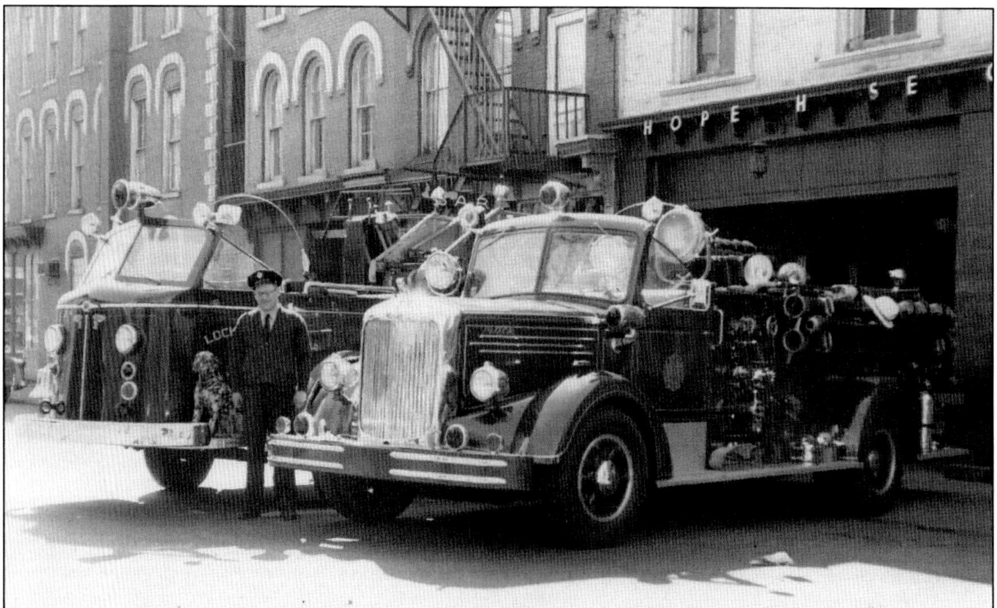

Bruce Bryerton, driver for the Hope Hose Fire Company, then located on Grove Street, poses with the Aerial Ladder Truck and Mack Pumper Truck. (Courtesy of Hope Hose Fire Company.)

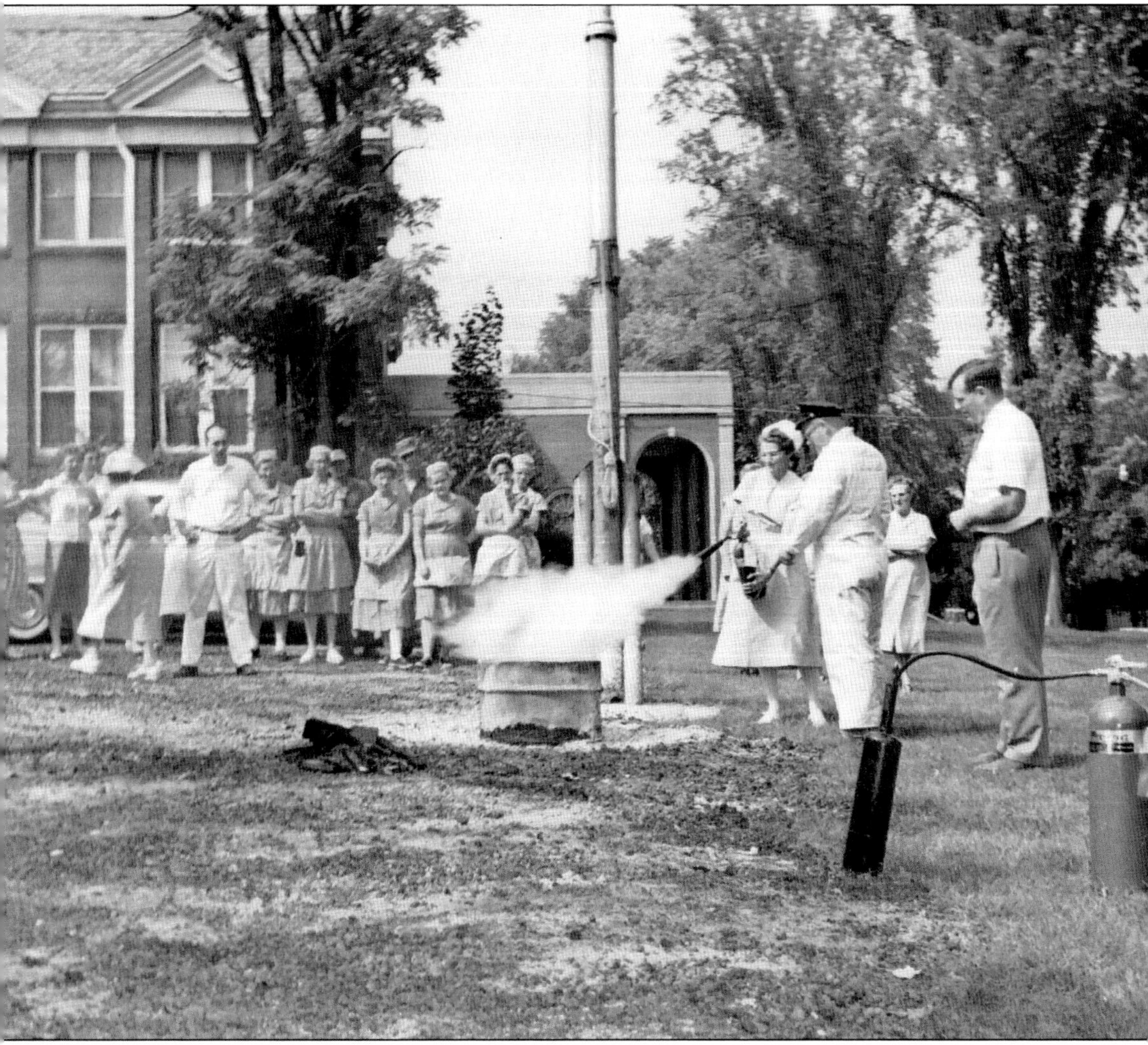

Lock Haven Hospital employees take fire extinguisher training in September 1959, on Susquehanna Avenue. Lock Haven Hospital's director Al Speth looks on as Bruce Bryerton demonstrates the use of an extinguisher. (Courtesy of the Hope Hose Fire Company.)

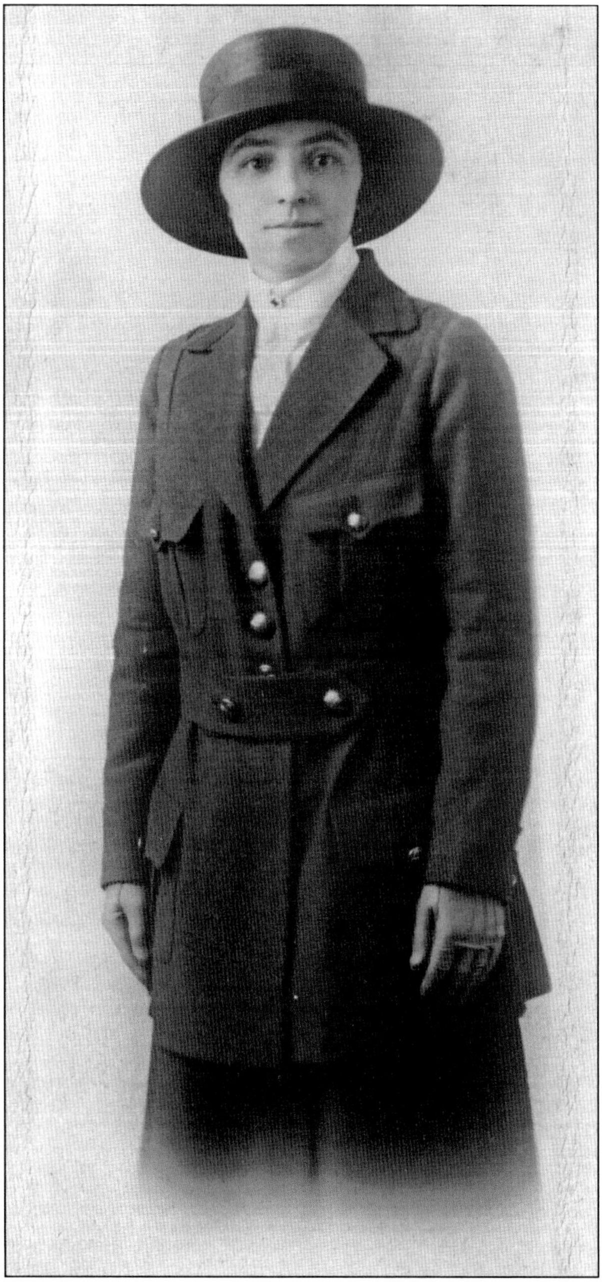

Maude Albright of Lock Haven served overseas during World War I. Maude met her husband Raoul Moquin while on duty. She is seen here in her World War I nurse's uniform. At the start of World War I, there were 403 active duty nurses and by 1918, there were 12,000 nurses serving at 198 stations worldwide. In 1917, more than 400 nurses left for France to serve in the British Expeditionary Forces. Army nurses during World War I did not have officer status—they were appointed. While some nurses were wounded during the war, none died as a result of the war, however almost 200 died from influenza and pneumonia. Army nurses were awarded numerous medals including the Distinguished Service Cross as a sign of their valiant contributions to the Great War. (Courtesy of the Annie Halenbake Ross Library.)

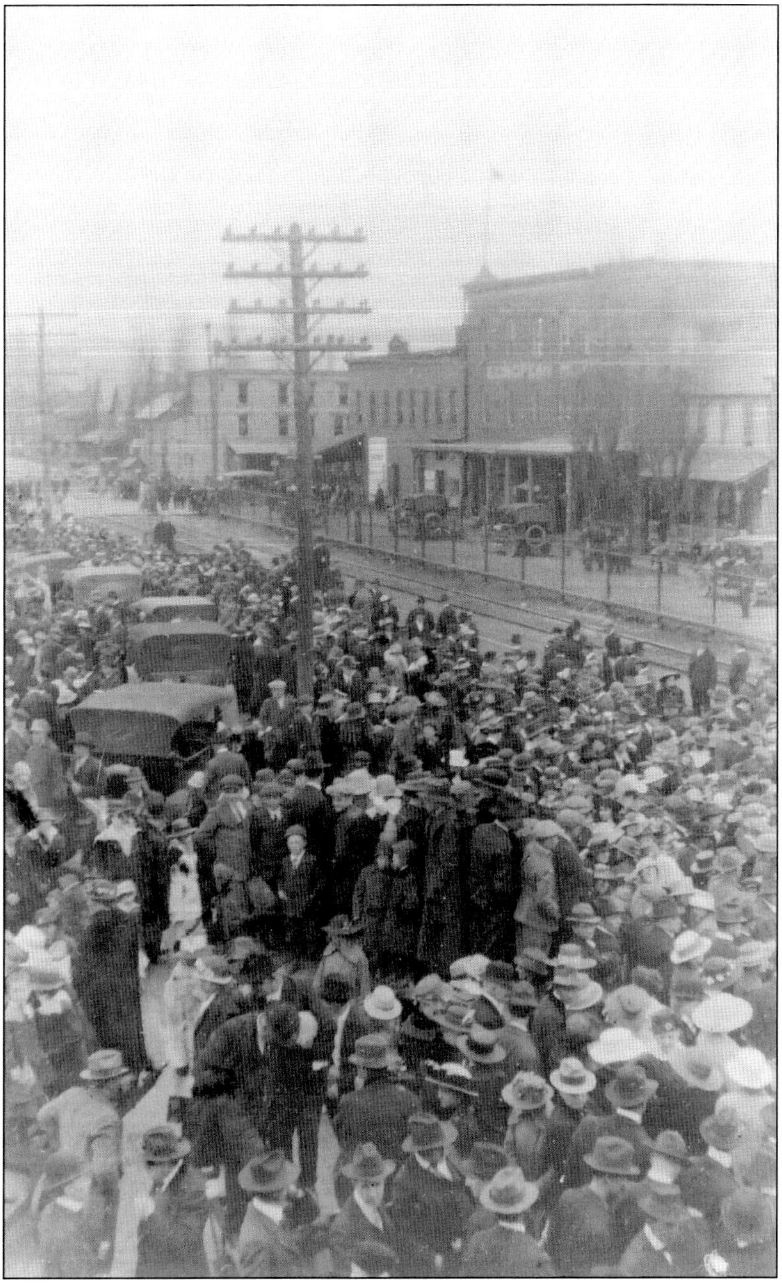

A large crowd of family and friends show their support as their loved ones prepare to leave the Lock Haven train station on Henderson Street at the beginning of World War I. More than 1,500 county residents either volunteered or were drafted for military service. On September 11, 1917, Troop K, 1st Pennsylvania Cavalry was the first volunteer unit from the county to be inducted at Camp Hancock in Georgia. Ambulance Company 41 started service at Camp Upton the following week. The first group of men drafted for service left home on September 19, 1917, for Camp George G. Meade in Maryland. At about 4:00 a.m. on November 11, 1918, the news of the Armistice reached Lock Haven. Businesses closed, and church bells and whistles called for celebrations throughout town. (Courtesy of the Annie Halenbake Ross Library.)

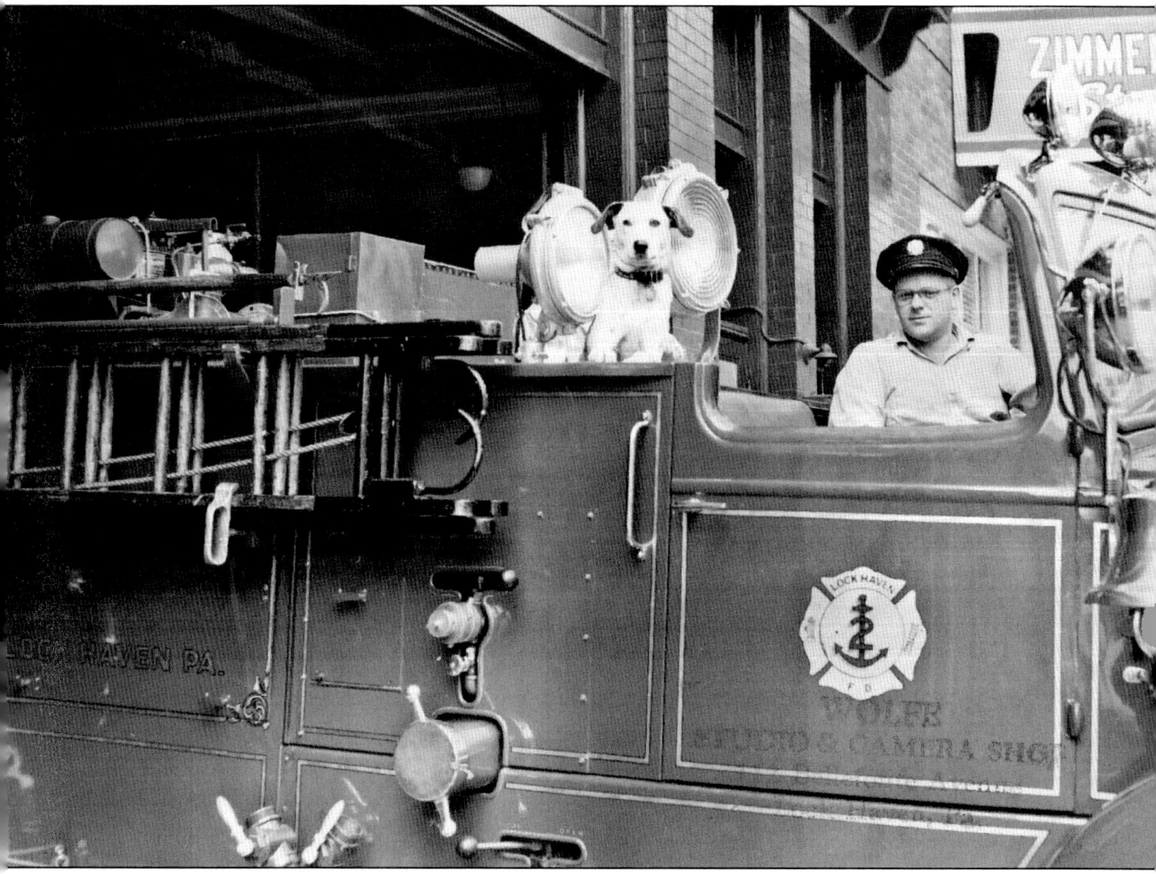


Bruce Bryerton, driver for the Hope Hose Fire Company, and a very attentive firedog, pose with the fire truck. Today the Dalmatian serves as a firehouse mascot to many fire companies, but back in the days of horse-drawn fire carts, they provided a valuable service. Dalmatians and horses are very compatible, so the dogs were easily trained to run in front of the engines to help clear a path and guide the horses and the firefighters to the fires. They are still chosen by many firefighters as pets, in honor of their heroism in the past. (Courtesy of Hope Hose Fire Company.)

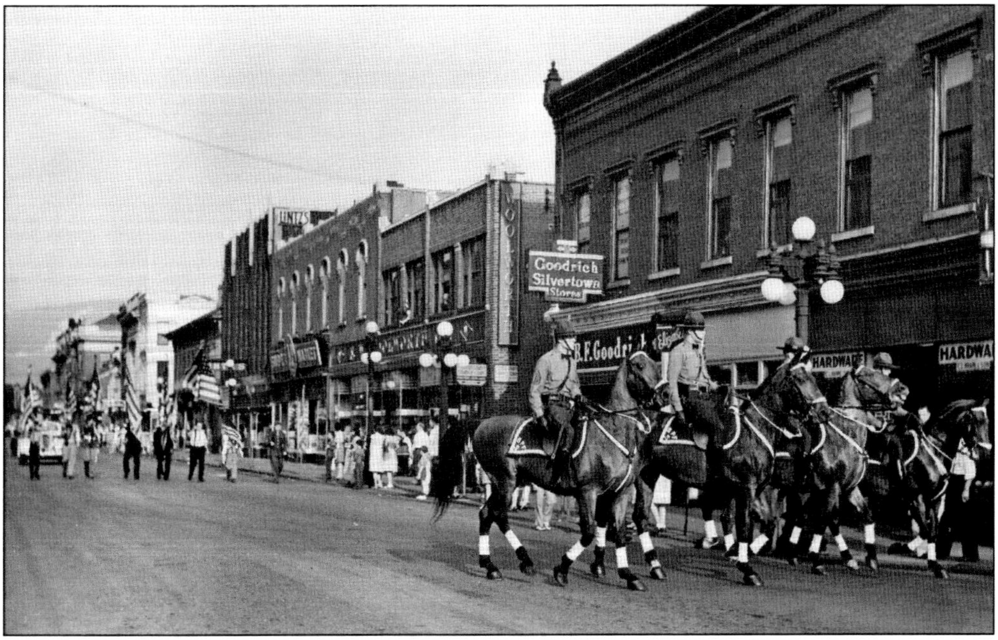


Lock Haven had spectacular parades throughout the years. This parade in 1917 was in honor of Flag Day. The city's police led the way, followed by the honor guard. Flag Day is celebrated on June 14, and commemorates the adoption of the flag of the United States on June 14, 1777. In 1916, Pres. Woodrow Wilson issued a proclamation establishing Flag Day. National Flag Day was established by an act of congress in August 1949. While Flag Day is not a federal holiday, Pennsylvania became the first state to celebrate Flag Day as a state holiday on June 14, 1937. (Courtesy of the Annie Halenbake Ross Library.)

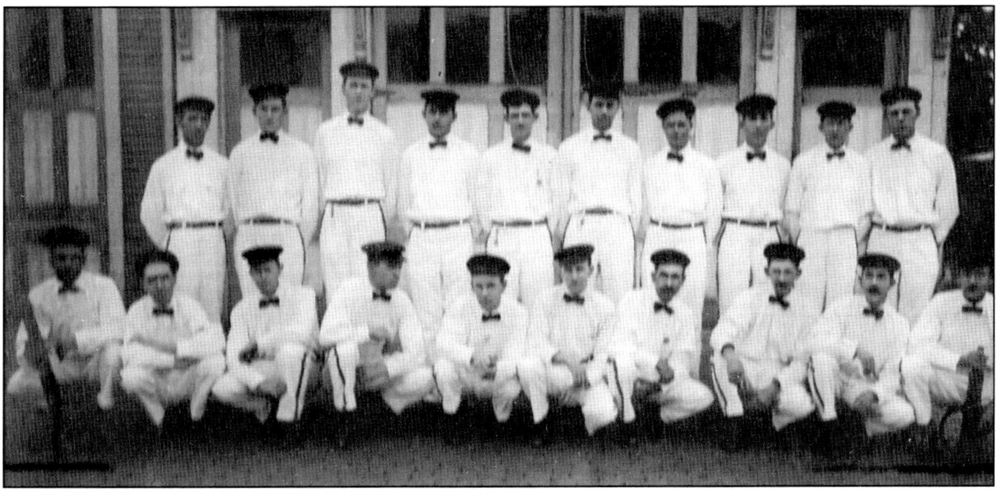

These gentlemen constituted the drill team of the Citizens Hose Fire Company in 1910 during a line-up in front of the firehouse on Bellefonte Avenue. The old hose house, which stood almost where the current firehouse is located, was damaged in a fire that also destroyed the old planing mill next door. Members of the company, from left to right, are (first row) H. A. Ferrer, C. E. Gross, C. A. Shaffer, Charles Kitchen, F. E. Ritter, and Ralph Harnish; (second row) John Devling, H. B. Rokenbrode, Charles Burd, Arthur Saiers, C. T. McGill, Charles Haussener, Earl Harnish, John Myers, Charles Kelly, and Harry B Bottorf. (Courtesy of Hope Hose Fire Company.)

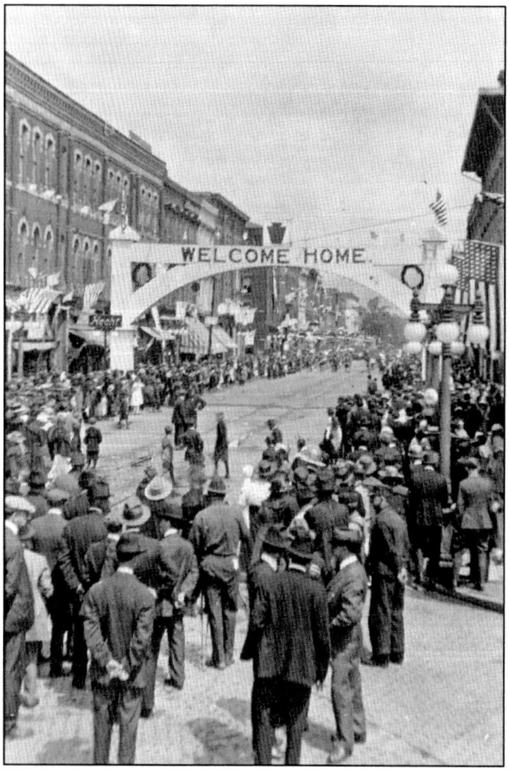


This welcome home celebration was held after World War I. In 1919, the community gathered on Main Street to celebrate the end of the war and the return of their loved ones. The parade wrapped around Main and Church Streets and celebrations continued into the evening. (Courtesy of the Annie Halenbake Ross Library.)

In mid-September 1901, crowds of mourners gathered along the railroad tracks in Lock Haven long before the arrival of the funeral train bringing the body of assassinated Pres. William McKinley from Buffalo. The 24th president, McKinley was elected in 1896 and reelected in 1901. The funeral train took his body to Washington and then to Canton, Ohio. (Courtesy of the Annie Halenbake Ross Library.)

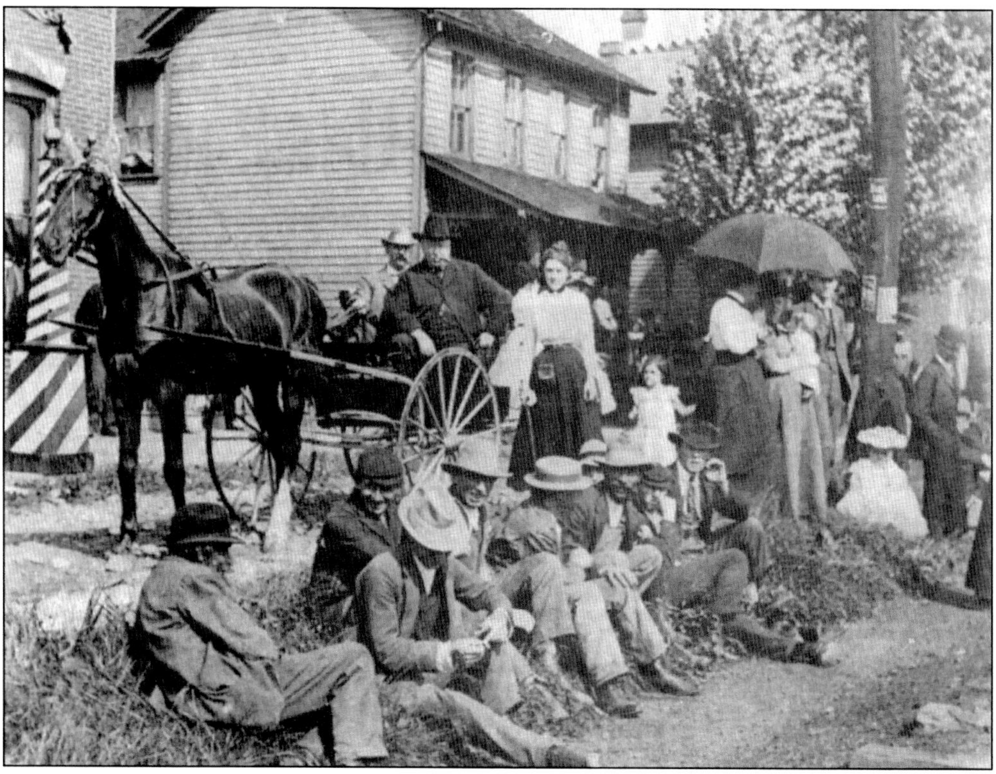

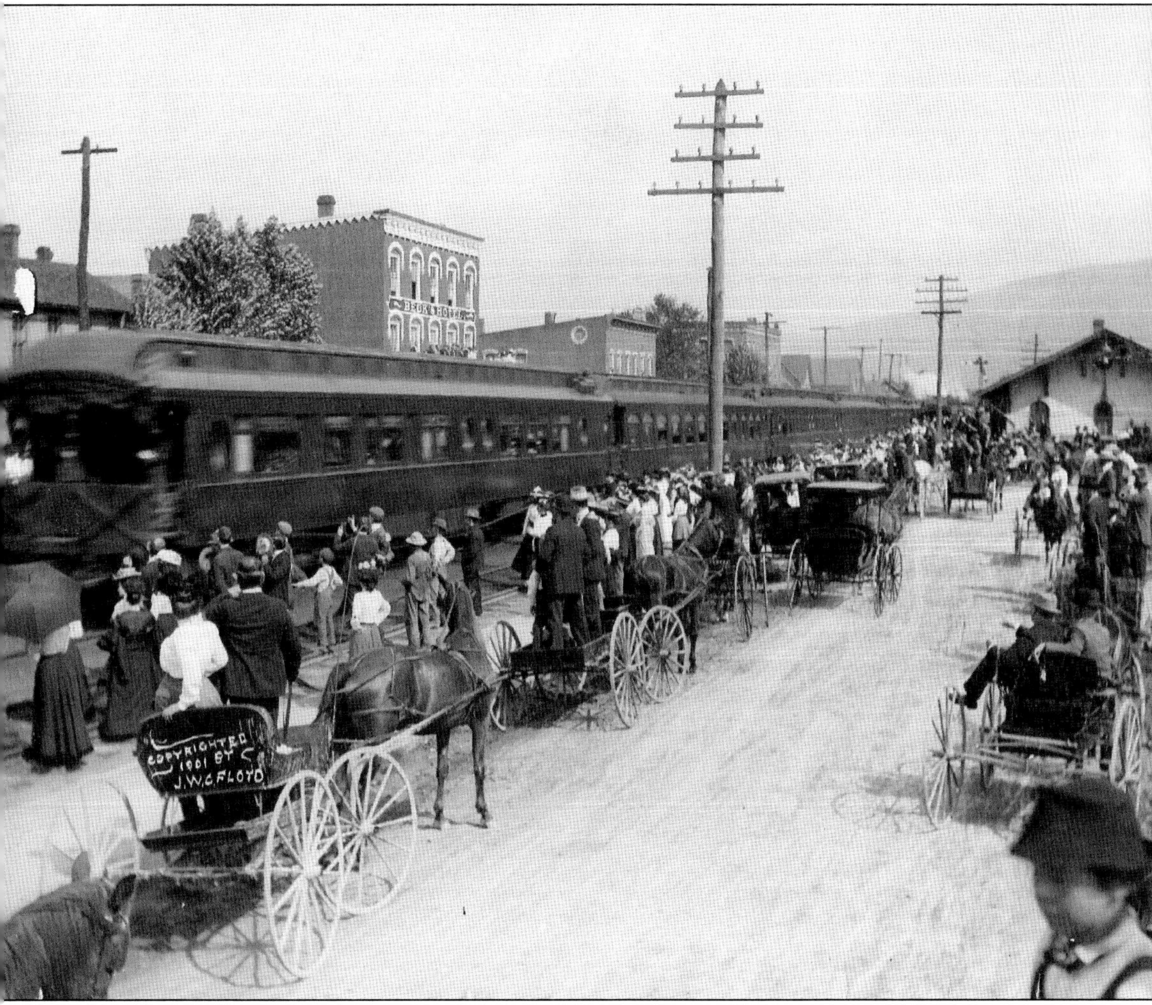


William McKinley died September 14, 1901. His coffin was described as being made of handsomely carved red cedar and covered with fine black broadcloth. The rear train car, Pacific, contained the body of McKinely, and Mrs. McKinley occupied the car immediately ahead of it. Pres. Theodore Roosevelt and members of the cabinet were in the third car from the rear. All merchants closed their stores from 1:00 p.m. to 3:00 p.m. in respect. Factories also shut down. Huge crowds gathered along the track, and schools were dismissed. When the train passed Farrandsville, a telephone message was sent to Robert McGhee, who waited at the Hope Hose Fire Company. He immediately began to toll the fire bell, which was a signal for all the church and school bells. Many people put coins on the track to keep the flattened pieces of metal as a memento of the solemn occasion. (Courtesy of the Annie Halenbake Ross Library.)

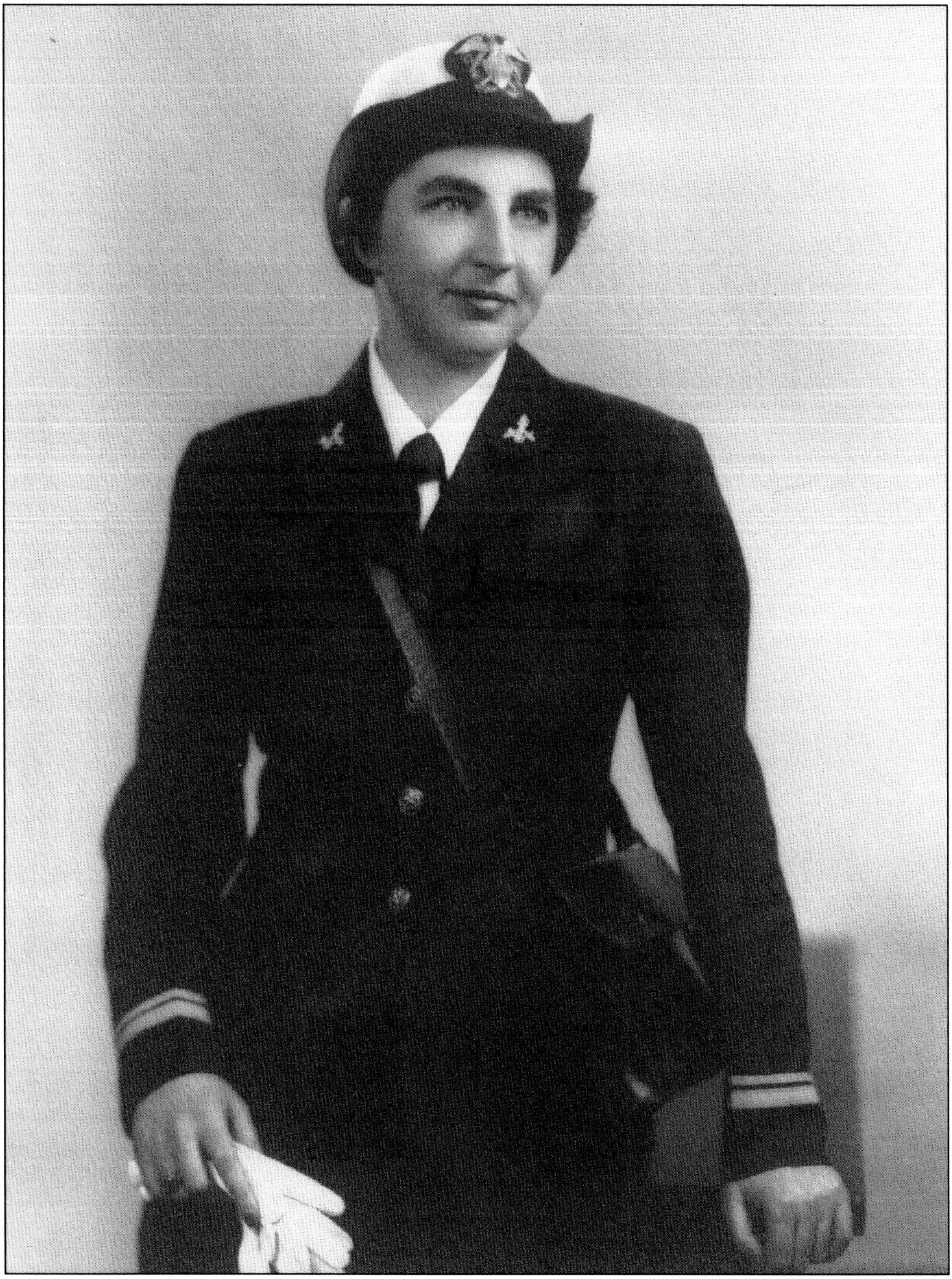

Born in Lock Haven on April 27, 1905, Rebecca F. Gross attended Temple University journalism school. After graduation she worked for the *Lock Haven Express* in 1925 and became managing editor in 1931 until her retirement in 1970. During World War II, she served in the navy and was editor of naval ordinance magazine *Firepower.* She served on the City of Lock Haven's recreation board, the board of directors of the Ross Library, and as president of the Lock Haven Civic Club. (Courtesy of the Annie Halenbake Ross Library.)

Members of Troop K, 3rd Squadron 1st Regiment Calvary stand in front of the Veterans of Foreign Wars building located on East Church Street. The picture was just prior to World War II. At center is Hall F. Achenbach, who became the National Guard general. (Courtesy of the Bland J. Rossman Post 1630 VFW in Lock Haven.)

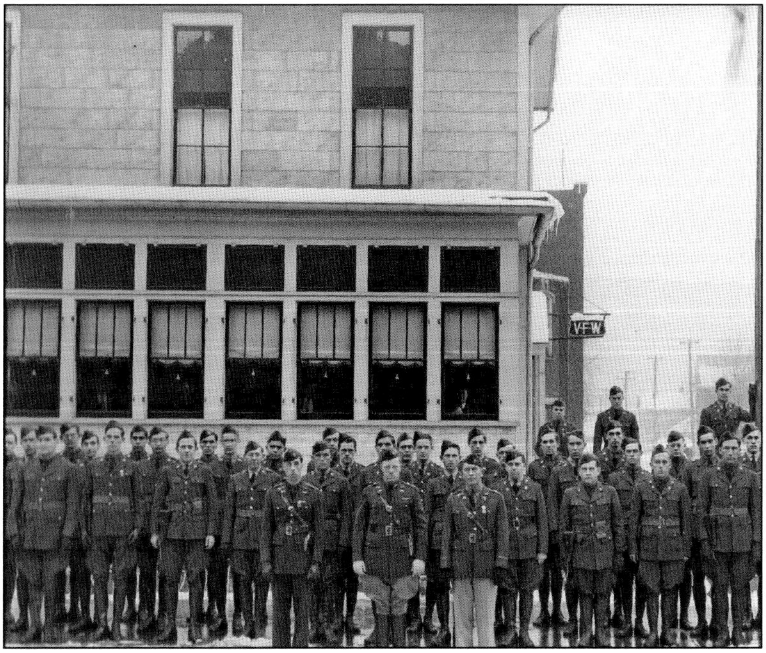


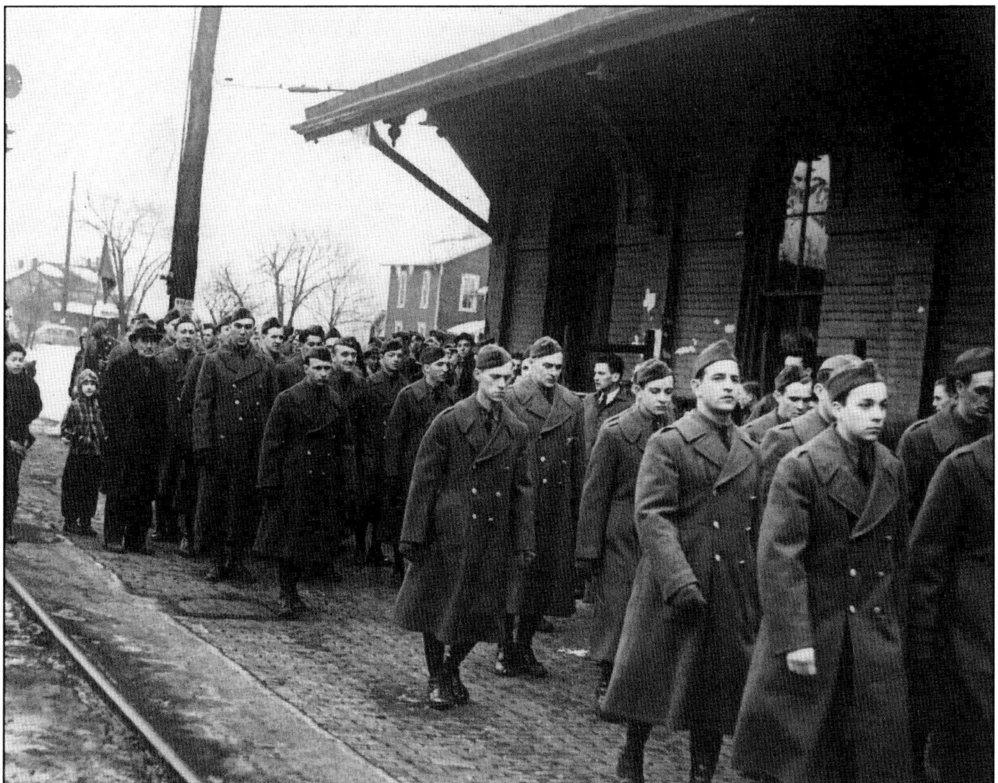

This picture was taken just prior to World War II. This troop of soldiers prepares to board the train in Lock Haven. (Courtesy of the Annie Halenbake Ross Library.)

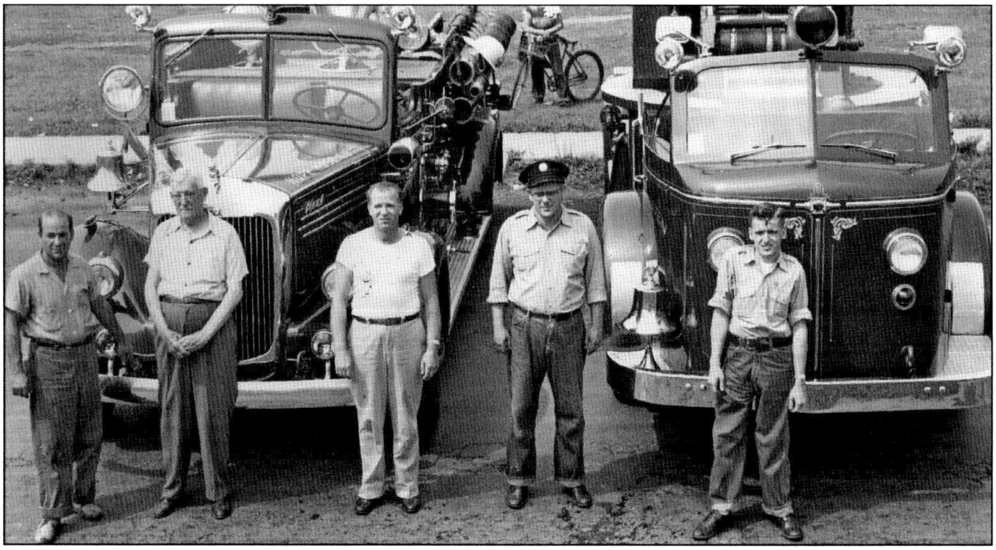

In 1954, the assistant fire chief for Hope Hose Fire Company was Joe Montovino, and fire company members included John Brownlee, Ralph Cummings, Bruce Bryerton, and Jimmy Swope. These men stood in front of the company's pumper and the Fire-Police aerial ladder truck. The ladder truck and the two city ambulances were housed at the Hope Hose Fire Company on North Grove Street. Founded in 1881, the Hope Hose Fire Company was one of the largest firefighting units in the county. The president of the Hope Hose Fire Company at that time was Paul Mack, and Bruce Bryerton was the Hope Hose Fire Company driver. Vincent Shay was the president of the Fire-Police. (Courtesy of the Hope Hose Fire Company.)

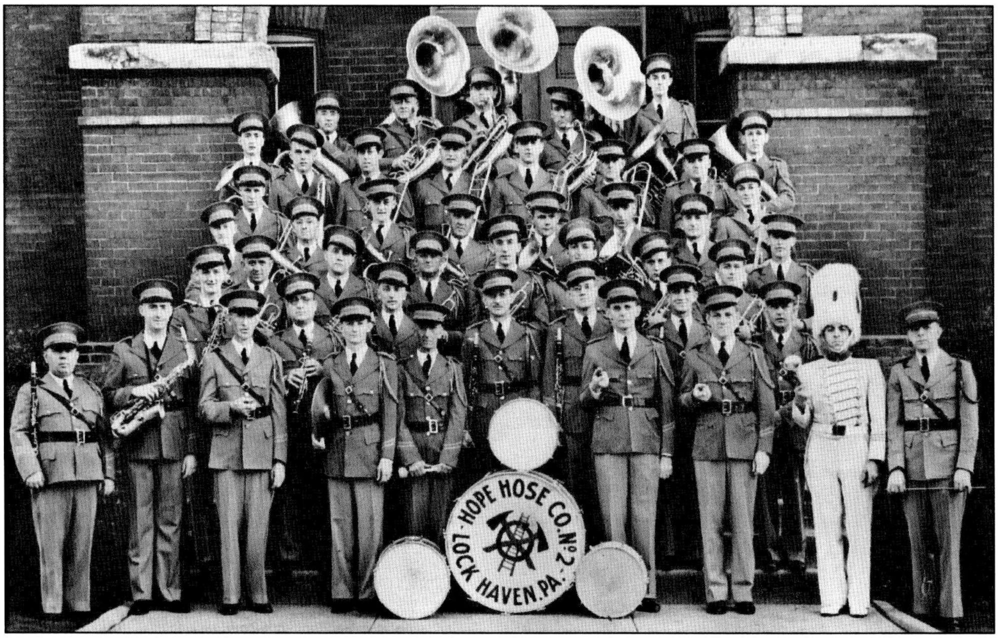


Members of the Hope Hose Company No. 2 Drum and Bugle Corp stand in front of the Penn School in the early 1900s. This band performed in many parades and community events. Standing to the right is Harry Pinge, a longtime dedicated member of the Hope Hose Fire Company and sergeant of the National Guard. (Courtesy of the Hope Hose Fire Company.)

# *Eight*

# Just for Fun

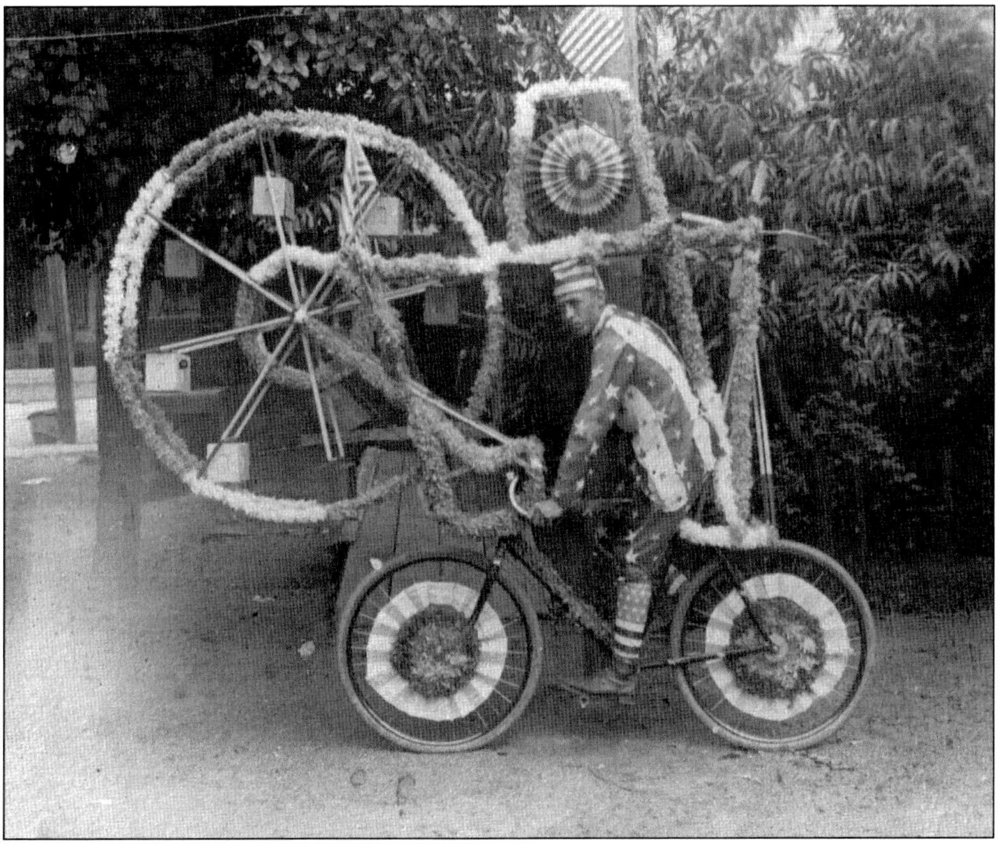

During the early 1900s, popular recreational activities included home drama presentations, balls, weekly dances, church socials, lawn tennis, baseball, and footracing. Picnics, turkey shoots, country-dances, housewarmings, and sleigh rides offered social outlets. (Courtesy of the Annie Halenbake Ross Library.)

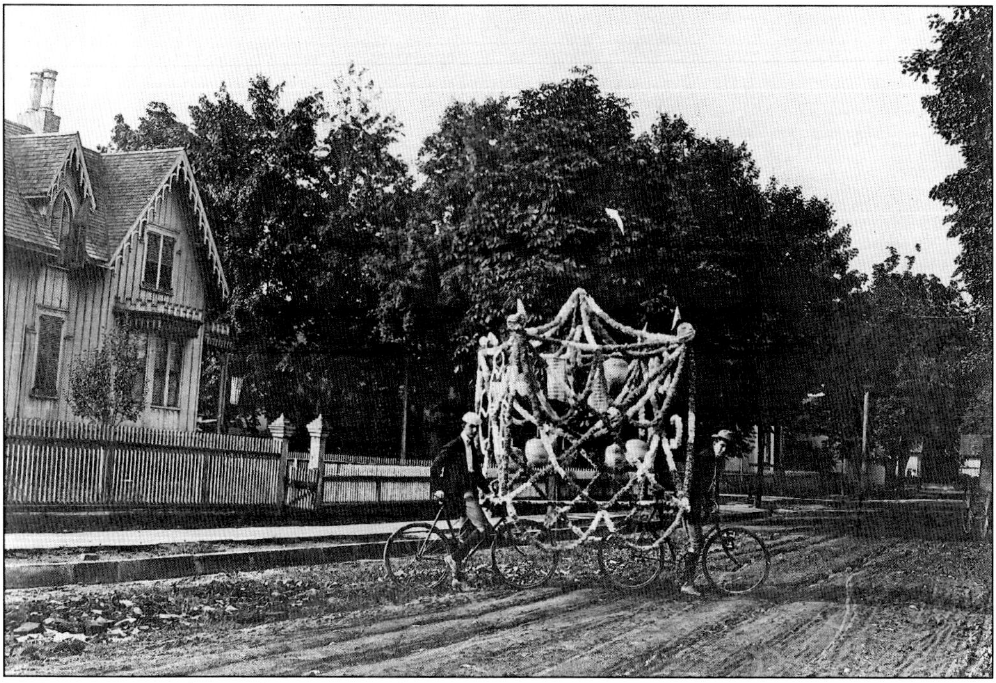

In August 1898, the Lock Haven Cycle Club hosted the Illuminated Bicycle Parade. Some of the finest wheels were Al Rote with the revolving umbrella, Charles Hamilton with an air ship, Annie Bickford with an umbrella, Annie Freed with a square float and arched top, and L. H. Miller with the Brooklyn Bridge. Undeterred by a threatening storm, the line formed at 8:00 p.m. at West Main Street. The parade was slow moving and took one hour. The judges were Mayor Mayer, T. M. Stevenson, Esq., and W. C. Franciscus. Parade prizes included $5 in gold, a carbide lamp worth $3.50, and $2.50. A separate ladies prize was either a lantern worth $3.50 or a pair of bicycle shoes. (Both, courtesy of the Annie Halenbake Ross Library.)

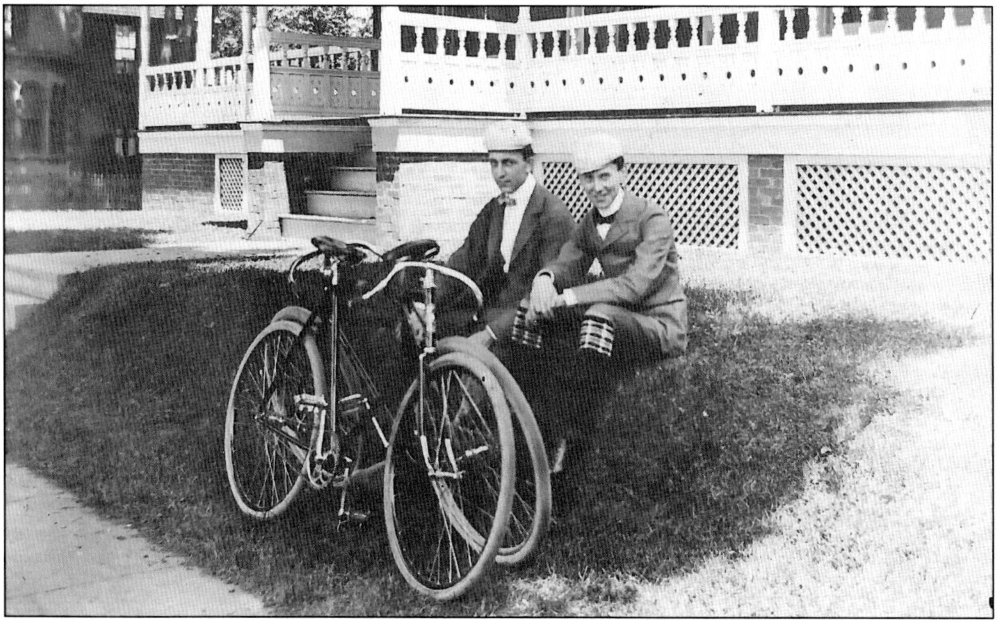

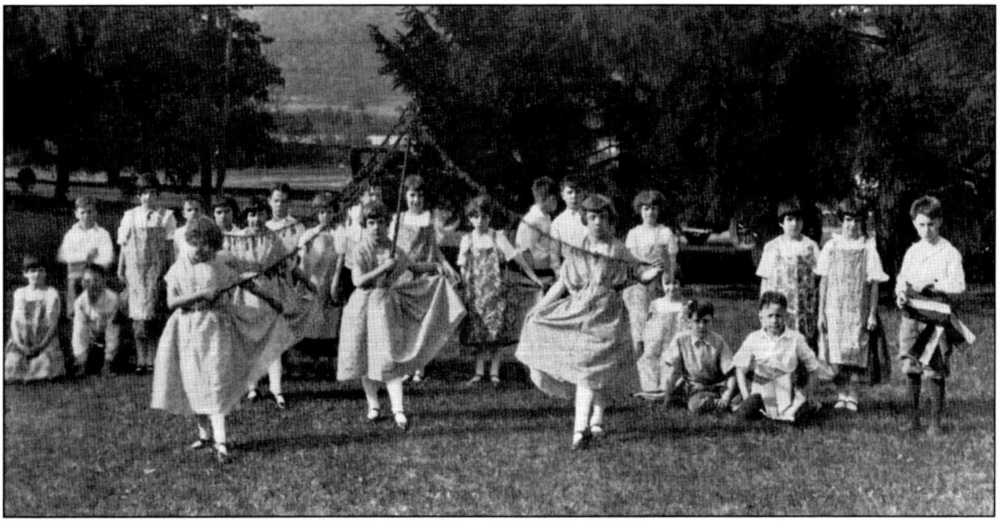

Children participate in May Day celebrations on the grounds of the Central State Normal School. May Day marks the end of the winter and a time for celebration. May Day events vary around the country and around the world. In some regions, maypoles are decorated with ribbons and pairs of girls and boys stand alternately around the base of the pole, each holding the end of a ribbon. Participants weave in and around each other, boys going one way and girls another, until the ribbons are woven together and all the merrymakers meet at the base of the pole. (Courtesy of the Annie Halenbake Ross Library.)

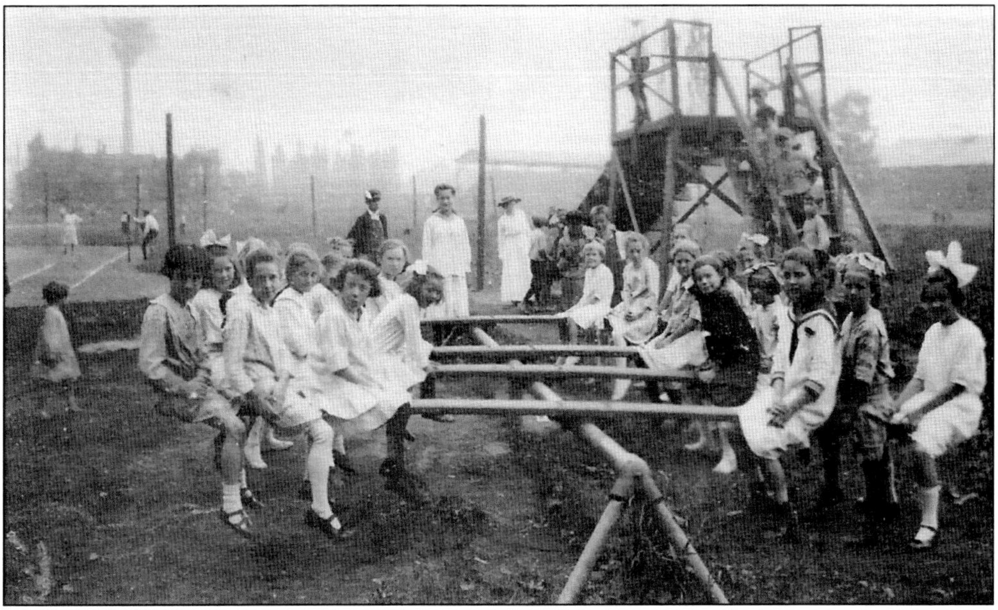

The Wilson Kistler Playground opened under the direction of the Civic Club. It was Lock Haven's first playground. Crowds of children attended the opening day in the city. Today the City of Lock Haven has a part-time recreation department that oversees the maintenance of four playgrounds and six parks. In cooperation with Keystone Central School District, a free summer recreation program is offered for area youth. Playgrounds include the Piper Harmon Playground, which was rebuilt in 2009 at a cost of $128,000, and the Bennage-Heights, Hoberman, and Hammermill Playgrounds. (Courtesy of the Annie Halenbake Ross Library.)

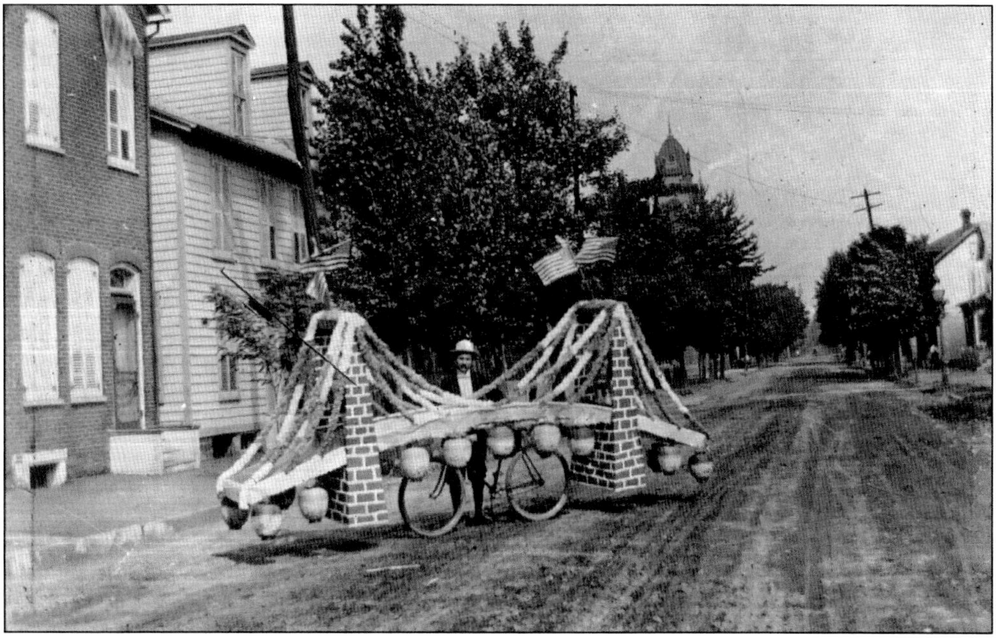

In August 1898, L. H. Miller was a participant in Lock Haven's Illuminated Bicycle Parade as the Brooklyn Bridge. The parade route moved down Main Street to Henderson, over to Water Street and up to Third Street, returning to West Main Street, and then to the paved portion of Jay Street to Church and then Grove Street and ending back at Main Street. It must have been a hot night—while there were 60 participants in the parade, some dropped out before they finished the route. Everyone was invited for a festival that followed with ice cream and cake. Prizes were awarded to winners of the parade. (Courtesy of the Annie Halenbake Ross Library.)

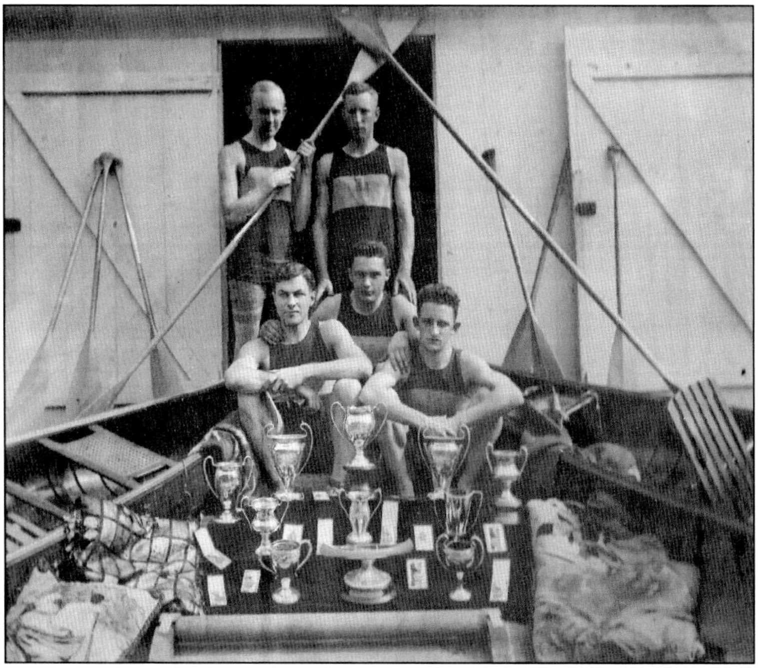

Some Lock Haven last names might seem familiar from this Bald Eagle Canoe Club picture taken in 1912. Surrounded by trophies are (first row) Bruce Kerns and Mallace Gast; (second row) Jim Hanna, Anson Bruner, and George Tidlow. (Courtesy of the Annie Halenbake Ross Library.)

There is no description left with this Floyd photograph to identify the adventurous gentleman. More than 100 years ago, ice sailing was one of many popular winter sports. It was not uncommon to see hundreds of people gather on the frozen river for skating. This iceboat was probably made of timber and canvas sailcloth. With all the right ingredients including ice, little snow, cold weather, and wind, these boats could travel at a nice speed. It took a skilled sailor to safely maneuver the sail and manage the unsmooth surface. (Courtesy of the Annie Halenbake Ross Library.)

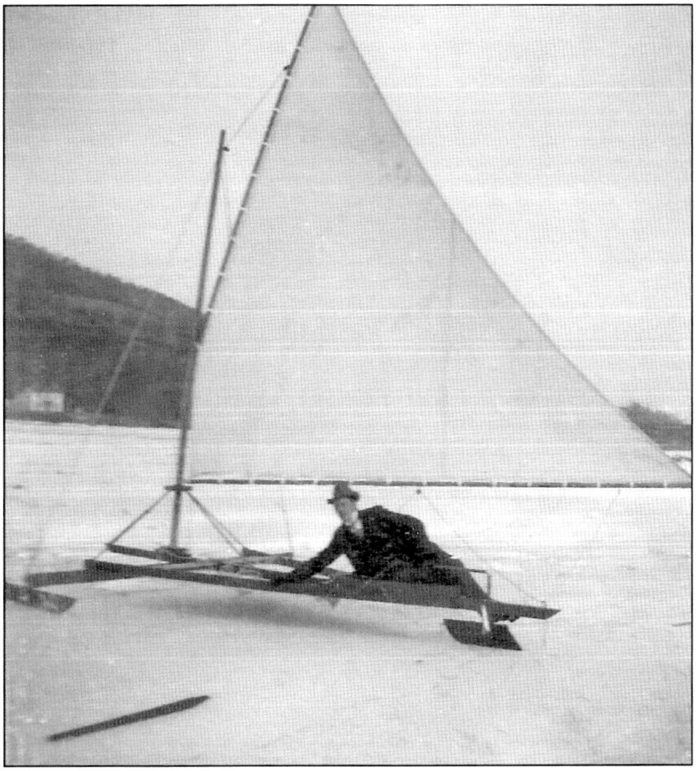

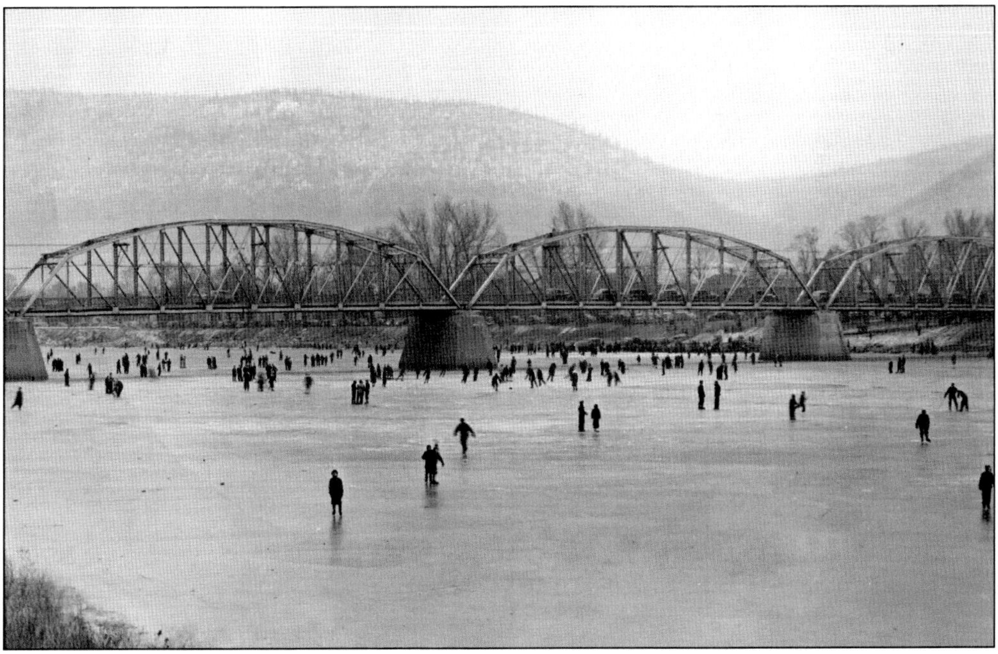

It takes some consistent cold winter weather to freeze the West Branch of the Susquehanna River. There are many photographs of scenes like this throughout Lock Haven's history. This picture was taken in 1939. Weather predictions that week indicated more cold weather was on its way, ensuring that skating would be possible for awhile. (Courtesy of the Annie Halenbake Ross Library.)

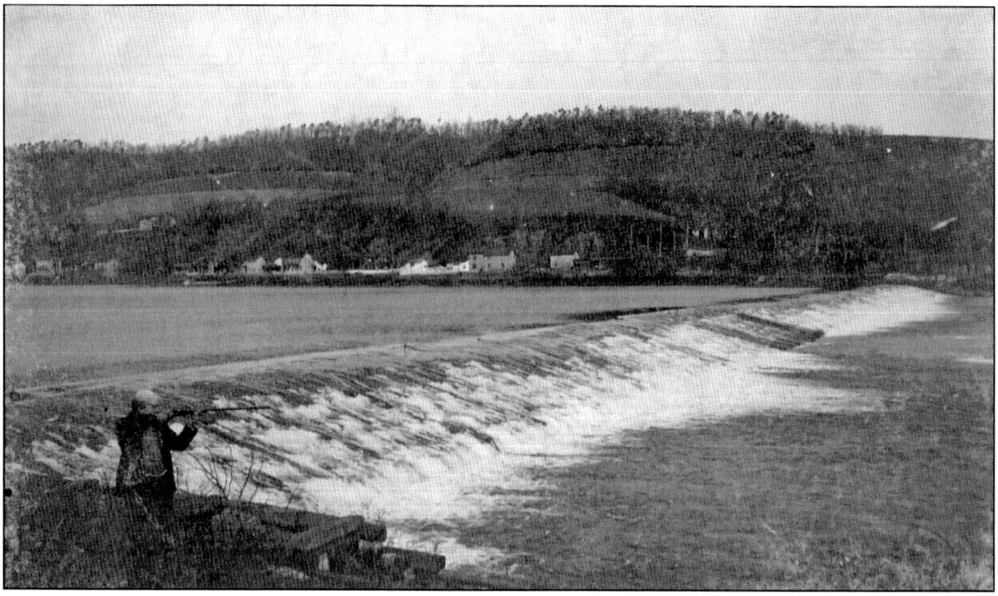

Striking a hunting pose at the dam on the Lock Haven side of the river, this gentleman was in several Floyd photographs. The river has always played an important role in leisure and recreational activities. Recreational use and tourism are now important sources of revenue for local businesses. (Courtesy of the Annie Halenbake Ross Library.)

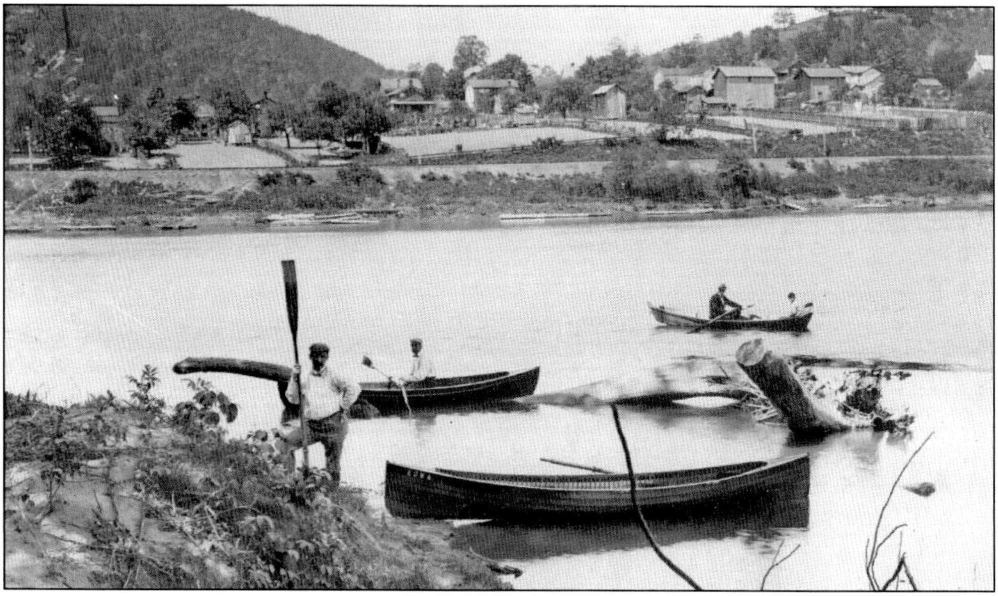

In the early 1890s, the Lock Haven Boat Club was founded by a group of people interested in water sports. A boathouse was located in the 200 block of West Water Street. The club was comprised of 150 members and became the social center of the city and the hub of activity. The boathouse was built along the river, and it extended to the edge of the water and could accommodate 100 canoes and cedar boats. There was a dance pavilion on the second floor, and large dances were held often. There were several tennis courts so that many people could play at the same time. Holidays on the river included a parade of boats with a judges' stand in front of the boathouse. (Courtesy of the Annie Halebake Ross Library.)

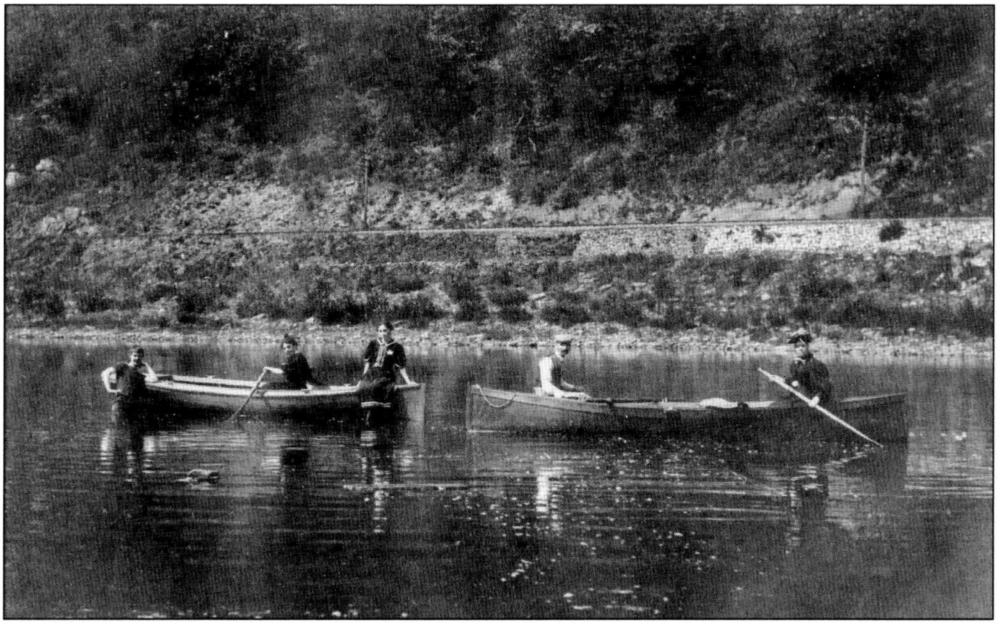

The boathouse was the center of Lock Haven's social activity before the Clinton County Country Club was organized and formed in 1901. The club remained active until the disappearance of the dam removed the placid body of water that fostered canoeing. The picture below shows a party of canoe enthusiasts on a boat trip to Riverview. The group includes, from left to right, Edward Bridgens, Elizabeth H. Peale, Thomas R. Weymouth, Mrs. George D. Green, Girard Williamson, Eleanor G. Galmon, Dr. L. P. Salmon, Grace MacVickar of Williamsport (now Mrs. Henry D. Brown of Philadelphia), Sedgwick Kistler, Florence Brown of Williamsport (now Mrs. George Atkinson of Washington, D.C.), Bruce Hayes, Mary Watson (now Mrs. Clarence Hall of Philadelphia), and Max Hayes. (Both, courtesy of the Annie Halenbake Ross Library.)

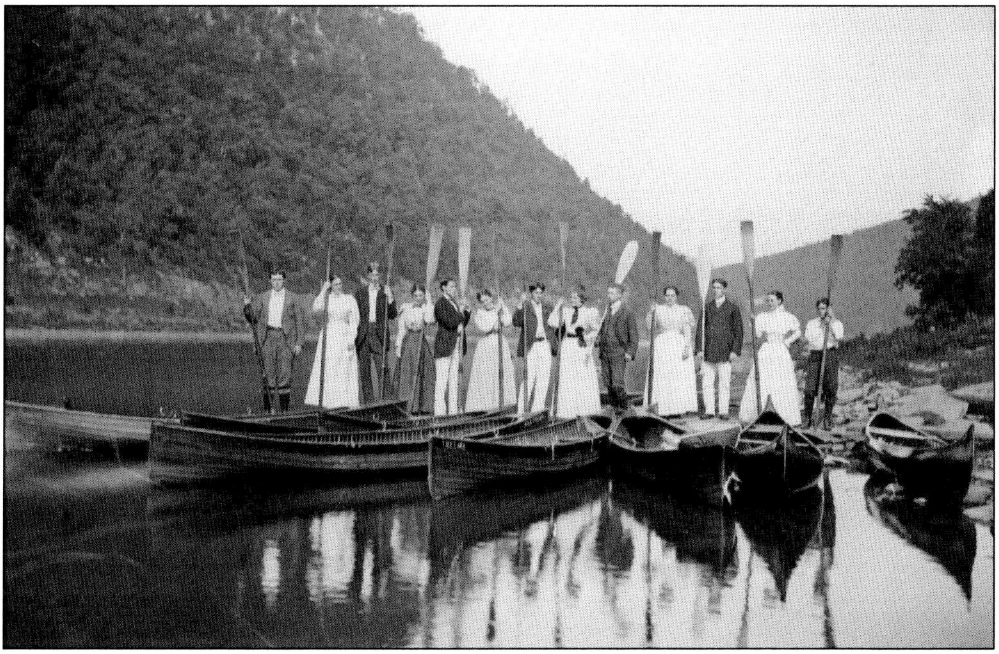

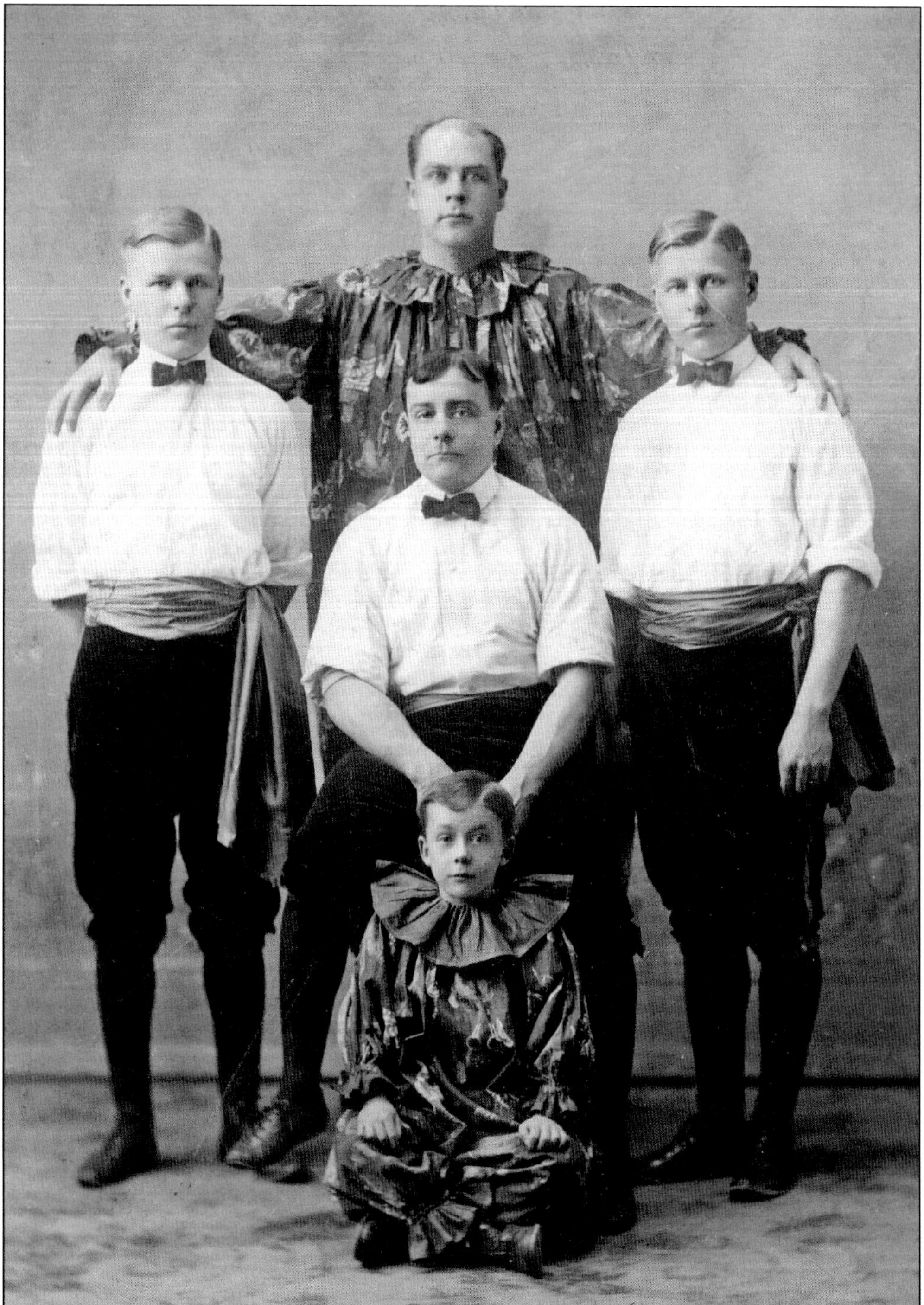

The Elks Minstrel Show was a popular show in town in the early 1900s. In this picture, the performers are the Stouck twins, Alvin and Mervin, Charles F. Poppy Strayer, and Max Hayes. Max was just 15 years old in this photograph. (Courtesy of the Annie Halenbake Ross Library.)

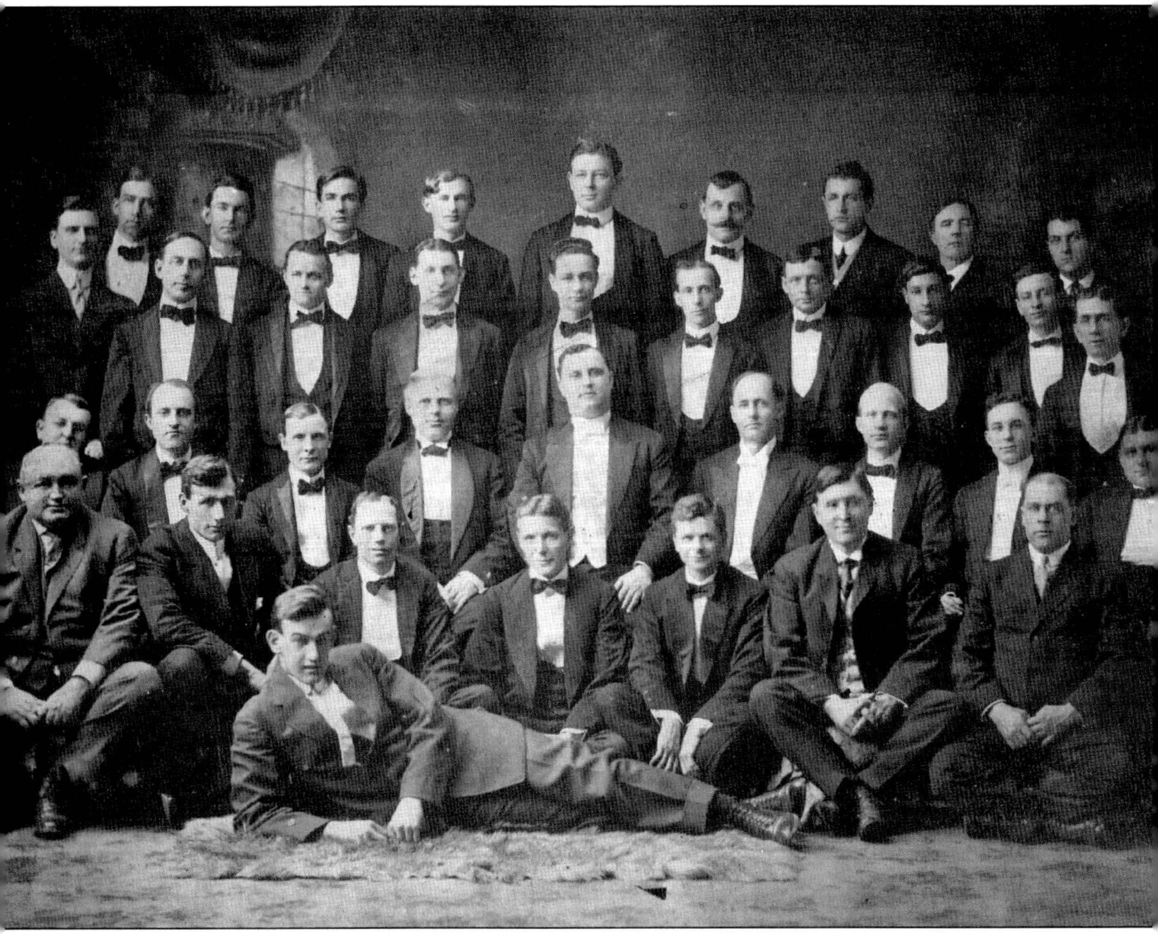

The Minstrel Chorus was one of the outstanding attractions of the famous Hospital Charity Minstrels who offered an annual charitable benefit show. Three of these men became mayor of the city. Staged at the old Opera House, there was always a rush for reserved seat tickets. Proceeds of the show went to improvements and additions of equipment to the Lock Haven Hospital. To stir added interest, the minstrels would parade up and down the business section. Judge Henry Hipple directed most of the music in the performances. (Courtesy of the Annie Halenbake Ross Library.)

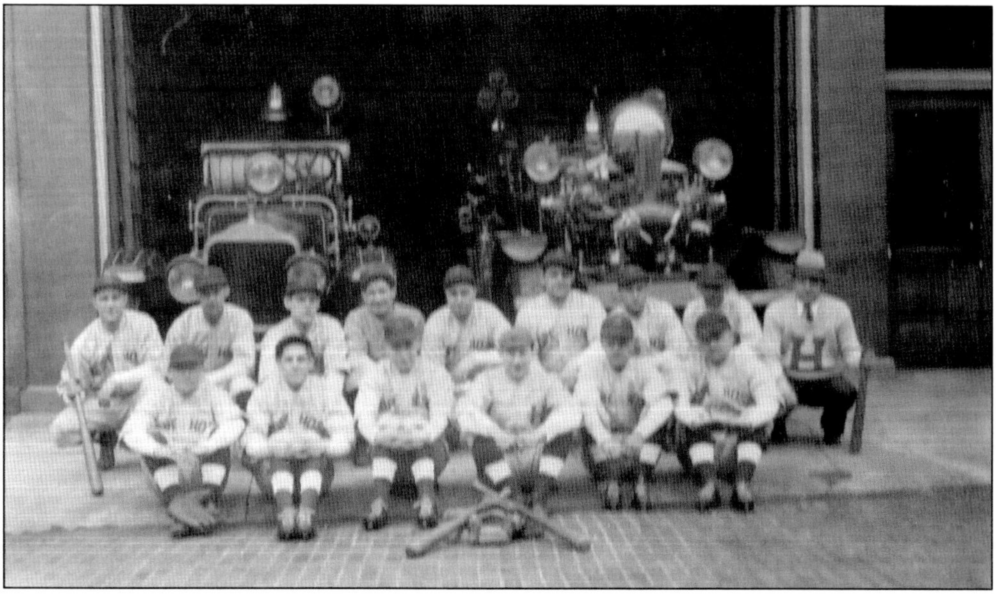

Pictured here are members of the 1938 Hope Hose Fire Company baseball team. Team members pictured are: Maurice Zettle, William Saiers, Harry Waterman, Charles Hain, Robert Lindsey, Robert Waterman, Dan Whitan, Fred Green, Frank Shuey, Al Wadswort, Harry Pinge, Wally Cowher, Mike Waterman, Watson Fowler, and Bobby Kunes. Notice the two fire trucks through the open doors of the fire station when it was located on Grove Street. (Courtesy of the Clinton County Historical Society.)

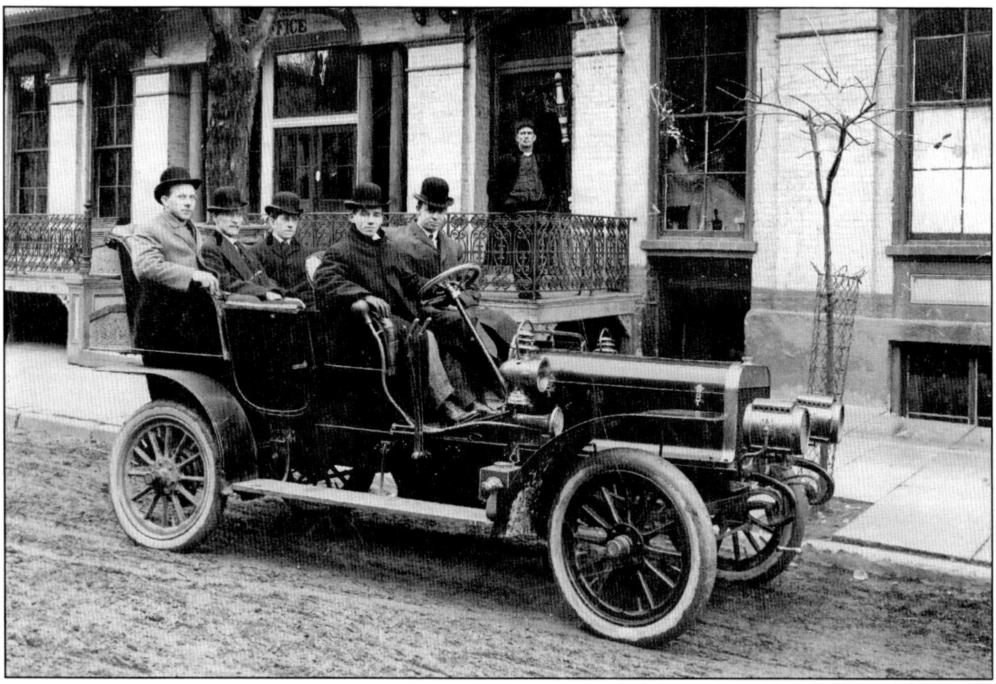

Roy E. Schuyler Sr. travels with Guy H. Achenbach. The car sits in front of the Fallon Hotel. At that time, the hotel housed a barbershop in the lobby entrance. (Courtesy of the Annie Halenbake Ross Library.)

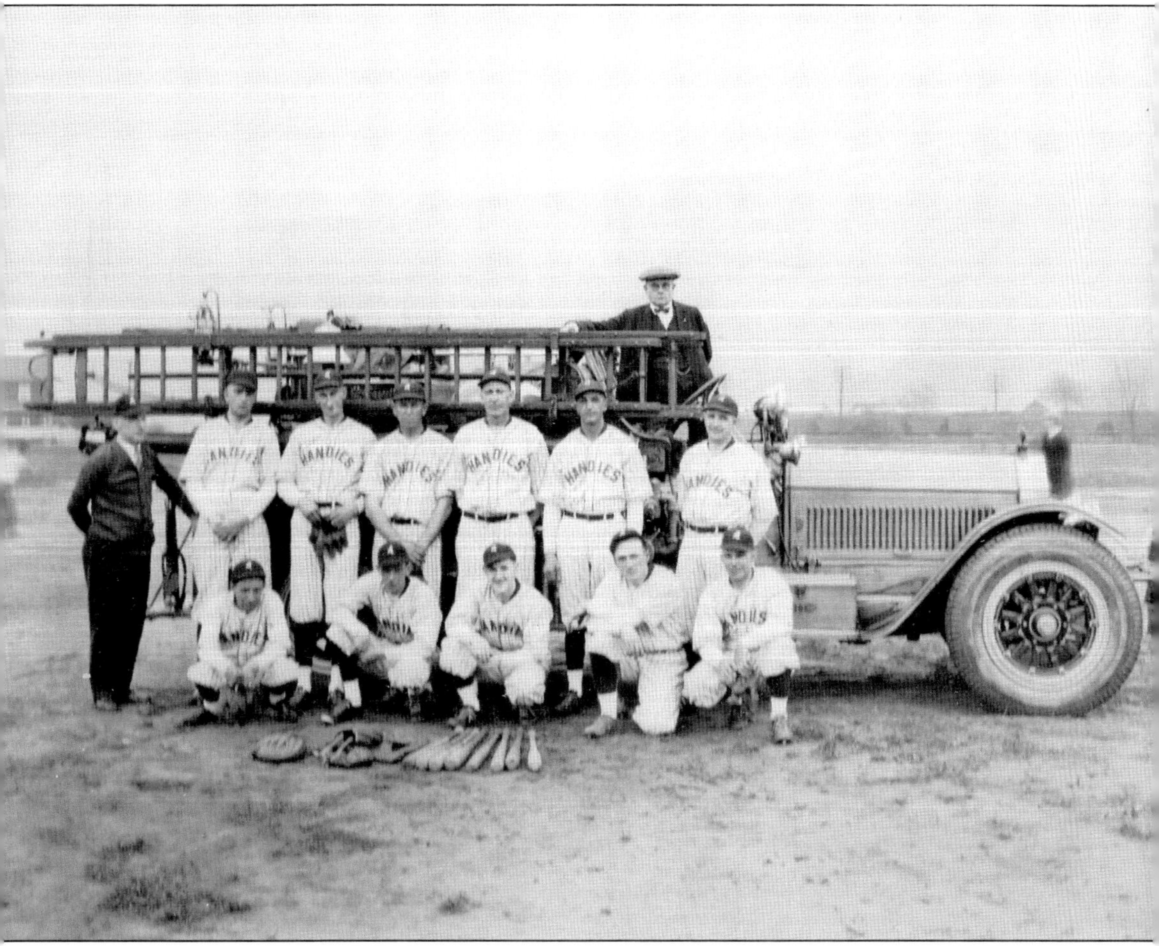

This Hand In Hand baseball team was the first team sponsored by the first ward firemen. This picture, taken around World War I, included, from left to right: (first row) H. A. Oberheim, Preston Bubb, Bruce McCormick, Stan Heydrich, and Scott Quiggle; (second row) Clyde Devling, Sam Vilello, Lester (Iron Man) Remick, Don Shaffer, Norval Remick, Chummy Hamberger, manager Fred S. Painter, and Dolly Barrett on fire truck. (Courtesy of the Annie Halenbake Ross Library.)

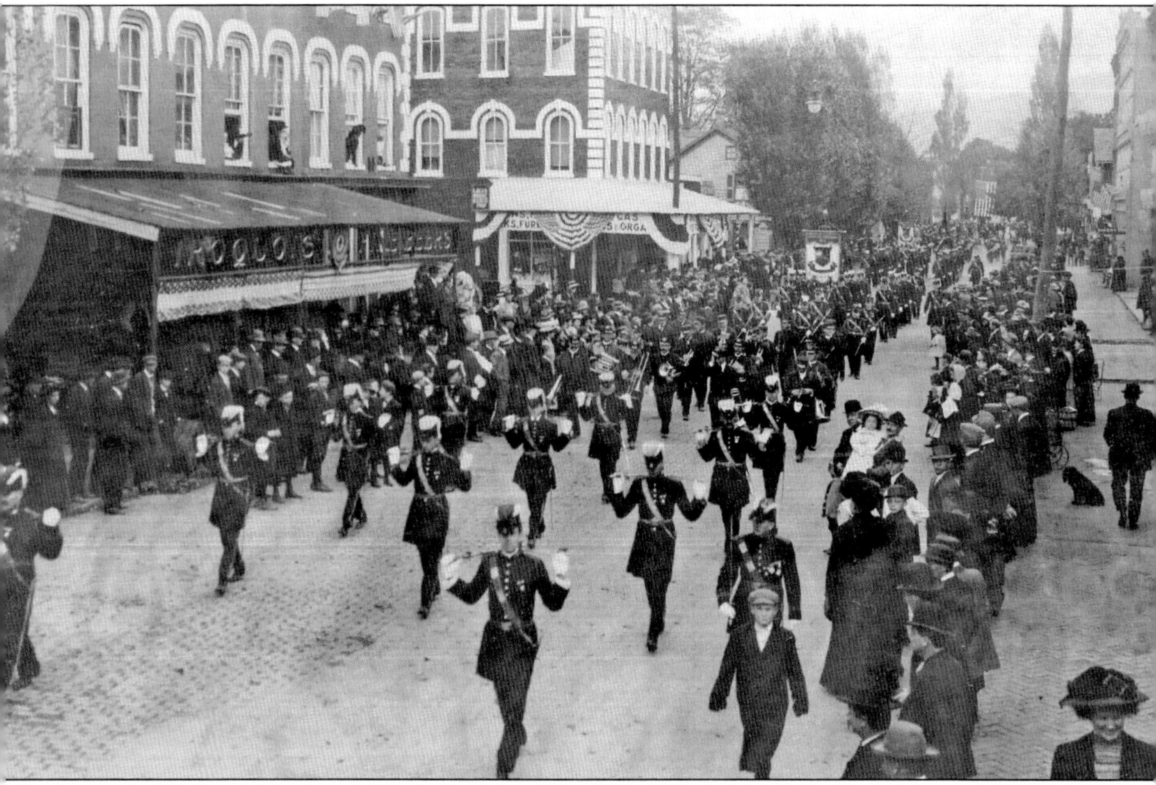

Parade routes in town were much more elaborate in the early 1900s. Hosted on October 18, 1909, the Independent Order of the Odd Fellows traveled not only on Main Street but also down Church Street near Grove Street. (Courtesy of the Annie Halenbake Ross Library.)

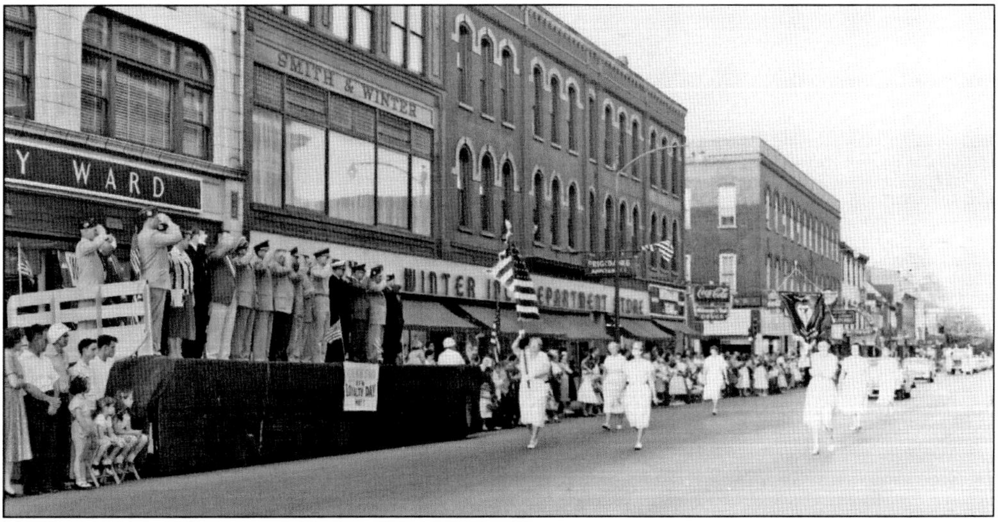


Members of the Veterans of Foreign Wars take the staging area on Main Street for a Loyalty Day Parade. Loyalty Day originally began as "Americanization Day" in 1921 as a counter to the Communists' May 1 celebration of the Russian Revolution. On May 1, 1930, approximately 10,000 VFW members staged a rally at New York's Union Square to promote patriotism. Through a resolution adopted in 1949, May 1 evolved into Loyalty Day. Observances began in 1950 on April 28, which culminated on May 1, when more than 5 million people across the nation held rallies. In New York City, more than 100,000 people rallied for America. In 1958, congress enacted Public Law 529 proclaiming Loyalty Day a permanent part of the nation's calendar. (Courtesy of the Annie Halenbake Ross Library.)

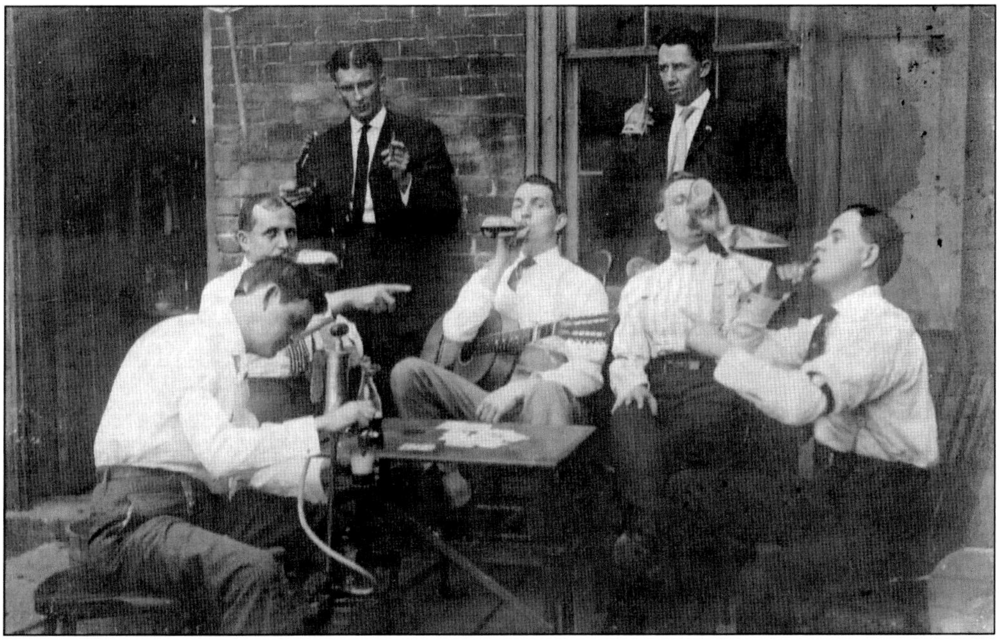

This photograph is believed to have been taken in the back of Maggs Barbershop, which was located at 101 North Henderson Street. D. Wasley Maggs is the fellow with the guitar—he was the leader in a string band at the time. Roy Maggs is tapping the keg. (Courtesy of the Annie Halenbake Ross Library.)

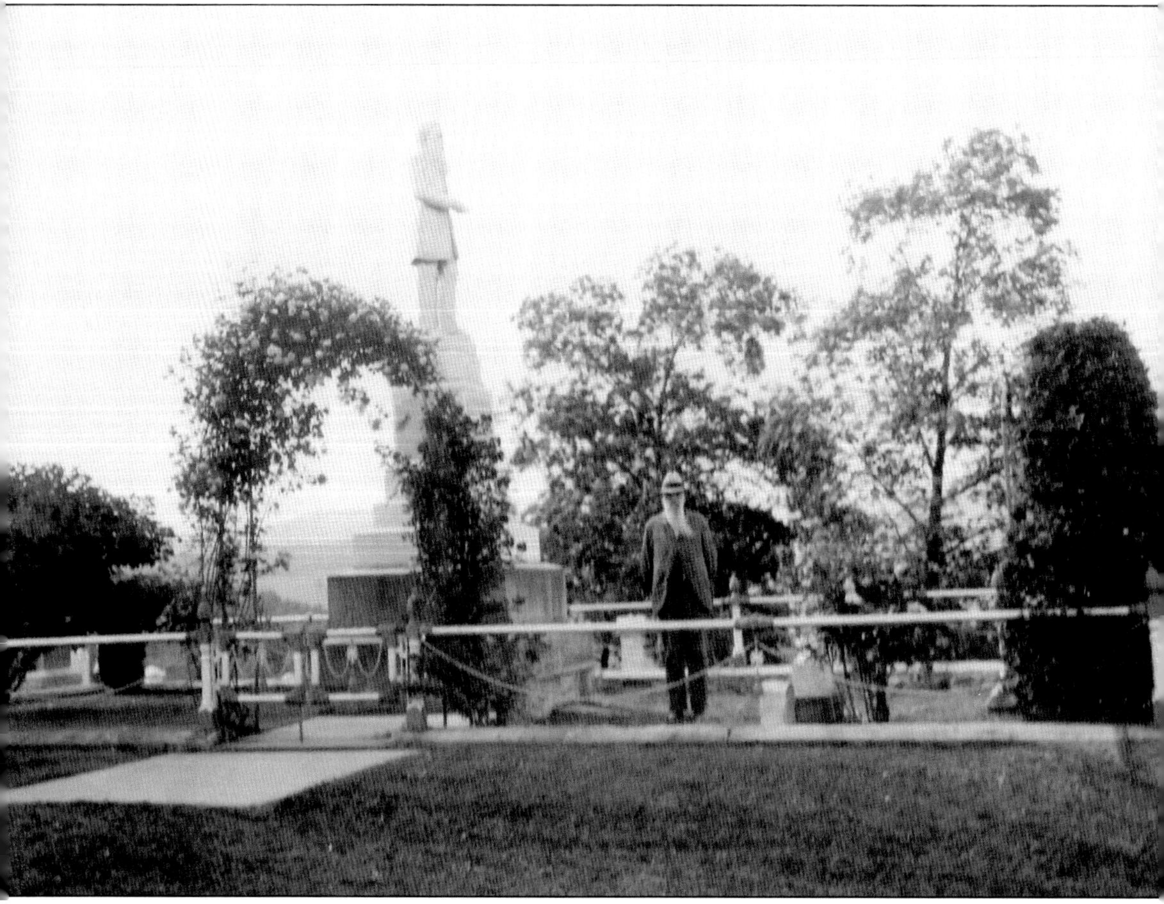

This statue of Peter Meitzler can be found at the top of Highland Cemetery overlooking the city of Lock Haven. Peter Meitzler was the owner of the Montour House, which is now Lindsey Place on Jay Street. He commissioned the statue and had it placed in the cemetery in his own memory. The statue depicts Meitzler holding out his right hand. As the story goes, he requested that the outstretched hand be carved holding a beer mug, which he felt was fitting for his position as owner of a bar. As seen in this picture, the arm appears to be outstretched in greeting, as the beer mug is missing. There are conflicting stories about how the mug disappeared. (Courtesy of the Annie Halenbake Ross Library.)

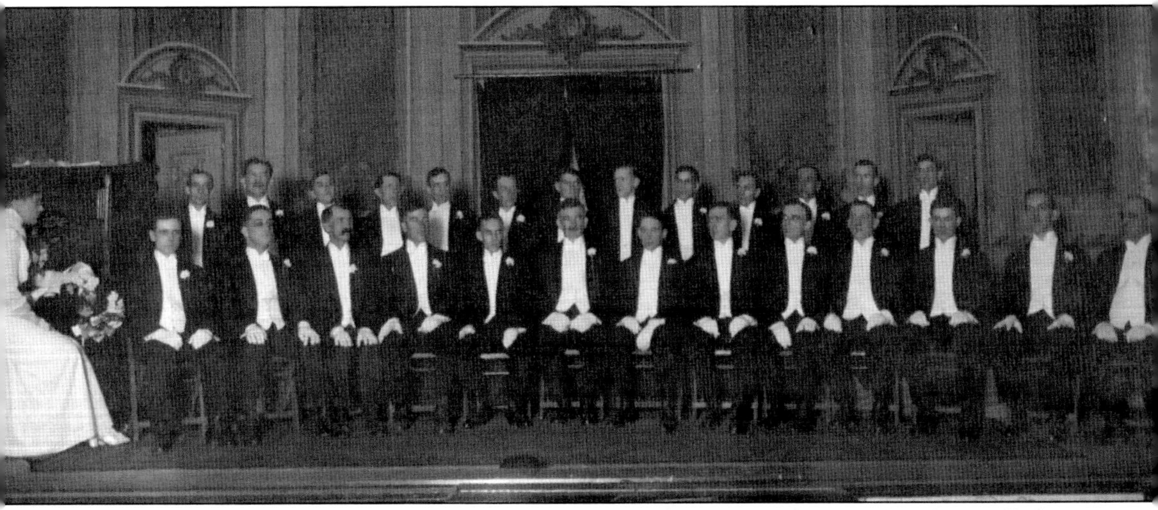

The Schubert Glee Club performed in February 1914 at the Martin Theater. Mrs. George Eadie, in the white gown, accompanied the group. Pictured from left to right are (first row) Milton H. Simon, Thomas H. Stover, Ralph Burd, Ralph Smith, Charles E. Harter, George H. Diack, Charles H. Herr, Thomas W. Bittner, Fred S. Painter, unidentified, William Murphy, and William G. Laye (director); (second row) Claude E. Miller, Frank Heydrick, Charles L. Keister, T. Mark Brungard, Rev. William E. Harr, Edward T. Miller, Raymond Adams, Harry W. Swope, Bruce Kerns, Charles D. Leitzell, Lynn Trexller, William T. Griffith, and Frank Swinehart. (Courtesy of the Annie Halenbake Ross Library.)

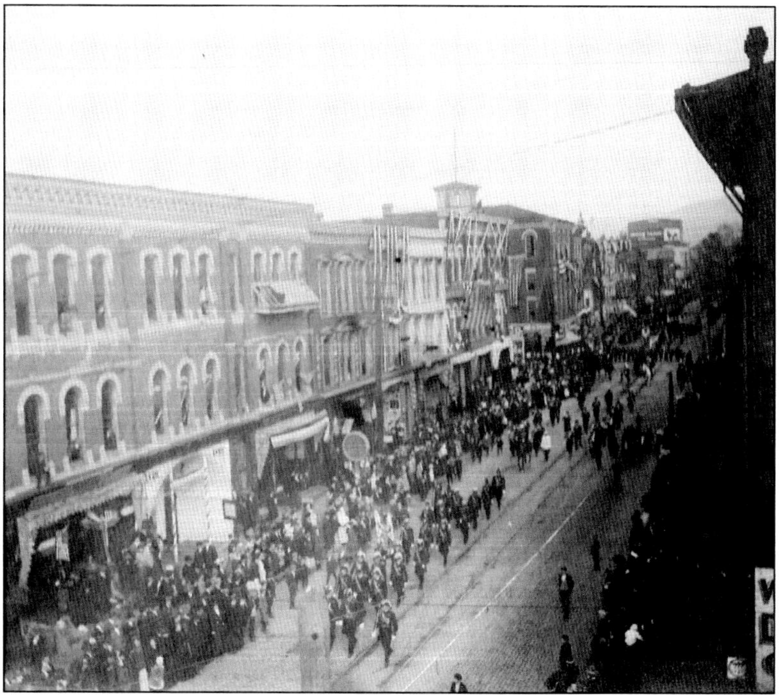

The community turned out for this parade on October 18, 1909. The Independent Order of the Odd Fellows parade drew large crowds of participants and spectators along Main Street. (Courtesy of the Annie Halenbake Ross Library.)

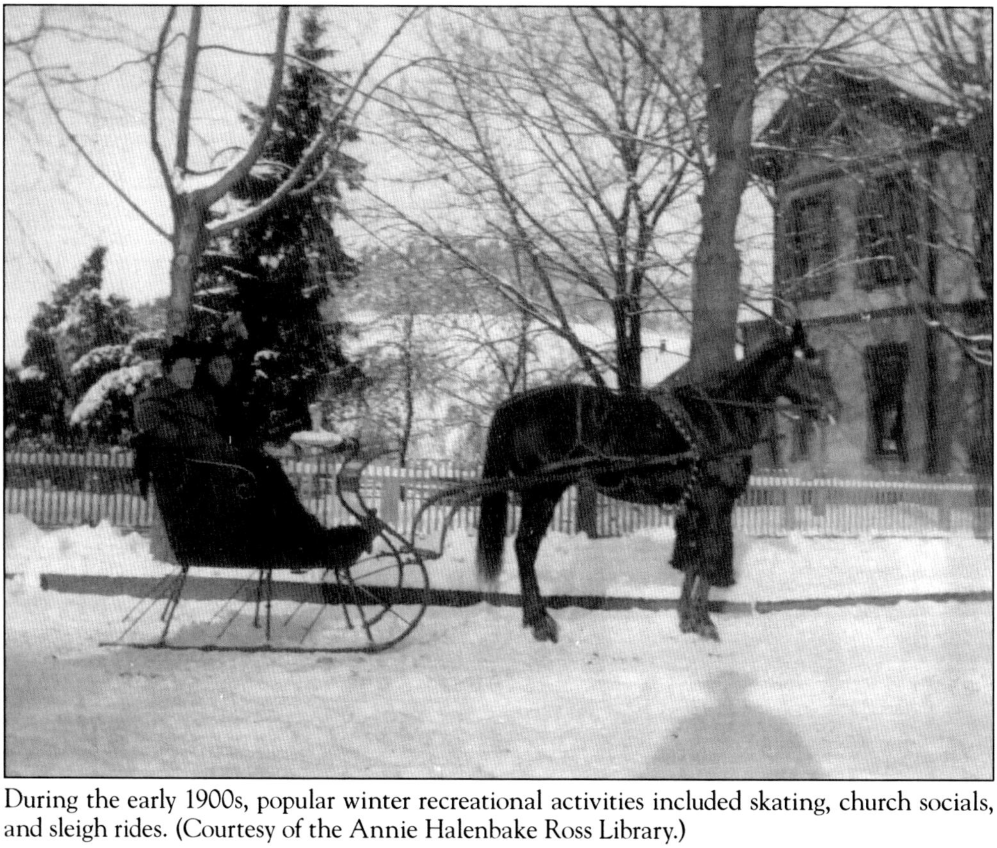

During the early 1900s, popular winter recreational activities included skating, church socials, and sleigh rides. (Courtesy of the Annie Halenbake Ross Library.)

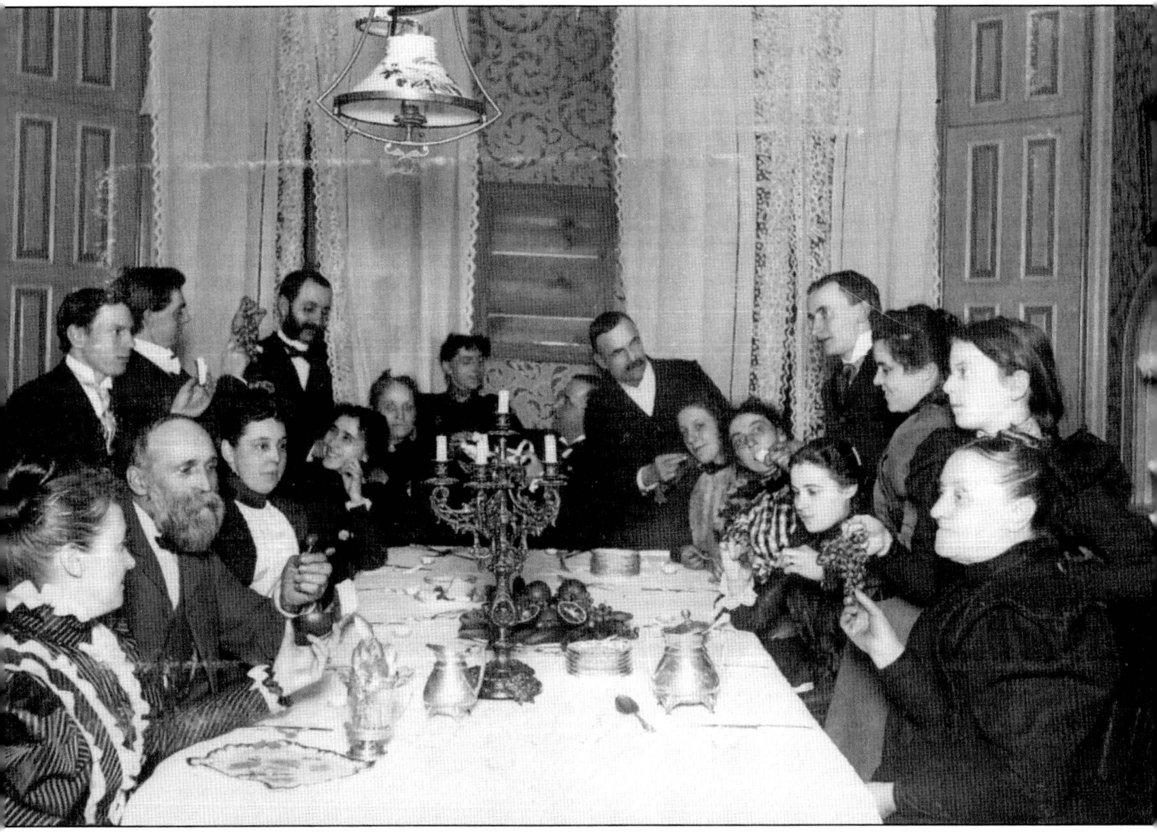

This is one of John Floyd's photographs of social gatherings at a residence in town. Early photographs took about 10 minutes to produce. During that time, people needed to hold their poses. Some movement did not matter, though some pictures do show it. Try standing, or even sitting, in one pose for that long. It is a strain, mentally and physically, as one begins to worry that they moved too much and that their pose is different. (Courtesy of the Annie Halenbake Ross Library.)

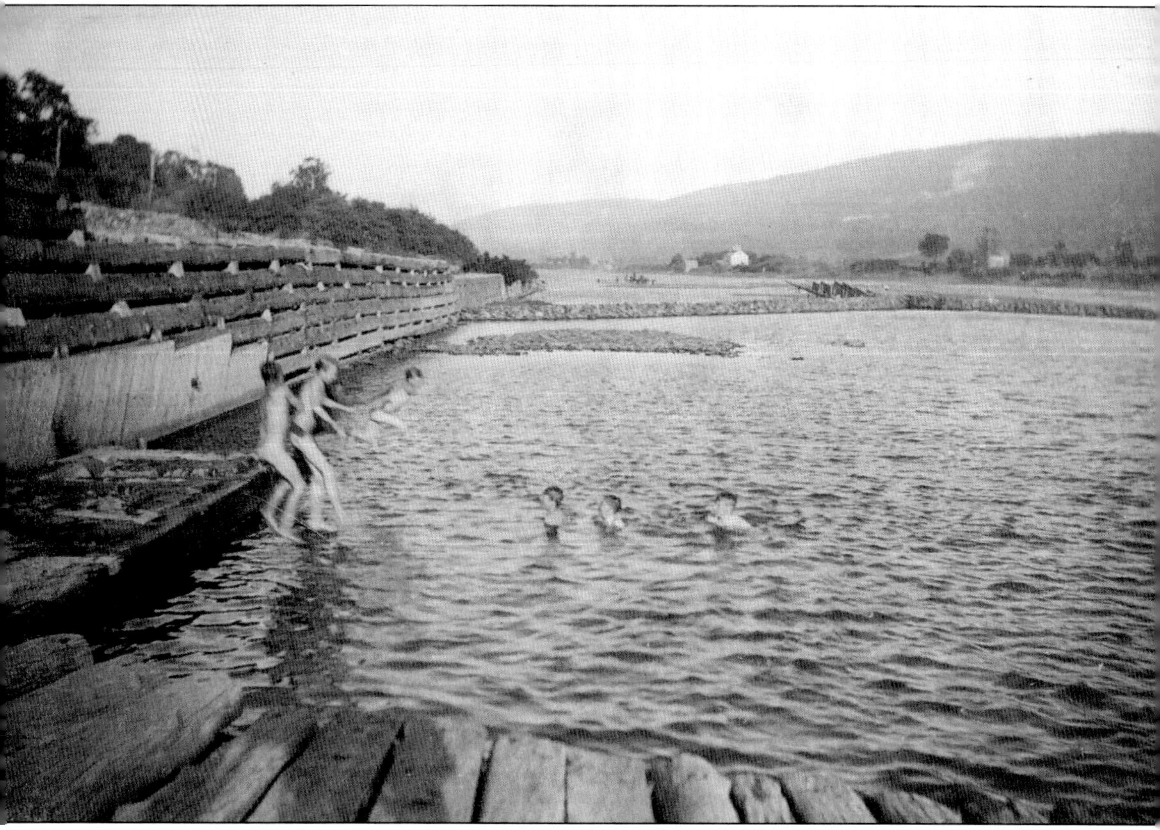

Swimming was another activity for summertime fun as these children jump in the Lockport side of the river. Today the City of Lock Haven operates a recreation program that is responsible for the swim program at the city beach along the Susquehanna River. The city beach operates from noon to 8:00 p.m. each day from June to August. (Courtesy of the Annie Halenbake Ross Library.)

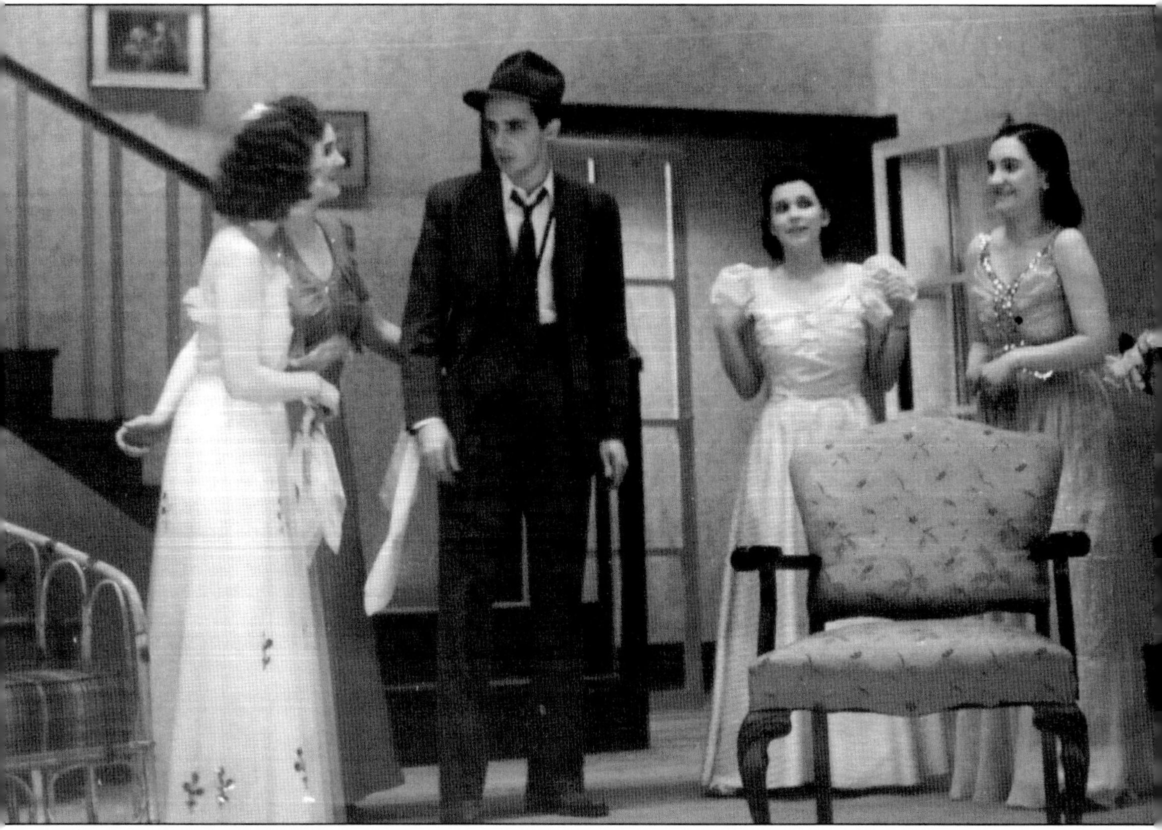

In 1941, the Lock Haven Players act out a production. Young entertainers developed an appreciation and understanding of the performing arts. Today Central Mountain High School offers two performances, one in the fall and one in the spring. The Lock Haven University Performing Arts Department offers a series of theater, music, and dance performances, which are open to the community. (Courtesy of the Annie Halenbake Ross Library.)

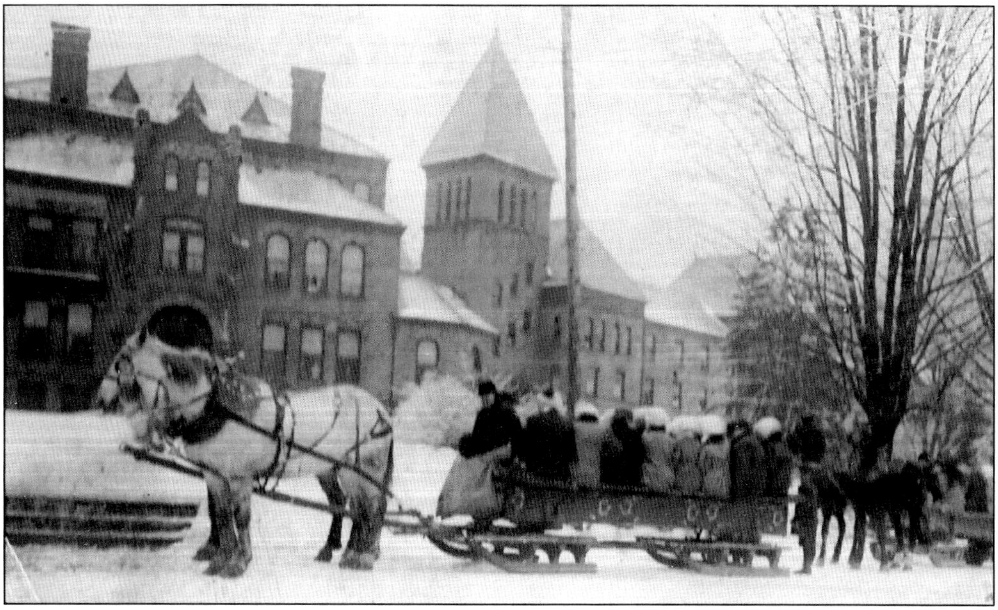

The Central State Normal School graduating class in 1910 takes a sleigh ride on campus. A charter was granted for State Normal School in 1870. The school was purchased by the state in 1914 and chartered as a state teachers college in 1927. The college focused on preparing students for kindergarten, elementary, and high school teaching. (Courtesy of the Annie Halenbake Ross Library.)

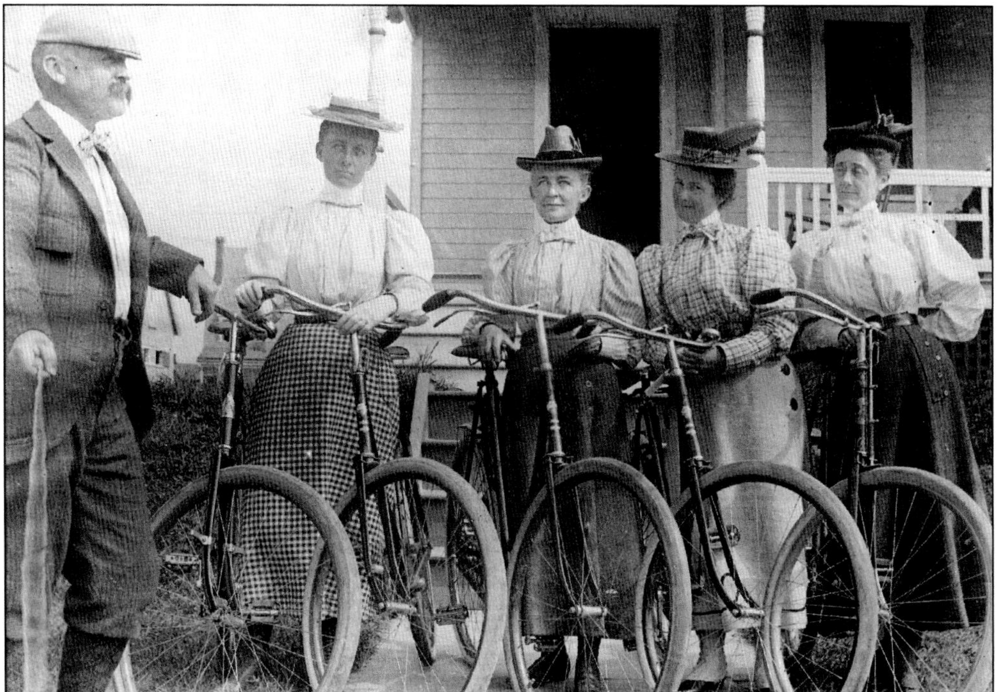

Bicycle clubs, such as the Lock Haven Cycle Club, were popular in town. Races and parades were held for all ages. (Courtesy of the Annie Halenbake Ross Library.)

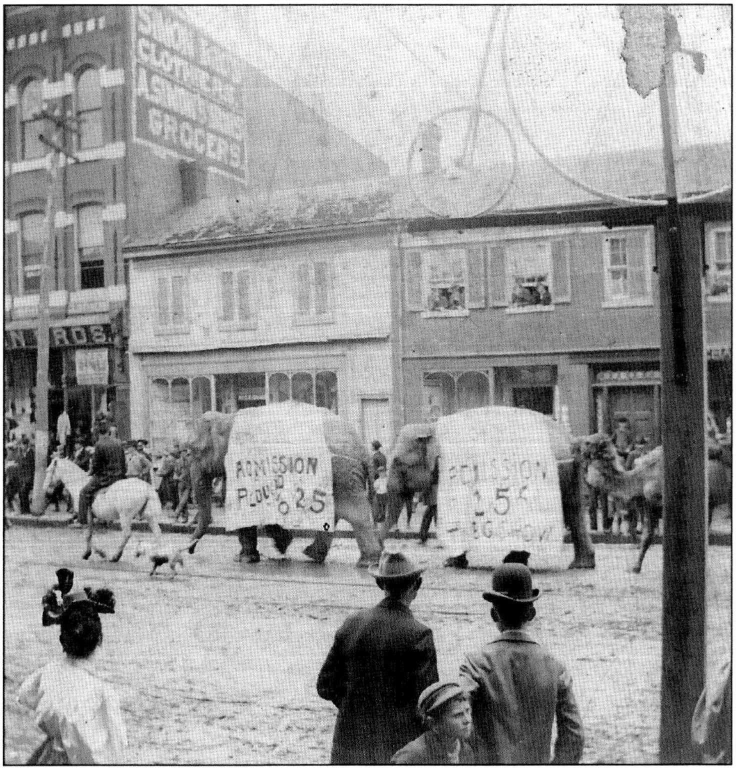


This parade is something special. Held in 1905 on Main Street, it included all kinds of attractions, even elephants. (Both, courtesy of the Annie Halenbake Ross Library.)

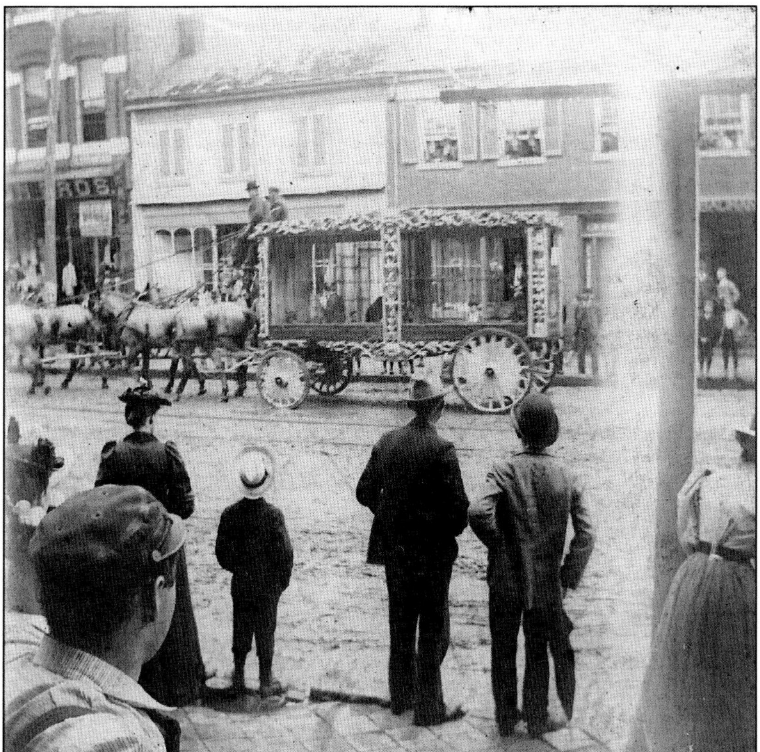

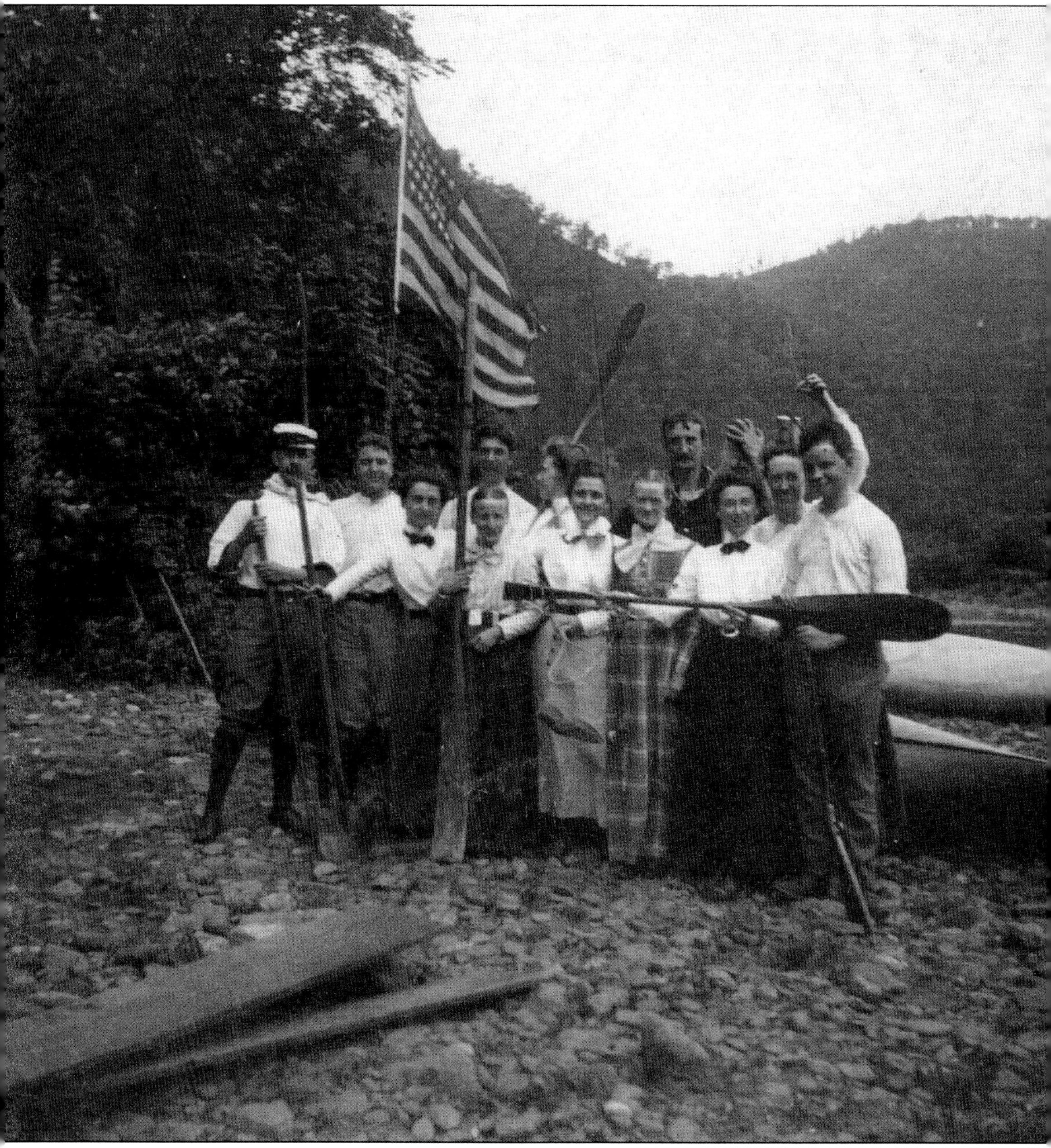

In the early 1890s, the Lock Haven Boat Club was founded by a group of people interested in water sports. At its height, the club had about 150 members. It became the social center of the city and the hub of many activities year-round. The boathouse was constructed along the banks of the river, behind the Presbyterian Parsonage and the residence of Mrs. Oscar Kreamer. It extended down to the edge of the river and was built to accommodate about 100 canoes and cedar boats. On the second floor a dancing pavilion was built and it was here that the members of the club held large dances. Members were able to use one of several tennis courts. (Courtesy of the Annie Halenbake Ross Library.)

On holidays, the river was the scene of much activity. On the Fourth of July, canoes were decorated, and a parade of boats was staged in front of the boathouse. A gala float was also built and fireworks were used. Prizes were distributed to the owners of the most beautifully decorated boats. (Courtesy of the Annie Halenbake Ross Library.)

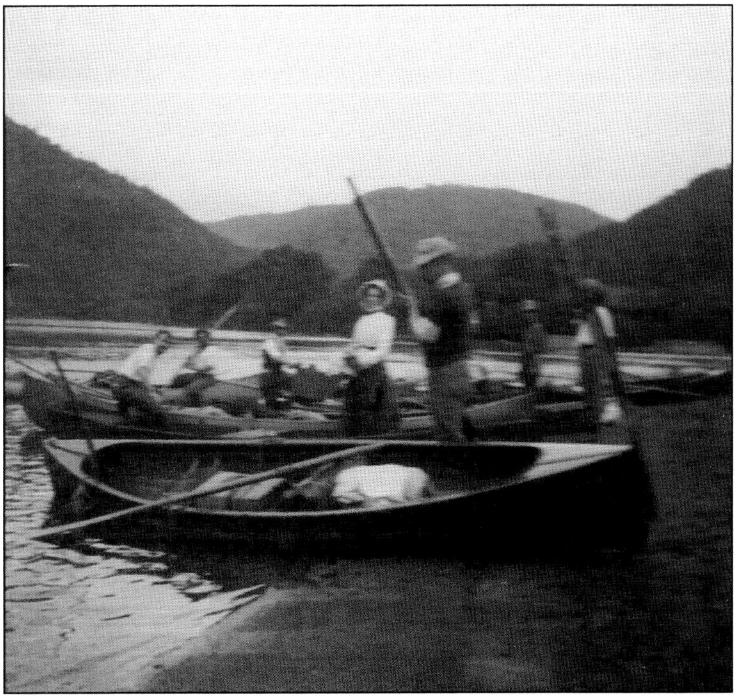

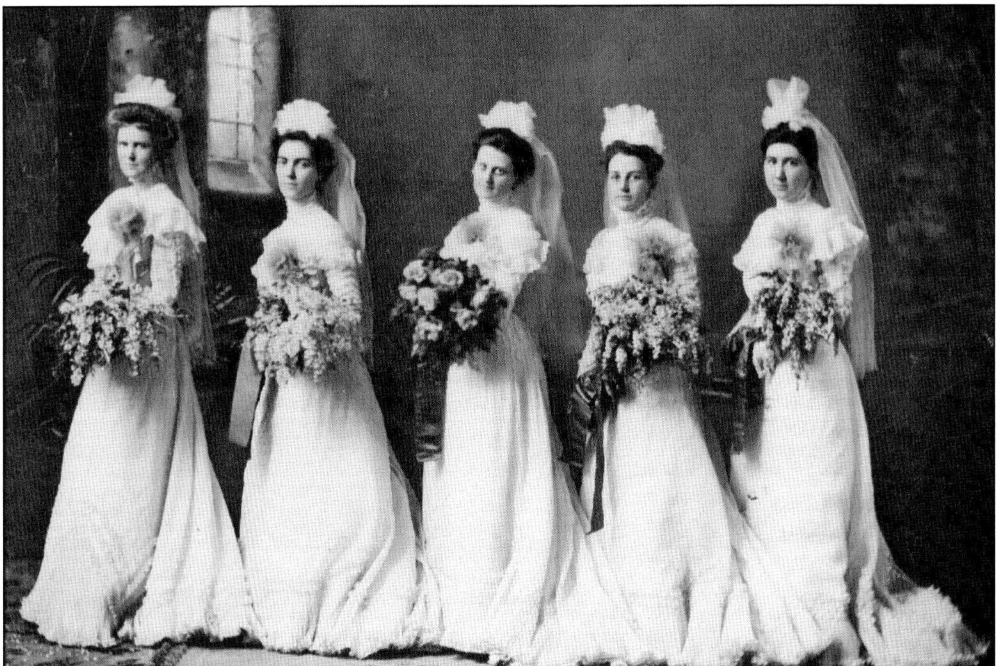

Pictured here are five debutantes from Lock Haven. No information is available about this photograph. Debutantes were usually from upper class families who had reached adulthood. To introduce them to society, balls or coming-out parties were held. The debutante might have her own debut or share it with a sister or relative. These balls were elaborate affairs involving escorts, ushers, flower girls, and pages. (Courtesy of the Annie Halenbake Ross Library.)

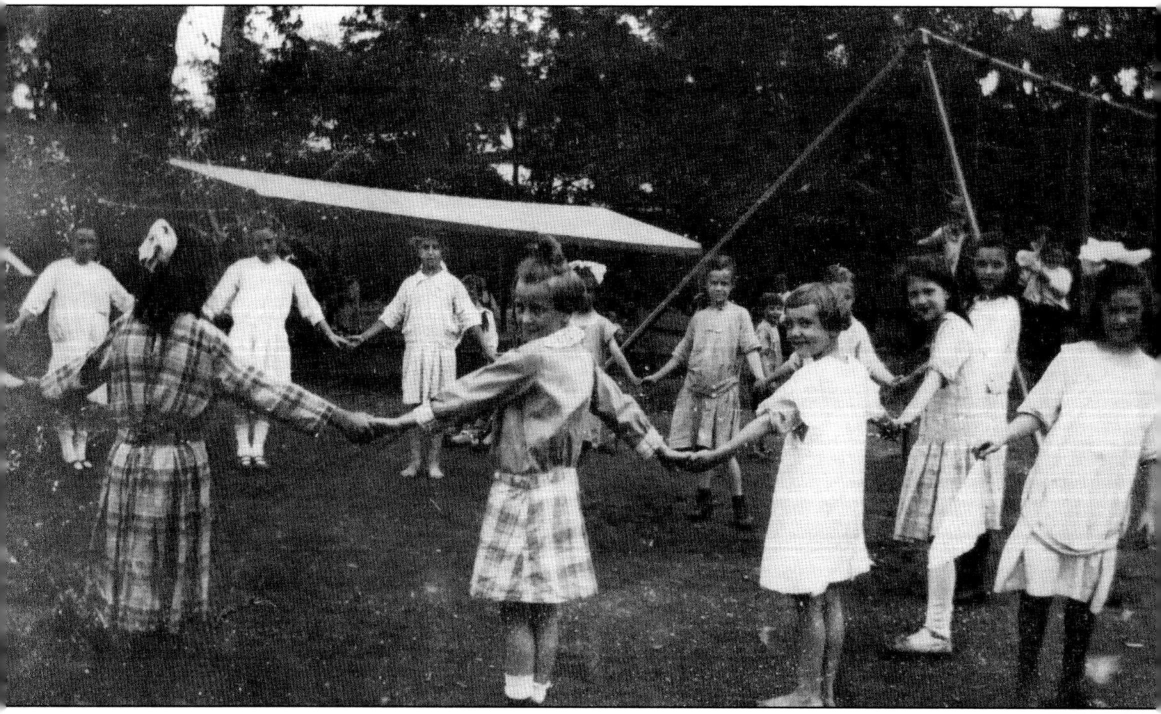

Children play games at the Wilson Kistler Playground, which was opened under the direction of the Civic Club. It was Lock Haven's first playground. Crowds of children attended the opening day in the city. The playground offered many activities and equipment such as swings, jungle gyms, and slides. Seesaws were made of plank boards laid over old logs. The Civic Club helped to promote the city's recreation resources. (Courtesy of the Annie Halenbake Ross Library.)

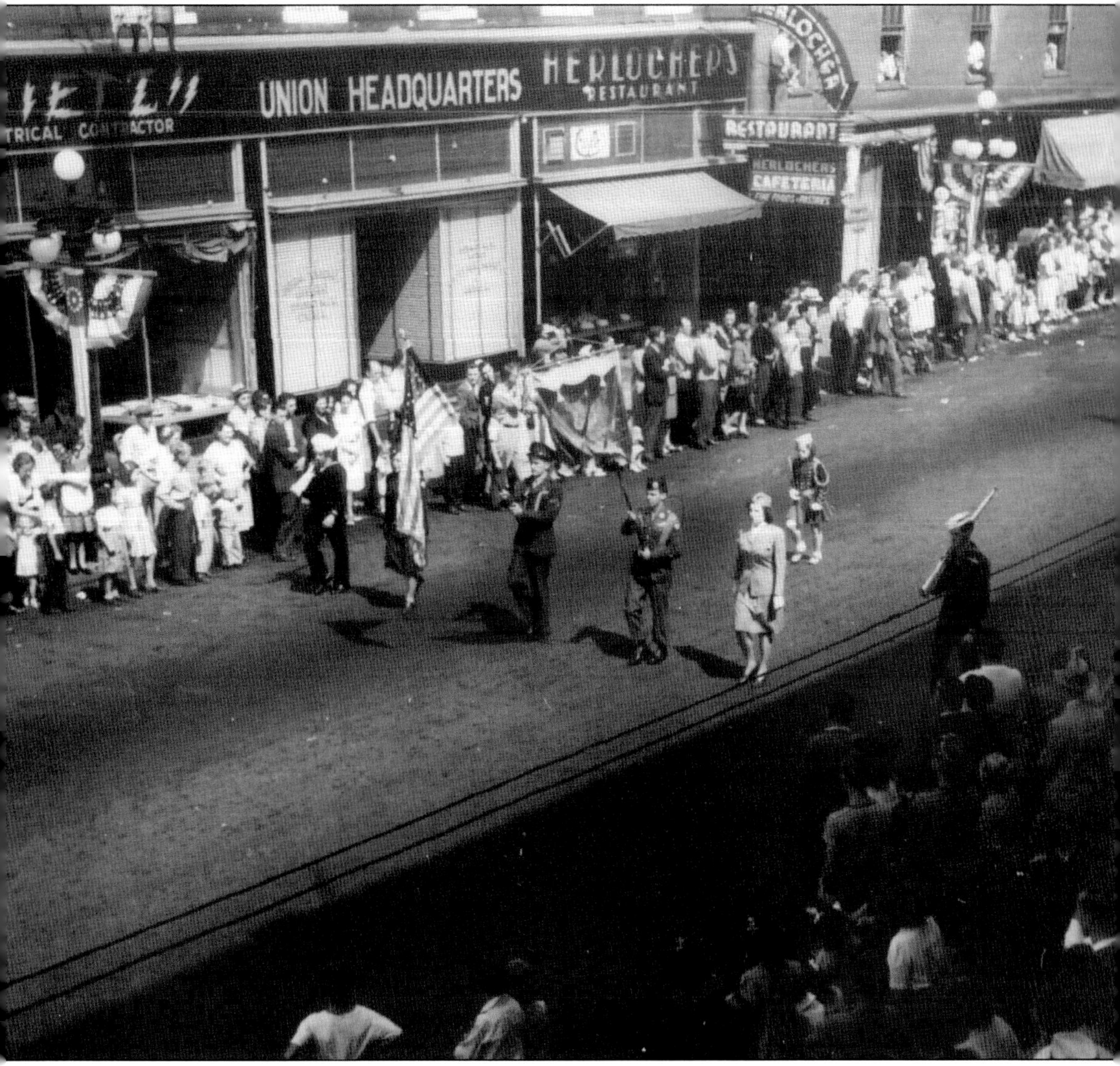


Military veterans participate in the 1939 fireman's parade on Main Street. The celebration was part of the Central District Firemen's Association Annual Convention. Thousands of firefighters attended this parade with over 200 units marching. (Courtesy of the Annie Halenbake Ross Library.)

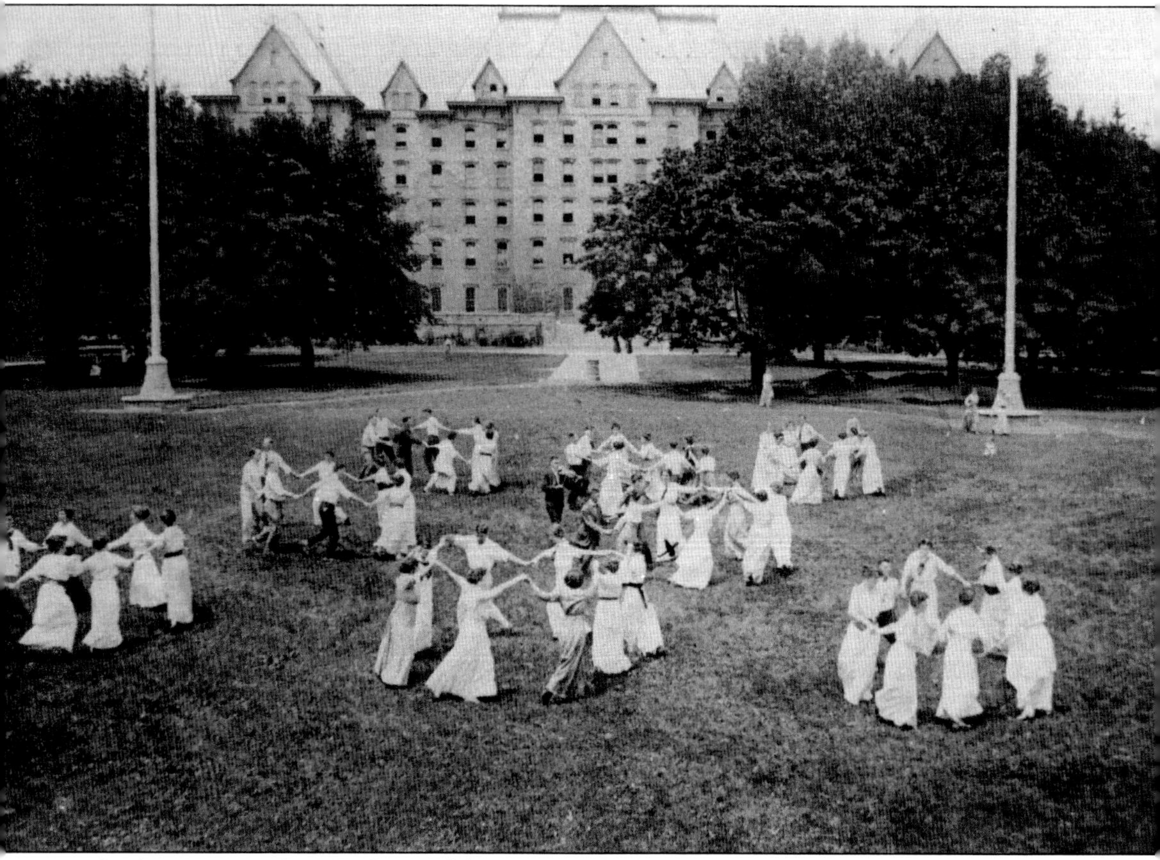

Students join in the May Day Celebrations on the lawn of the Central State Normal School. May Day marks the end of the winter half of the year, and it has traditionally been an occasion for popular celebrations. In some parts of the country, May baskets are prepared. The baskets are filled with flowers or treats and left at a doorstep. The gift-giver would ring the door bell and run away. The person receiving the basket would attempt to catch the giver. If they were caught, a kiss was to be exchanged. Celebrations included dances, food, maypole competitions, and music. (Courtesy of the Annie Halenbake Ross Library.)

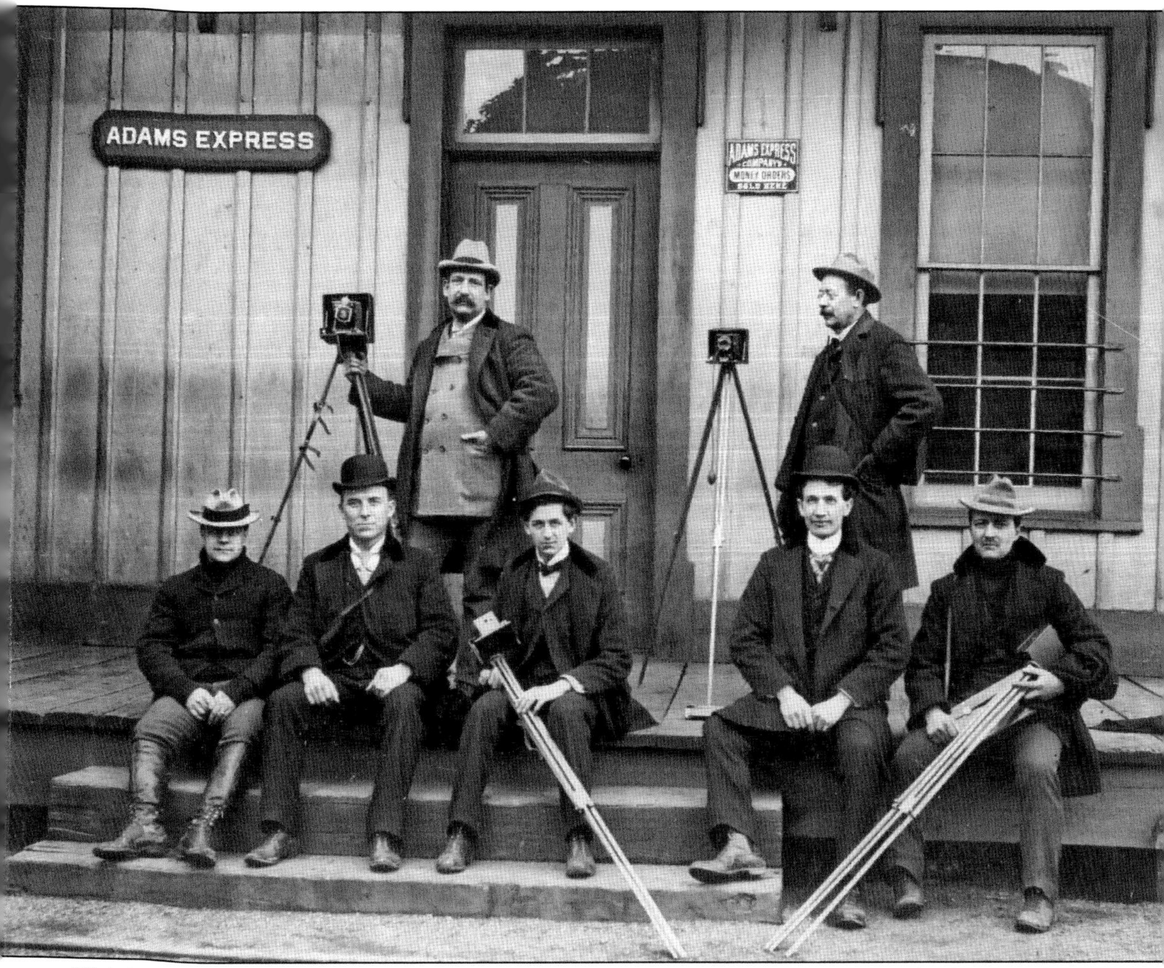


This is probably the Camera Club from the late 1800s. John W. C. Floyd was an early photographer who lived and worked in Lock Haven in the 1880s. He married twice; his first marriage was to Erma L. Gast, who died at age 25. Floyd married again in 1892 to Jessie Batcheler. Jesse died in 1896 after a brief illness. Floyd left the area in 1898. His photographs were predominantly scenes, points of interest, and portraits. He maintained a studio in the Kreamer Building on Main Street. Thanks to the dedication of the Annie Halenbake Ross Library, much of his work is included in this book. (Courtesy of the Annie Halenbake Ross Library.)

www.arcadiapublishing.com

Discover books about the town where you grew up, the cities where your friends and families live, the town where your parents met, or even that retirement spot you've been dreaming about. Our Web site provides history lovers with exclusive deals, advanced notification about new titles, e-mail alerts of author events, and much more.

MADE IN THE USA

Arcadia Publishing, the leading local history publisher in the United States, is committed to making history accessible and meaningful through publishing books that celebrate and preserve the heritage of America's people and places. Consistent with our mission to preserve history on a local level, this book was printed in South Carolina on American-made paper and manufactured entirely in the United States.

This book carries the accredited Forest Stewardship Council (FSC) label and is printed on 100 percent FSC-certified paper. Products carrying the FSC label are independently certified to assure consumers that they come from forests that are managed to meet the social, economic, and ecological needs of present and future generations.

FSC
Mixed Sources
Product group from well-managed forests and other controlled sources
Cert no. SW-COC-001530
www.fsc.org
© 1996 Forest Stewardship Council